The
MILE END
MURDER

The MILE END MURDER

The Case CONAN DOYLE Couldn't Solve!

SINCLAIR McKAY

Aurum
Press

Rotherham MBC

B54 026 511 7	
Askews & Holts	23-Jul-2018
364.1523	£9.99
WAT	

First publish...
an imprint ...
The Old Br...
6 Blundell S...
London N7...
United King...

www.Quart...

This paperb...
© 2017 Quarto Publishing
Text © 2017 Sinclair McKay

Sinclair McKay has asserted his moral right to be identified as the Author of this
Work in accordance with the Copyright Designs and Patents Act 1988.

A catalogue record for this book is available from the British Library.

ISBN 978-1-78131-804-1
Ebook ISBN 978-1-78131-734-1

10 9 8 7 6 5 4 3 2 1
2022 2021 2020 2019 2018

Typeset in Caslon by SX Composing DTP, Rayleigh, Essex, SS6 7xF
Printed by CPI Group (UK) Ltd, Croydon, CR0 4YY

Note from the author

Across that abyss of time – and in the absence of surviving forensic evidence – it is
impossible now to deal with certainties. But it is possible – taking on board some salient
points made by Arthur Conan Doyle – to theorise about the person who killed Mrs Emsley
and to make a well-reasoned deduction based on the evidence available.

Contents

'All these details I observed afterwards. At present my attention was centred upon the single, grim, motionless figure which lay stretched upon the boards, with vacant, sightless eyes staring up at the discoloured ceiling.'

A Study in Scarlet, Arthur Conan Doyle

Preface: Conan Doyle and
the Bloody Riddle

The creator of Sherlock Holmes understood the streets of London as a dark, gothic maze. Away from the mist-haloed gaslight of the wealthy West End and the bright clatter of fashionable parades, there was another world: twisting alleys, damp wharves and odorous passages. And in the distance, rising from the foggy river, were shadowy, wooded hills, upon which stood houses filled with murderous secrets. Holmes' London was a city of seemingly perpetual night.

Arthur Conan Doyle had a fascination with the city's uncanny possibilities. Where others saw dreary streets with identical yellow-brick housing, bitter smog, a shuffling mass of tightly-packed humanity, clerks and labourers pushing their way past horse-drawn vehicles, Conan Doyle observed London's sinisterly divided heart. In his fiction, this was a city in which fantastical killers, moving among ordinary people, committed seemingly impossible crimes: locked rooms were penetrated, unknown poisons were administered, supernatural prophecies were apparently fulfilled. When Holmes

1

and Watson ventured down to the docks, the darkness became an almost physical presence, pressing in on the figures who moved through the slimy, slippery passageways between the warehouses.

Even when the great detective travelled to Switzerland and was consigned, with his mortal enemy Moriarty, into the roaring abyss of the Reichenbach Falls, his creator could not let his obsession with London rest. Doyle continued to write fiction for *The Strand Magazine* and *The Cornhill Magazine* – everything from wild, storming adventure to eerie tales of the macabre. As he did so, the author found himself brooding on real stories of the city – on news reports he had read and remembered, on events that had passed into memory, and on episodes of extraordinary violence.

Conan Doyle turned briefly to writing short essays about real crimes: notorious cases and the circumstances surrounding them. In the spring of 1901, at the point when he was preparing to resurrect Holmes for *The Strand Magazine*, Conan Doyle examined an unsettling case that, to his mind, was never satisfactorily solved.

It was a murder that had been committed in the East End some forty years previously in 1860. At the time, the killing and subsequent police investigation had caused a national sensation; the repercussions had been felt all the way up to Whitehall and the Treasury. There was a particular ferocity about the slaying of a rich old lady called Mary Emsley that seemed, to some, to symbolise a wider savagery about the streets near the docks. This was a world of pitiless landlords and rent collectors, of labourers who were never more than a few pennies away from the workhouse, of stolid, uninspired policemen, and of highways haunted by violent predators.

As Conan Doyle saw it, there was a seemingly inexplicable aspect to the case: the victim had been secure inside her comfortable terraced house, and the killer had somehow entered and left without leaving any signs of breaking in, or having been seen by another soul.

The author was also fascinated by small, macabrely incongruous details that came up in the subsequent trial for murder – mysterious hands seen opening windows and holding torn strips of wallpaper, just steps away from the sickening, blood-drenched carnage – that were so bafflingly odd that the judge and jury simply ignored them.

Most importantly, Conan Doyle was gripped by this particular murder case because it had, at its heart, another hideous question: did the authorities convict and hang the wrong man?

He was greatly exercised by the police's use of circumstantial evidence and mused on the dark possibility that certain clues which may be used to convict someone could equally be interpreted in quite the opposite direction; the result being that the innocent might hang.

Conan Doyle took a passionate interest in cases where he felt, as here, that the eventual verdict was 'debatable'.[1] In the mystery of the widow of Mile End, the author was haunted by the boiling fervour and certainty of the police and public alike.

There was something else in this murder case, the very element that had suffused so many of his Sherlock Holmes stories: the violent intrusion of frightening and malevolent forces into ordered and wealthy domestic scenes.

Like so many Holmes stories, this was a shocking murder that also came to unearth old family secrets and scandals; an act of bestial violence that could have been triggered by a poisoned inheritance.

In Conan Doyle's resulting essay, titled 'The Debatable Case of Mrs. Emsley', he described the police discovery of the horror, with the first sight of a footprint 'dimly outlined in blood'. He gave pen portraits of the victim ('a grim, stern, eccentric woman') and of the man who would eventually be accused and convicted of her murder

---

[1] In one famous example in 1906, Conan Doyle involved himself heavily in the case of Anglo-Indian lawyer George Edalji, who was accused of mutilating animals and sending malicious letters; some attribute the eventual founding of the Court of Criminal Appeal to the author.

('respectable-looking . . . well drilled'). He described the trial and the fate of the defendant. Crucially though, having raised his own doubts about the conviction, Conan Doyle left the story of this murder dangling without a final conclusion, leaving it to his many thousands of readers to make their own deductions. It was as if he was just as bewildered as the judge had been at the Old Bailey. After the article was published in the May 1901 number of *The Strand Magazine*, the author returned once more to the fictional certainties of Holmes and Watson.

Over a hundred and fifty years later, now is a crisply pertinent moment in London's history for us to return to the strange mystery of Mrs Emsley. The city in which the victim dwelled was one that sharply mirrors today's London and its East End. Then, as now, we see rapacity and insecurity; wealth and ostentation coexisting with deprivation and slums.

Through a more distanced examination of all the archival material, some of which was not available to Conan Doyle, the story offers up many more credible suspects. Finally – possibly – an answer to the enigma of who descended into psychotic, murderous frenzy that warm summer night, and then evaded detection, might be found.

The bloody tragedy also throws a startling light on to the texture of life in the Victorian East End; a world where the pressing darkness was balanced by outbreaks of extraordinary colour and vivacity. There are some killings that seem to capture, in their murk, the flavour of a time and place. This is one such case.

1

The Woman at the Window

❧

Her neighbours never seemed to wonder if the sharp-tongued old lady might be lonely. As the London sky darkened each evening, and the pale cream of her defiantly old-fashioned candle light appeared in the widow's second-floor bedroom window, the people who lived opposite, with their newly installed gas lighting – the blue-yellow aura glowing on brightly coloured floral wallpaper – could glance through their windows at the old lady, sitting there gazing out towards the sunset.

Mrs Emsley lived in a terraced house with a back garden that was big enough for pear trees, and a small front garden that, in the summer, had daubs of purple and yellow, a tangle of determined wildflowers and unruly green ivy. She was by no means a recluse; during the day, there would be visitors coming and going up and down the front path. Some of these were relatives or acquaintances of her late husband. Others were handymen she employed, or the children of the handymen running errands. Very much less frequently, there were visits from her two stepdaughters and their husbands.

She was extraordinarily active for a lady of seventy. Rare was the day when she would not be seen walking down the street, basket on her arm, preparing to make an extensive tour of the neighbourhood. Mrs Emsley was noted for her direct, sometimes harsh, manner. There was nothing remotely frail about her; instead, she seemed filled with caustic energy.

However, once the daylight started to fade, Mrs Emsley withdrew into solitude, into the shadows of a house that smelled of homemade broth. She was very reluctant to receive people after sunset. Sometimes, however, she had to.

Her reticence about the night might simply have been due to the wisdom of age. Mrs Emsley lived in a district of the rapidly expanding East End that was, by the standards of neighbouring parishes, relatively genteel. Yet just a few streets away, a matter of mere yards, lay quite another realm. Mrs Emsley – having spent her entire life in Stepney, close to the rough clamour of the docks, and very familiar with the enclosed courtyards that hid so much deprivation – would have known better than most about the possibility of violence.

In 1860, violence was part of the grammar of life in many of the streets of the East End. Though she was reluctant to have dealings with anyone after sunset, one curious thing was this: during the daytime, the old widow always set out to walk down some of the most rundown roads of Bethnal Green, Limehouse and Whitechapel – pavements punctuated with puddles of sewage co-mingled with rotting vegetable waste, broken windows stuffed with grey rags. The air was constantly thick with threat. Mrs Emsley was met with aggression quite frequently. On those poor streets, in the daylight, the anger of others appeared to amuse and stimulate her. During those hours, she seemed to have an appetite for confrontation – possibly even a relish for it.

Mrs Emsley was very rich, but had given no indication she had thought of retiring to enjoy her ever-increasing wealth. A couple of her neighbours had the impression that each evening, before she closed the shutters on her windows, she was counting out her money. While they were not concerned about her emotional wellbeing – she was defiantly self-sufficient – they might have had some concern about her apparent physical vulnerability. For all her pugnacity, she was small. For some time, there had been local rumours about foreign gangs carrying out house burglaries involving knife-slashing; some said the thieves were Frenchmen.

Whenever the old lady did have occasional callers after the sun had gone down, she would spend a long time looking out of her window and questioning them, before she would assent to going downstairs to let them in.

The other curious thing – the detail that constantly piqued her neighbours' interest – was the fact that Mrs Emsley refused to have servants. There was plenty of room in her three-storey terraced house for a maid and a cook; her neighbours certainly employed domestic staff. The most she would allow herself was a charwoman who came once a week, during the daytime.

Come the evening, as she took up her usual position at the window, Mrs Emsley gazed out past the houses opposite towards a prospect of manufactories on the canal; of brick-built institutional workhouses; of vast breweries, with their elegant chimneys rising into the sky.

If a summer's evening was fine, with the sky streaked red and indigo, she would see further yet to the tops of the steeples and spires of the old churches of the City, some two miles off, silhouetted against the deepening night. It was rare for her ever to travel that far, aside from an occasional errand to the banks; her business dealings were conducted very much closer to home. As she sat there, the sounds of the old and the new city could commingle. If the wind was right, one might hear the two peals that sounded each quarter-hour from St Anne's Limehouse, blending with the distant plangent orchestra of steamboats blowing and whistling on the river.

The brightly painted onrush of progress was everywhere. In 1860, the nature of new commerce meant that work and leisure now kept irregular hours. There were well-established public houses on the corners of the road where she lived, with benches outside in the warmer evenings for drinkers to enjoy their pipes in the fresh air. There was an eel pie house on the main road nearby, together with an establishment called The Coffee Pot. (This was an early coffeee chain – there was another branch in Limehouse.) On that busy junction there were stalls selling hot potatoes and hot wine, which would often be there until midnight in the summer months. In the other direction, a little to the north of the old lady's house, the road was bisected by a railway bridge. The Eastern Counties Railway, which ran trains from Shoreditch to the countryside and coast of Essex and Suffolk – and which had been a source of legal grief to the widow's late husband – was now well-established. Indeed, these rail routes, and all the construction work that had come with them, had added to the old lady's wealth.

The bulk of that wealth was in property and it was this that had made Mrs Emsley notorious locally. When she looked out westwards from her second-floor window towards the sloping loose-tiled roofs and crooked chimneys of Stepney, of Mile End Old Town, of Bethnal Green, the old woman was surveying a world of which she owned a large share. Dozens upon dozens of those houses belonged to her, and she rented them out to countless tenants.

Mrs Emsley was not born an heiress; she had been brought up half a mile to the south in Limehouse. Much of her younger life had been spent in precarious conditions. But now, entire streets, through which she had once walked in poverty, were hers.

In the fast-swirling tides of those changing times, some swam and prospered: the young engineers, helping to effect the new miracles of gas pipes and ever more railway lines; the sharp City clerks and trainee solicitors, required to deal with ever-increasing amounts of record-keeping. For them, the expanding East End offered smart, affordable housing and a rich culture, not merely of amusing music hall, but also grandly staged theatre and opera. For these new East

Enders, there were cafés, dance academies and pleasure gardens. But further down the chain of employment – and quite literally around the corner from these prospering new middle classes – there were streets in which the possibilities of civilised life were circumscribed horribly. Part of the reason for social tensions in 1860 was the resentment felt by previously well-paid manual workers (many now casualised), for the new generations of poor incomers who were thought to be bringing down streets by being prepared to live in squalid and even dangerous housing, and in far greater numbers: anything to get a foothold in London.

The widow, a landlady on a grand scale, was not oblivious to the ever-present proximity of calamity. Yet there was also a side to her that was utterly unyielding. The tenants over whose lives she had such sway could never appeal to her for help.

Mrs Emsley knew the people intimately. She was one of them. There was something curiously modern about her. But even with her knowledge and experience, she couldn't see the terrifying threat and the frenzy that was moving so fast towards her.

She was quite right to be afraid to open her door at night.

2

'Down Among the Dead Men'

❧

The teenaged boy running through the streets, his clothes spattered with mud, had no inkling or sense of the darkness that was soon to steal over his family.

He had been sent from his home in Bethnal Green by his father with a message for the old woman early on the morning of 14 August 1860. That wet summer had made dark mulch of the road and the new paving stones around Mile End; the hooves of horses that had echoed on cobbled and surfaced roads were now muffled and crunched in the gravelly dung. The heavy clouds above moved fast; the breeze brought throat-catching tangs of bittersweet chemicals from factories on the canal and on Bow Common Lane, and from the jute and soap works on the River Lea.

The boy wove his way through a range of narrow streets, past the squeals and stench of backyard abattoirs, and past two handsomely built establishments, elegant in brickwork, three storeys high, that could perhaps have been mistaken for hospitals, or even – in another part of the city – for government or civil service buildings. These establishments had large windows and cultivated gardens. To anyone unfamiliar with the area, it would have been strange to learn that the poorest people in Bethnal Green passed the buildings with a quiver of unease. These were the local workhouses. The landlady of Grove Road would have seen a few of her former tenants finally giving up the uneven economic fight and submitting to becoming inmates of these establishments.

The boy was fortunate to have been brought up in a household where the terrors of the workhouse seemed just far away enough; he, his two siblings and his mother and father lived, if not in ease, then certainly not in hunger.

The messenger knocked hard on the door of 9 Grove Road, waiting patiently. There was no reply. The boy, Edwin Emm, was familiar to the old woman's neighbours; he was a more respectable prospect than many of the young men who sometimes formed gangs in the area. This was the son of one of Mrs Emsley's most trusted handymen.

No one came to the door.

Since the old lady was notably active, this was no cause for concern. It was more than possible that she was out attending to business, or financial matters, or simply shopping. The neighbours observed that despite her enormous wealth, Mrs Emsley showed a determined preference to ask at the open-fronted butcher's shop for scraggy cuts of meat and offal that they personally would not have had in the house. Greengrocer Archibald Mann, who had a stall on the corner, was familiar with Mrs Emsley; she would wait for the most opportune moment late in the day to make her own modest choices of fruit and vegetables that were older, less fresh and therefore cheaper. There was little local admiration for her thrift; rather, it was viewed as perverse.

It was possible that the old lady was out visiting friends – a rarer occurrence, but known. One particular friend styled himself as a pastor. Joseph Biggs had been hoping to take rather more prominent a place in her life than she seemed keen on. There were occasions when they shared a glass of beer together. However, Mrs Emsley was sharp and adept at keeping people at a distance.

She might have been out visiting her niece who lived three-quarters of a mile west in Whitechapel, close to the teeming street market with its second-hand clothes merchants crying, 'Clo! Clo!', its sellers of pea soup, fried fish, Persian sherbet and strawberryade, and its 'Gallery of Varieties' – a ghoulish waxworks exhibition featuring tableaux of real-life murders, at the door of which a harmonica player enticed people in with continual renditions of 'Down Among the Dead Men'. The niece, Elizabeth Gotz, seemed to be one of the few blood relations for whom the widow had any patience or time. Despite years of marriage to Samuel Emsley, she didn't have a great deal of affection for the children from his first marriage. There had been suggestions that she and Emsley – a Yorkshire businessman who made a great deal of money in corset-making in London – had not been happy together. Certainly, Mrs Emsley had not seemed prostrated with grief after his passing in 1856.

Mrs Emsley had been widowed twice; her first husband, John Jones, died in 1833. She had borne one child of her own, but the infant died at the age of eighteen months. Mary had no children thereafter. When Edwin Emm knocked on that door in Mile End, there would have been little sense of anything untoward. Mrs Emsley was, by and large, in good health. In an area of London that had been darkened more than most by mortality and the filthiest of diseases, her spryness was quite unusual.

The boy returned the next day, and then the next. Still, there was no answer at the door. Nor did the open window shutters appear to have been moved. It was only now that mystification began to set in. The boy's father, Walter Emm, knew about the precision of Mrs Emsley's life and, more particularly, the nature of her routine when it came to collecting rents.

Mrs Emsley's property was not just based on inheritance from her rich second husband, as her neighbours assumed. Strikingly, she was independently wealthy at a time when it was extremely rare for women to have any sort of claim on property at all. If a woman was married, then it was conventionally the case that her husband had dominion over all her interests. Mrs Emsley was reckoned to own over a hundred properties over a vast area, stretching from Whitechapel out into the marshes of Stratford-At-Bow, Barking and even the coaching town of Romford. All her houses were filled with tenants, a great many more than would have been comfortable. In many cases, these were not happy houses. Indeed, they were the types of property that were beginning to attract the outraged attention of campaigning writers and journalists. Rents were collected on a weekly basis. Some of this work was delegated to trusted agents – men such as Walter Emm. However, the old lady preferred to attend to many of the addresses within walking distance of Grove Road herself.

In this respect, Mrs Emsley showed what some might have seen as remarkable bravery, if not utter foolhardiness. Behind the main roads of Bethnal Green and nearby Ratcliff lay small close-built streets and courts. These enclosed courts consisted of a few houses subdivided into many dwellings, with grubby whitewashed or whiteboarded exteriors and dark, airless, close-smelling, creaking interiors, jammed with families and lodgers, built around small courtyards, which could only be entered and left one way: beneath low arches. These were patches of London – moist, rotting, stinking, often burning with feverish disease – into which the police were reluctant to venture; once one had entered through that low archway into the darkness of the court, there was only a single way back out if one had to make a speedy exit. The families who lived in such places frequently viewed the police as enemies, complicit with landlords and employers in persecuting them.

It was into these areas that Mrs Emsley would plunge, apparently with gusto. She would visit her properties, collect the rent owed, place it in her basket and move on to the next property. The landlady would no doubt have presented an extraordinarily tempting target for a desperate thief.

After several return visits to Grove Road, young Edwin told his father on the Friday morning that there was still no response from the house. Mr Emm, an intelligent and skilled tradesman, indicated to his family that he thought something was wrong. It might be asked why it had taken this bright man several days to start feeling uneasy. Mrs Emsley, although generally robust, had told him a few weeks beforehand that she had had 'a swimming in the head'. Concern for her health and a rather speedier raising of the alarm might have been expected. Why did Mr Emm apparently not wonder rather more quickly what lay behind that unanswered door?

On that Friday morning, Mr Emm understood the lines of authority he would have to consult to take action. His first step was to raise Mrs Emsley's solicitor, William Rose, who knew more than most about her financial dealings.

Mr Rose, who lived about a mile away in a handsomely appointed square in Bethnal Green, immediately made his way to 9 Grove Road and, like Edwin before him, tried the door. A sense of foreboding would have been quite natural; Mrs Emsley was, after all, seventy years old. It was more than possible that she could have fallen or had been taken ill. She may have been lying alive, but helpless, anywhere in the house.

Perhaps Mr Rose felt a chill of premonition. Instead of taking matters into his own hands and trying to effect a forced entry – which would have been a perfectly justifiable course of action for a trusted solicitor – he withdrew from the door and made his way to the nearby police station on the busy Bow Road.

Whatever was behind that door, he wanted to be sure that a constable was there to witness it immediately. Mr Rose was quite right to have done so. The solicitor also summoned Mrs Emsley's stepsons-in-law John Faith and Henry Whittaker, who both lived nearby.

'I beg to report that at 12 noon this day, Mr Rose, Solicitor . . . informed Sergeant Dillon, K19, that he had called at the home of Mrs Hemsley [sic], Widow, No. 9 Grove Road, Mile End Road, Stepney, for the purpose of seeing her, but could not make anyone hear, & that he thought something was wrong. The Sgt went through the next house & over the garden wall, when he found the back door & window shutters of No. 9 unfastened,' ran the official police report from Inspector Hayes of K Division, dated 17 August 1860. [1]

It was the absence of forced entry that struck the first uncanny note. Judging by the later testimonies it seemed that the solicitor and sergeant had, between them, expected to find all the exaggerated roughness of a burglary: broken locks, smashed windows, marks of violence on the door.

Instead, the house was open to all. The men entered. The first thing that appeared to strike them was that inside the house all the doors were wide open.

The second uncanny note was sounded by the uncertainty in that silence; was there anyone in there? Was Mrs Emsley home? Would she be scandalised or even amused to see how her own solicitor and the police had crept in around the back? Even in the daylight, it was a shadowy house.

The heavy thump of footsteps on boards and rugs; the echoes filling the quiet rooms. It was the dark and stillness of a house with no living occupant. And gradually, as they moved through that ground floor, the foul and unmistakeable smell would have become increasingly pungent. The solicitor and the police officer did not waste time downstairs; they must have known immediately, staring upwards, what they were going to find.

Sergeant Dillon was methodical. He took a few minutes to thoroughly examine the 'parlours' and 'first and second floor', as he later testified.

'He proceeded upstairs,' continued Inspector Hayes' report, to 'the front room [second floor]'. [2] There, he and his companions first saw the bloody footprint on the landing. Then, turning to the lumber room, Dillon, Rose, Faith and Whittaker found the source of the nauseating stench.

3

'The Expression Lost'

❦

It was as if there had been an explosion of blood, extending out across the room 'in three directions'. [1] The corpse of Mrs Emsley was, as stated in the police report, 'lying on her left side, with her head against the door-post'. Her head, as one journalist described the scene the next day, had been 'forced in'. [2]

The 'splashes' of blood had hit the 'surrounding furniture' as well as the doorpost. They were, as the doctor was to note later, 'dry, hard and shining'. [3]

Mrs Emsley was lying face-down, one arm outstretched towards the door, almost obstructing it; the back of her white-haired head had been pulverised, the skull smashed, the blue-ish brain exposed. It was not just the furniture: the walls of the parlour were also sprayed with gouts of blood. The wooden floorboards were crusted with thick dark coagulation. It had not taken the flies long; maggots were writhing in and around the lurid crater in her skull.

Curiously, the old lady's long skirt and outer petticoat had been raised up, revealing her lower legs and thighs. The hitched clothes partly covered her back and the lower half of the back of her bloodied head. Oddly, the weird obscenity of this did not find its way into the very first police report, almost as if it was too strange and incongruous a thing to relate. The brutal murder was one thing, but who would then defile the body of an old lady in this fashion?

There was an indentation in the wainscoting which looked as though it could have been produced by a heavy instrument. Indeed, it seemed to those in the room that the mark signified the spot where the assailant had taken an initial swing at Mrs Emsley and missed, the weapon crashing into the wall. A swift, brutal death was one thing, but the idea that Mrs Emsley might have had even a slender chance of escaping her murderer was another.

Yet there cannot have been very much noise. In a street as relatively peaceful as Grove Road, any prolonged struggle would have been heard and would surely have aroused one of Mrs Emsley's neighbours.

The corpse was holding a roll of wallpaper; indeed, the room was full of such rolls. The police made enquiries into why the old lady had seen fit to buy such huge quantities of 'paper-hangings'. That day, as they examined the crime scene, they also sought medical expertise. 'Dr Gill, of Bow, who was passing at the time examined deceased & stated that death had been caused by the fracture of the back part of the skull,' continued the first police report. [4] No photographs were taken of the murder scene. While cameras were just starting to be used to photograph convicts, no one had yet considered how they might help at the scenes of crimes. Such techniques would not be pioneered for another two decades.

However, the men who found Mrs Emsley's corpse had no difficulty recalling the horror of gazing on the brain-exposed wound and, as the police report stated, 'the great quantity of congealed blood'. They also remembered the greenish hue of her face and the way that it contrasted with the mottled purple around her neck where, as she lay dead, the blood had gradually settled. It was noted that 'her face was swollen . . . and the expression lost'. [5] The doctor also noted that 'a large pool of blood extended from the head across the room, saturating the upper portion of her dress'. [6]

The shock of examining that head wound further was great; it was, as Dr Gill later testified, 'very deep'. The skull was so comprehensively broken that there were fragments hanging next to 'portions' of the brain. The floor around the body was sticky.

'It is supposed that deceased had been lying where found for – at least – 2 or 3 days,' the report continued. 'The deceased was last seen alive on Monday afternoon last.

'It cannot at present be ascertained whether anything has been stolen or not.' [7]

In the sickening atmosphere of that warm, quiet house, the idea of theft must have been among the first things that occurred to Mrs Emsley's solicitor. Mr Rose knew every detail of his client's neurotic handling of the great quantities of money generated by the rents. Mrs Emsley was known to dislike banks (this was an age in which banks crashed: there had been crises in the City in 1847 and 1857, and one followed in 1866). She preferred to invest surplus funds into acquiring even more property. Any bigger lump sums remaining would be looked after by the solicitor, who would deposit them temporarily with banks. Whenever Mrs Emsley collected rent cash in her covered straw basket, she would take it down the road and round the corner to the New Globe Tavern. She knew and trusted the landlord, so instead of keeping the money in her house overnight, she would instead place it in the pub's safe and get a receipt.

As he looked down at Mrs Emsley's body, the solicitor would have known that it was unlikely she would have kept anything much of value on the premises.

Nor did the house, at first glance, seem to have been ransacked or even systematically searched. The sense of relative calm and order was more disturbing than if the place had been turned upside down. If this had been a burglary, there surely would have been chaos.

There was not.

In those cracked puddles of congealed blood were footprints – more precisely, the prints made by a boot. They led out of the murder room and on to the landing.

Once Dr Gill's preliminary examination of Mrs Emsley's body was complete, there were a couple of immediate necessities for the police. The local station acknowledged that they needed the help of an experienced officer. To this end, a young policeman called Sergeant Tanner was assigned to the case. In addition, they had to ensure that a guard was placed on the house to protect the integrity of the crime scene, and to deter thieves and ghoulish sensation seekers who had heard the news.

The ghouls arrived swiftly. By that evening, an excitable crowd had formed outside 9 Grove Road. It is certain that some in the assembly had been Mrs Emsley's tenants.

Largely through picking up on local talk, it wasn't long before the police were beginning to understand something of the victim's character and movements.

They knew that on Monday 13 August, Mrs Emsley had spent some time collecting rents around Lamb's Fields in Bethnal Green. Some of those houses were 'very dirty' and were bitterly over-crowded, with 'four to five families' living within them – properties to which the Board of Health might be alerted. The police also learned that Mrs Emsley had met one of her property maintenance men and had been seen in The Vicar of Wakefield public house, but had not stopped for refreshment. When she went home to Grove Road, she had a basket filled with collected rent money. They knew that Mrs Emsley employed rent collectors, that she had poor relatives and wealthy in-laws, and that if tenants fell behind with rent even by a single week, she was ruthless about throwing them on to the street.

'The deceased was about 70 years of age,' stated a police report written by Inspector Thornton 'resided quite alone in her house and was possessed of considerable house property situated in [the] very low neighbourhoods of Bethnal Green, Ratcliff, Stratford, Barking, Dagenham, etc., and she was in the habit of personally collecting the greater portion of her rents on a Monday, and in consequence of her frequent litigation with the tenants, her very plain way of dressing and living, she became well known at the East End of London.

'On the 2nd August last the deceased purchased a large quantity of paper hangings at an auction . . . the main portion of which was put into the room where the deceased's body was found, and I am of opinion that some person or persons called on the deceased on Monday evening last [13 August] under pretence of buying some of the said paper hangings, and she went upstairs to the top room to show it when she was murdered and robbed of 3 or 4 rings from her fingers and whatever rents she collected on that day estimated at present at about £40, which is all the property that at present can be ascertained to be stolen.

'I directed a thorough search of the Coal Cellar, privy, etc. of the house in order if possible to find the weapon with which the deceased was murdered but it cannot be found, but a tin box containing £32 in gold, and £16-2-0 in silver has been found among the Coal in the cellar, and now is in the hands of the police.' [8]

In other words, if the sole intention had been purely to rob Mrs Emsley, then the murderer had made an extraordinarily bungled job of it. After the old woman had been fatally struck, the burglar would have been at liberty to conduct a thorough search of the premises, including the coal cellar, which would strike most as an obvious hiding place for valuables.

It transpired, however, that some curiously random items had been taken. As well as a cheque for ten pounds, there were a few small objects – lenses, spoons, a pencil case, hardly of any value in themselves – which would later come to acquire totemic significance. However, at the scene of the crime there was nothing that looked obvious or straightforward.

That first weekend after the discovery, Scotland Yard sent a small team of men to make a close examination of the house. A 'commodious' house of 'eight rooms', there was, apart from the spot where Mrs Emsley was found, remarkably little sign of disorder. The pattern of the blood splashes was studied and there was a minute examination of the wainscoting. The search for anything, any item at all that the murderer may have accidentally dropped, for instance, was exacting.

Frustratingly, the curious absence of any forced entry and the apparent lack of any attempt to ransack the property meant that there were initially few physical clues with which the police could work. The technique of fingerprinting had not yet been developed. A couple of years before, the British chief magistrate in the Indian town of Jungipoor demanded that the local population put their fingerprints on to contracts – the idea was that they were even more of a guarantee than a written signature. Fingerprints being kept on police files did not begin until an official in Argentina in the 1890s saw the value in these unique identifiers.

There was the bloody boot mark on the landing outside the lumber room; this, at least, could be examined more closely. Inspector Thornton arranged for its preservation. The stained floorboard was carefully covered with oilcloth, then cut out with a saw. When detached, the oilcloth was then secured tighter to the bloody area so that the distinct boot print would not be touched or marred. The section of floorboard was then taken back to the police station at Arbour Square.

A few steps down from the landing was a long, torn strip of wallpaper, smeared with blood. This too was taken to Arbour Square.

In an age before the science of pathology had been formulated to any great degree, it was impossible for the doctor to say with any certainty when exactly Mrs Emsley had died. By using the logic of the first witness statements, the police tried to narrow down the hours.

'There is no doubt the deceased was murdered on Monday evening as she was not seen alive after that time,' stated a police report, 'and it was not discovered until about 12 noon the following Friday.

'At present there is no clue to the perpetrator of the crime a length of time having elapsed since the commission of the offence and its discovery,' continued the report, 'and there is nothing stolen which can be traced beyond a Ten pound cheque which has been stopped, but I am of opinion the murderer will not make use of that. No weapon left behind, no person seen near the house on the evening in question.'

There may have been no clues as to the perpetrator, but there were numerous suspects, starting with those Mrs Emsley employed to assist in collecting rents or to do other jobbing work for her. They knew her custom of living alone, and of collecting and taking home her money on a Monday. This was also well known among her tenants, who numbered, as the police report said, 'some hundreds, some of whom are of the most depraved and lowest class, and who have frequently threatened her'.

This fury had been on show just two months before. In a case brought before Bow County Court, Mrs Emsley had claimed that some fifteen tenants in one of the streets there owed her rent. She was mistaken. The magistrate found against her and awarded each of the aggrieved tenants ten shillings and sixpence costs.

An editorial in the *Morning Post* was already suggesting that this hideous crime might have had its roots in deprivation and slum dwellings. 'If the law has power to punish,' it wrote, 'society may do something to prevent: and the condition – both moral and material – of large classes in this country must be improved before we can hope for a much more cheering state of things.' [9]

Thornton's subsequent police report also noted that Mrs Emsley's solicitor, 'Mr Rose, a very highly respectable man, informs me that he has frequently told the deceased that he thought she would be murdered, going about as she did about [sic] among such bad and dangerous characters. (10)

'The deceased has also a number of very poor relations who have all a great interest in her death, and she had made up her mind to make a will to build Almshouses with the whole of her money and not leave anything to her relatives which fact the deceased had talked publicly about and all the relatives knew it.' (11)

On 21 August, Inspector Thornton wrote from the Metropolitan Police's detective department about one promising lead.

'I beg to report that I have this morning received information that a nephew of the deceased Mrs Emsley who was murdered at Bow is a Soldier at Portsmouth and has a very bad character he has often enquired by letter to his sister to know if his Aunt was dead and has appeared anxious for her death as he believes he will have considerable property at her death.

'I beg to ask the Commission if I should send Sergeant Tanner down to Portsmouth to make the necessary enquiry respecting him as to whether he has been absent or not – or whether I should telegraph.' (12)

(A telegraph was sent to the barracks of this nephew, Edward Jackson, and elicited this reply from his commanding officer, M Barber: 'Edward Jackson was not absent but obtained leave today to go to London about the murder of a Relative'.) (13)

The possibility of the murderer being a psychopath posing as an interested buyer of wallpaper could also not be ignored. Very quickly it was decided to monitor potential suspects from the streets and the houses that Mrs Emsley owned. Inspector Thornton wrote a letter to Scotland Yard on 21 August: 'I beg the Commissions' sanction to employ two police constables of K Division in plain clothes to keep observation on persons suspected to be implicated in the murder of Mrs Emsley at Stepney.' (14)

Despite these suspects, *The Times* noted the following on 22 August 1860: 'Up to yesterday evening, nothing had transpired positively tending to implicate anyone in the murder of the unfortunate woman Mrs Emsley.' In addition: 'some of the most experienced detective officers from the headquarters of the metropolitan police in Scotland-yard ... are actively engaged in endeavouring to throw fresh light upon it.' [15]

Indeed, the murder of Mrs Emsley became a sensation that late summer not merely because it was a tantalising mystery in its own right, but because both the victim and those suspected of her foul murder seemed to stand at the edge of a harsh new world that was already being written about and portrayed on the stage and in novels. This was a killing that seemed a consequence of an amoral new age: a city in which an old lady, who by custom ought to have been cherished by family and neighbours, instead died alone in hideous circumstances. A rich widow who could never bring herself to leave the streets in which she herself had been brought up. Streets that now appeared to have swallowed her up in their darkness.

4

'A Most Sickening
Spectacle'

❦

This modern city had still not quite developed modern responses to bloody violence. Local inquests often came before arrests and formal trials; the most socially superior of the parishioners, generally self-appointed, would gather to conduct the initial examination of the body and witnesses, usually in a makeshift location.

By the Monday morning of 20 August, almost a week after the time that Mrs Emsley was presumed to have been murdered, a jury was brought together in the backroom of the Railway Hotel, at the north end of Grove Road, just a few doors up from the old lady's house.

The murder of Mrs Emsley had the unexpected result of bringing a sharp upswing in business to this and other local pubs.

The 'investigation', as it was termed, started at noon, led by the coroner John Humphreys. 'The large club-room of the hotel was crowded,' reported the *Evening Standard* on Tuesday 21 August, 'and amongst those present were some of the most influential residents of the district.' [1] In addition to this, there was, 'a large crowd of persons assembled in the road both around the hotel and the house in which the outrage was committed'.

'The police, under Inspector Kerresey and Serjeant [sic] Coppin of the K Division, and Inspector Thornton and Serjeant Sawyer of the metropolitan detective force, have been unremitting in their endeavours to obtain some clue to the perpetrators of the fearful crime,' the article continued, 'but unfortunately little has been gathered to elucidate the mystery which surrounds the whole affair. It would appear that the whole of the old lady's property was not stolen, for on a further search being made by Mr Serjeant Tanner a tin-box was found amongst the coals in the cellar, and on being opened it contained 32*l.*[1] in gold and 16*l.* 2s in silver. A diamond mourning ring was also found in her bedroom.' [2]

This, as it turned out, was one of Mrs Emsley's mourning rings; but she had been married and widowed twice. The police had not yet realised this, and the whereabouts of the second mourning ring was soon to prove one of their more elusive investigatory strands.

'The jury having been sworn, the Coroner addressed them,' added the newspaper report, 'and said that, as they lived in the neighbourhood, no doubt they knew something of the case. All he had to ask them was to pay attention to the evidence which would be submitted. It was a case of extreme suspicion. An old lady was found dead in her house under peculiar circumstances, which they would inquire into, but first they would view the body and the premises.' [3]

Mrs Emsley's body had been returned from the mortuary to the house and restored to the position in which it had been found. The coroner and jury marched out of the hotel, along the slippery paving stones and entered the dark house, climbing the stairs to the lumber room.

'The jury then proceeded to view the body,' the newspaper explained, 'which lay in the room where it was first discovered, only having been removed for the purpose of making the autopsy.

---

[1] '*l*' was a widely used version of the pound sign (£) at the time.

'The body presented a most sickening spectacle, not only from the frightful nature of the wounds on the head, but also from the extremely advanced state of decomposition ... the jury, at the suggestion of the Coroner, made a minute examination of the premises, and the various spots on which the slightest traces of blood occurred.' [4]

It must indeed have been utterly nauseating, even for those jurors familiar with the sight of death. Under the grey, wet August sky, the manoeuvring to and fro of Mrs Emsley's body was striking in its macabre theatricality.

Once the jurors had taken in the discoloured and decaying body stretched out in that warm top room still filled with wallpaper rolls, they were directed downstairs, along the street and back to the hotel.

There, the first witness was called. In the first spasm of confusion in the case – the result of labyrinthine family connections that would have repercussive effects through the courts throughout the following decade – John Faith was thought to be a distant relation of Mrs Emsley. In fact, he was a stepson-in-law who was married to Betty, one of Samuel Emsley's daughters. The jury and the onlookers would have observed this well-dressed young man with the keenest interest; all would have wondered where he stood in relation to the inheritance, and by how much he might stand to benefit from the old woman's passing.

'I live at Park House and I am of no occupation,' Mr Faith told the jury. Nor apparently did he need any; the money that had cascaded down from his late father-in-law was more than sufficient. Park House was (and still is today) an elegant Georgian property on the Mile End Road facing Stepney Green. It was a great deal more handsome – and valuable – than Mrs Emsley's terraced house. 'The deceased was my stepmother,' explained Faith, for the benefit of the jury. 'She was the widow of the late Samuel Emsley who kept the Octagon Stay Manufactory. He was the owner of considerable house property.

'He was always known to be a very respectable man,' Faith continued. 'He was commissioner of taxes, and held other positions. I should think it was about three weeks since I last saw Mrs Emsley. She appeared then to be in remarkably good health and spirits. Although she was so advanced in life, she was of particularly active habits and well able to take care of herself.'

Faith's knowledge of her business affairs proved to be limited, however.

'She inherited considerable property from her husband, which consisted mainly of houses,' he told the jury. Yet this wasn't entirely the case: many of those houses already belonged to her. Faith's statement suggested where he believed the line of inheritance to lie: the wealth had been Samuel Emsley's and it should remain within the immediate family.

He told the jury that the Emsley property interests, 'would bring [Mrs Emsley] into connection with people who sell things for the repair of houses, such as paper-hangings, and these she used to buy herself to keep her property in order.'

'I know nothing of her death or how to account for it,' added Faith. The coroner interjected at this point, telling Faith to, 'never mind that'.

The witness was now available for questioning by the jury. One member, with a striking disregard for sombre pieties, leapt straight in with the most pertinent financial question.

'I believe you say the deceased held a large amount of property,' he began. 'To whom, on her death, would that property go?'

'That which she had from Mr Emsley would go to his two daughters,' answered Faith, 'and the other – her own property – to anyone to whom she pleased to leave it.'

'Has she made any will with regard to that property?' continued the juror.

'I do not know whether there is a will or not,' Faith replied. 'She has no relatives that I know of, beyond those two daughters. She had no children of her own.'

At this, the coroner interjected, clearly confused: 'Then these daughters are the daughters of Mr Emsley by his first wife?'

Faith confirmed this to be the case, but he was incorrect about the relatives; although she had no surviving children of her own, Mrs Emsley did have plenty of nieces and nephews.

The ambiguity about the existence of a will was vital at that stage for the authorities, who were looking for any kind of motivation for the crime.

The next witness to be called was one of Mrs Emsley's tenants. Catherine Weir lived in Jamaica Place in Limehouse, a few yards from the river between Limehouse Basin and the larger West India Dock. This was an area in sharp decline; just a few years later, it would be marked out on Charles Booth's famous poverty map of London as black, to denote the direst distress. Mrs Emsley could easily have walked the area blindfolded, so well did she know those streets. Some thirty years previously, she and her first husband were the ones struggling to make a living themselves in the same district.

'I am the wife of William Weir, a labourer,' the eyewitness told the coroner. 'I knew the deceased woman. I last saw her alive between half-past-four and five on the afternoon of Monday last. That was at 3, Jamaica Place. She called on me for her rent. She then appeared as well as ever. She said "are you ready for me?" and I said: "Yes: I am ready and willing". I then gave her the money and she went away.

'My husband,' added Mrs Weir, 'was at home at the time. He has no certain master, but he did not work for the deceased.'

The plight of Mr Weir was widespread at the time. With a surplus of labour flooding into London from Ireland and continental Europe, the large employers could operate on the most casual terms; men turning up outside the vast walls in the darkness of the pre-dawn hoping there might be a morning, or even a full day, of work. The effect on so many labourers was debilitating. Mrs Emsley would have seen many at-home husbands while she conducted her rounds.

Mrs Weir testified that the rent payments were entered meticulously in a book.

Now the coroner called upon a witness who was to prove, in the following weeks, to be an absolutely pivotal figure. In this backroom, there were no stands for the witnesses to take, so Walter Thomas Emm emerged from the general hubbub and started his testimonial.

'I live at Emsley's brickfield, Mile End and I am by trade a shoemaker. I collected rents for Mrs Emsley.'

In that one sentence, Emm had conveyed to the coroner and jury that he had a measure of respectability; more than this, he had the stability of some job security. He was a working man who could be trusted to collect money on behalf of a rich lady and to make sure all that money was delivered to her. Given her own compulsiveness on the subject, it is reasonable to imagine it took a long time for Mrs Emsley to fully trust anyone.

'I last saw her alive on the afternoon of this day week,' continued Emm. 'She was then in Barnsley Street, where she had just collected her last rents.'

From the point of view of the local jury, this would have been a source of some grim wonder. Visiting houses in the still semi-respectable Limehouse was one thing, but an old widow subjecting herself to the sights and roughness of Barnsley Street near Bethnal Green was another. It was not the lowest, by any means; the slums of the Old Nichol, a few streets further west, were even worse. Still, Barnsley Street was louring enough. It was a prospect of small, yellow-bricked terraced houses, each packed with tenants, sometimes sharing rooms. It was here that Mrs Emsley had got into a bitter dispute with one of her tenants, a mother with several children and no apparent father, just days before her murder. Walter Emm was accustomed to seeing hardship, yet there was an effort made to maintain standards in Mrs Emsley's various houses.

'We had a conversation about some brass taps which I had been putting on the water butts,' explained Emm. 'I told her I wanted more taps, and she directed me to send to her house for them. On the Tuesday I sent for some. My son, a lad of 16 years old, went, but he did not obtain them. I sent him again at night, and he came away without them.'

One of the jurors interrupted this careful testimony: 'Did you pay Mrs Emsley any money when you saw her on the Monday afternoon?'

'No,' replied Emm.

The coroner leant in: 'Did you go or send again to the house?'

'I went on Wednesday,' answered Emm. 'But I got no answer. I thought she might be at Stratford, as she usually went there to collect on a Wednesday. I went to Stratford; but I did not find her. I called at the house on the Wednesday evening and did not see her. I waited about till late that night. I sent my wife with the money on Thursday and she brought it back.

'My wife went to collect her own rents at Bromley,' continued the witness. 'And I went myself to Mrs Emsley's in the evening at eight o'clock. I could not get to see her and I went to Barnsley Street, thinking she might be there; but I did not find her.

'I went again to the house in Grove Road as late as eleven o'clock on Thursday night with the same result,' Emm then added. 'On the Friday morning, at about six o'clock, I sent my daughter, about eighteen years of age, to see if the parlour shutters were still open. She returned without gaining admission and said the shutters were in the same state as they had been all the week. I sent my wife down to the house and told her not to let anyone go in, as I was alarmed, and should go to Mrs Emsley's legal adviser.'

It is interesting that Emm's first priority was ensuring the presence of her solicitor, rather than a doctor. This suggests that Mrs Emsley's property was instinctively the chief concern.

'I went to Mr Rose,' continued Emm, 'and he said that perhaps she had gone for a holiday. I said I thought not, as she had asked me to go to Brighton with my wife and herself. Mr Rose and his son met me at the premises and the police were called.'

It was at this point that a juror asked Emm why it only occurred to him then to seek the assistance of the police.

'I did not speak to a policeman before that as I was not apprehensive of anything being wrong,' Emm responded. 'I should think that she would receive 25*l*. or 26*l*. on the Monday. She would come home about six or seven o'clock in the evening. She was not in the habit of showing large sums of money. Indeed she was very close in that respect. She was ill with a swimming in her head about two or three weeks back and I thought she might have died. That is why I sent my daughter on the Friday morning. I had a doubt about the state of her health on Wednesday evening.'

This caught the interest of one of the jurors.

'It seems strange to me that you should have had that doubt,' the juror interjected.

The coroner caught this swiftly.

'It is better for you not to offer any opinion in the presence of the witness,' he replied. 'You can call him again presently if you wish.'

'Very well, sir,' answered the juror. 'I think I shall have to.'

In his testimony, Emm had laid out a striking portrait of an independent elderly widow. With a sense of foreboding about the state of her health, it seemed not to have occurred to him to have contacted or consulted with Mrs Emsley's step-daughters or their husbands, all of whom lived close by.

Emm had also conveyed an impression of a rich lady who, while employing a shoemaker to collect up money, also suggested a seaside excursion with him and his wife. That was not the social connection one would expect of a woman of such means; Emm was her employee, but the portrait he offered the jury was one of respect and a certain friendship. The truth was more shaded.

The next witness to appear before the local jurors was Sergeant Dillon.

'From information I received I went on Friday, about twelve o'clock, to the house, no 9 Grove Road, in company with Mr Rose and there saw some other gentleman,' recounted the officer. 'The door was fast, and we obtained an entry through the next house. There were no marks on the door.

'I examined the parlours, first floor and second floor, but found nothing,' Dillon continued. 'In the third floor, front room, we found the deceased lying on the floor, with her head against the partition. The door was wide open. She was dressed, but one slipper was off. A doctor was sent for, and Dr Gill came and said she was dead and that she had been murdered.'

'Never mind that,' responded the coroner, adding that it would be for the jury to make that judgement when they had heard the medical testimony.

Sergeant Dillon returned to the detail of the many pieces of wallpaper, or paper-hangings, that filled the room. There were, he said, 'two pieces under her arm'. What had also struck him was the fact that there did not appear to be a forced entry to the house.

'I examined the place,' said the sergeant, 'and found no signs of violence, nor could I find marks indicating that any person had got over the wall.

'The back window of the basement was a little way open and the shutter was unfastened but there were no marks of the window having been forced,' added Dillon. 'The front door was simply on the lock, and the back door on the latch. Every door in the house was wide open. I searched the room but found no marks of the door having been forced.'

The jury was being asked to consider that this was not a burglary carried out by a violent stranger. Yet here was an old lady lying in a welter of blood. How much, asked the coroner, had been spilt as a result of Mrs Emsley falling to the floor? Sergeant Dillon was of the view that the 'blood on the doorpost' was the result of her head cracking against it as she collapsed.

'Was there,' asked the coroner, 'any more blood?'

'Beside the blood on the doorpost and the pool in the middle of the room,' replied Dillon, 'there were some slight marks on the landing outside and on the middle landing. There were some marks of blood, as if made by boot-nails, on the outside of the room.'

At this point, one of the jurors remarked on 'an indented mark near to the bottom of the wainscoting', as if it had been struck by something heavy.

'Yes,' agreed Dillon, 'as if someone had hit at her and the blow had missed. And there is another one higher up.'

Now it was time for the assembled jurors and spectators in that hotel back room to hear expert medical evidence.

'I am a member of the Royal College of Surgeons and registered,' began Dr Lawrence Gill. 'I am practising in Bow-road.'

The area of Bow had an interesting mix of tenants: poorer workers who lived in cheap houses (many owned by Mrs Emsley) and who had jobs in the stinking crude oil and coal tar distilleries a little further up the road on the banks of the River Lea at Fish Island. But there was also a number of slightly more well-to-do residents living just off the main road in the relatively gracious surrounds of Tredegar Square, in houses that architecturally echoed the properties that had sprung up in the more fashionable streets of Belgravia. The square and the whitewashed terraces that led off from it were still largely rented properties owned by the Morgan estate, but the tenants were in professional occupations.

'I was called on Friday last,' Dr Gill told the coroner, 'between twelve and one in the afternoon to the house no 9 Grove Road. On the third floor, in the front room, I found the body of the deceased woman. The odour of decomposing matter was almost unbearable, leading me to the opinion that she had been dead three or four days. The body was lying at full length on the floor, with the head towards the door post, and on the left side. The gown and upper petticoat were turned upwards over her head.

'A portion of the gown was in a slight twist,' he continued, 'with blood smeared upon it, as if fingers had been wiped upon it.

On removing the gown and petticoat I found two rolls of paper by her head.'

Dr Gill testified to the enormous quantity of blood on the floor and splashed on the walls. The blood on the walls was 'bright'. The corpse, he added, was grasping a table leg.

'I caused the body to be stripped,' continued the doctor, 'and found the dress to be sound, excepting a lace cap which was lying under her head, and from that the ornaments had been torn.

'There was a circular hole in the back of the cap corresponding with the hole, which was also circular, on the back of her head. The body was pale, excepting the chest, neck and abdomen, which were slightly purple, owing no doubt to the position in which the body had been lying.'

At this point, Dr Gill informed the jurors and onlookers that he had since made a much more thorough examination of the body.

'There was a lacerated wound, about an inch long, on the left ear,' he reported. 'A straight wound, an inch and a half long, on the left eyebrow, which I think was occasioned as she fell against the door-post. The whole of the scalp at the back of the head was displaced.

'On removing the scalp I found extravasated[1] blood universally over the whole of the skull, with a larger accumulation on the right side, above the right ear,' explained Dr Gill. 'The temporal bone on that side was broken into many pieces. Nearly the whole of the occipital bone was driven in, through the membranes, into the brain. I removed the skull-cap and found it much injured; the membranes on the left side were much congealed, corresponding with the fracture of the occipital bone. The external portions of the brain were filled with extravasated blood.

'The base of the brain was the same and the centre of the brain was unusually healthy for a person of Mrs Emsley's time of life.'

Added to this, the 'organs and contents of the chest and abdomen were healthy', said the doctor.

---

[1] 'Extravasated' simply means fluid forced out of its usual place or vessel.

The coroner wanted to know if it was possible to say what style and description of instrument was likely to have 'produced the wound on the head'.

'I think the wound ... was produced by some heavy circular blunt instrument,' replied Dr Gill.

'It might or might not have been a life-preserver,' interjected one of the jurors. In 1860, the term 'life-preserver' was given to a form of wooden telescopic truncheon which was a long-shafted instrument with a heavy flexible wooden ball at the end, marketed as an item of domestic self-defence. Such instruments were also used by violent offenders.

Finally, the coroner asked the doctor what, in his opinion, was the actual cause of death.

'Compression of the brain from a blow,' he answered.

'Could a fall have produced the wounds which produced death?' asked another juror.

'No,' responded Dr Gill. 'Nothing but a blow.'

The next to take the stand was Inspector Walter Kerressey, of K Division and based at Bow police station.

'From information I received, I went to the house no 9 Grove Road,' he began. 'I was admitted by the front door by Sergeant Dillon, 119K.'

Even in these reasonably early days of large-scale, citywide policing, the legal niceties of establishing even the smallest details were well-entrenched.

'In the back-yard, I saw Mr Rose and his son and Mr Whittaker,' continued the inspector. 'I went upstairs to the third floor and saw the deceased as previously described. The left-hand window was raised up about six inches.

'I came downstairs, and found the back-shutters on the basement door unclosed and unbolted and the window raised about a foot. I examined very carefully the shutters and the front door but could discover no marks of violence. I then searched the back part of the premises and went along the walls into the next garden but I could discover no marks of violence whatever.

'I afterwards searched the pockets of the deceased,' Inspector Kerressey added, 'and found a knife, but no money. On the first floor landing I found a small piece of paper, used for papering walls, with blood upon it. There was a little blood on the floor alongside of it. On the steps going upstairs to the top room, I found some marks of blood. It was about three steps up where I found the pieces of paper.'

'What part of the house was this?' asked one of the jurors.

'On the first floor landing,' replied the inspector. 'It was on the edge of the tread of the steps, close to where the deceased was lying. On the landing of the top floor, I also found blood.'

'And these marks,' asked the coroner, 'had the appearance of what?'

'Of foot marks,' answered Kerressey, 'as of a person in coming downstairs. That I have carefully preserved by nailing oil-skin over it. I have since examined the drawers and the bed and have had the water closet emptied, but I have not found any instrument whatever with any blood upon it. I immediately took possession of the premises.'

The jurors were fascinated by the murderer's means of entry.

'The back leads to Grove Street [sic] and any person to get into the garden from that direction must come through one of the houses,' declared one.

In other words, the homes of Grove Road and the neighbouring streets were built in a square pattern with all the back gardens enclosed within that square. There were no walls or fences to jump over; no passages to edge through under the shadows of night.

Another jury member wanted to hear more about this point – about how, in the opinion of the police, a killer might gain entrance to an otherwise secure property? At this stage, the coroner felt that the witnesses had contributed as much as they could for the moment with the evidence available. He had no choice but to adjourn the inquest.

The inquiry was yet to unfold more aspects of Mrs Emsley's unusual sensibility, and the coterie of male helpers that she kept around her. On the very day that the inquest was adjourned, there had been a new police search of 9 Grove Road. The constables had delved further through Mrs Emsley's cellar; as well as a quantity of firewood, they came across the half-hidden sum, in cash, of £48.

The question had been there from the start: if her killer had been an ordinary thief or burglar, perhaps surprised in the act by the unfortunate old lady, surely more would have been missing from the property? What was the nature, then, of this murderer who had effected entry via mysterious means and had left seemingly without leaving any trace, save for several footsteps in the blood? Did Mrs Emsley know her killer? Could it be that she – and her step-family – had made enemies in the course of amassing that extraordinary wealth?

For Conan Doyle, this was an important point: an old lady, fearless by day but suspicious by night, must have had an awareness of people who bore ill-will towards her.

'She showed . . . that extreme timidity and caution which are often characteristic of those who afterwards perish by violence,' he wrote, 'as if there lies in human nature some vague instinctive power of prophecy.' [5]

5

This Was Her Domain

❧

IN that 1901 essay for *The Strand Magazine*, Conan Doyle observed of Mrs Emsley's territory: 'The stranger in London who wanders away from the beaten paths and strays into the quarters in which the workers dwell is astounded by their widespread monotony, by the endless rows of uniform brick houses broken only by the corner public-houses and more infrequent chapels which are scattered amongst them.' [1]

The inquest jurors, locals and wider reading public were enthralled by the unfolding details of the shocking case, publicised not only in *The Times* but also in the more demotic local press. They had also been given a glimpse of the source of Mrs Emsley's wealth. Among those who had packed into the Railway Hotel were men of property. In 1860, there was a building boom throughout the capital, especially in the East End. Men from humble backgrounds, themselves builders or engineers, had seen the soundness of housing as an investment. Those who owned or part-owned several properties would have been curious to know exactly how many houses Mrs Emsley owned, and how she had acquired them.

The tide of wealth Mrs Emsley had enjoyed was directly linked to the economic bounty that was sailing into the vast docks.

Imperial trade brought rich silk and fur, wines, tobacco and vivid, fragrant spices, all stored in the huge warehouses which needed large numbers of men to handle the cargoes. These cheap labourers needed to rent dwellings close by.

For all the riches to be made by the merchants, London was a city of implacable economic ruthlessness for the less fortunate. Work for many, in the docks and across the East End in a variety of industries, was unpredictable and irregular. An income could disappear without warning. For those who were not nimble enough to learn new skills and trades, life was unceasingly fraught.

The shifting landscape of streets was disorientating. Incomers to this fast-growing city, and those who had always lived here, all had to make huge adjustments; few had ever lived in this way before. The momentum of the day had given way to a new cacophony of night: the roaring furnaces of the molten gasworks in Poplar, Bethnal Green, Limehouse; bakers at glowing ovens in Shadwell deep into the small hours; steamboats bringing fish up the Thames to Billingsgate by moonlight; night-soil men, almost delirious on gin, descending into backyard privies to dig out the excrement, piling heaps of ordure on to wagons, singing as they did so. For so many, unbroken sleep became a luxury.

Until fairly recently these streets had still been small villages surrounded by fields, orchards and market gardens; the growing city had swallowed them all. The parish churches remained, but these new, denser communities could not maintain social cohesion amid such transience.

The dark streets were evolving at speed. Since the start of the century, London's population had more than doubled to well over two million. This was reflected sharply in the East End. The population of Stepney in 1840 had been around 45,000; by 1860, it was closer to 100,000. Similar inflations occurred in Bethnal Green and Whitechapel. Parishes were filled to bursting; surrounding villages all around were being subsumed. The streets around the docks had been built up for longer; when the Regent's Canal and Limehouse Basin opened in 1820, the streets were already filling with industry and dwellings.

Close by in Whitechapel were several houses in Mrs Emsley's name. These handsome Georgian terraced properties on Philpot Street, built in the early years of the nineteenth century, with three storeys and courtyard back gardens, were just yards from the London Hospital. When they were originally built, the first tenants would have been retired sea captains, merchants, or senior clerks working at St Katherine's Dock or Shadwell. Although close to the rougher streets frequented by sailors and stevedores, these houses were a little removed from the clamour. The outdoor privies were emptied regularly.

By 1860, their bourgeois nature had fallen away dramatically. Where properties were once occupied by a single family, they were now filled with four or five. Children slept with parents, siblings shared beds (sometimes little more than covered palliasses). The courtyard privies, now emptied much less frequently, produced a terrible stench. Even so, no matter how harrowing these conditions might have seemed to the original occupants of the houses, for the poorer tenants who succeeded them, even the squalor and overcrowding were better than the conditions out in the countryside – or indeed in the remoter regions of the Continent – from which they had come.

Among the area's new inhabitants were immigrant Jews who had arrived from the farthest corners of Europe, and who brought a new energy to Whitechapel. In the early years of the century, there had been small Jewish communities in and around the city; now they were more familiar, woven deep into the economic life of the area. It would be a few years before Philpot Street got its own synagogues following the great immigration influx of the 1880s, but the street's Jewish residents were among those transforming the area.

In 1853, journalist Henry Mayhew caught some of the colour and atmosphere of the market in Petticoat Lane that the Jewish population had helped to alter.

'Wherever persons are assembled there are certain to be purveyors of provisions and of cool or hot drinks for warm or cold weather,' Mayhew wrote. 'The interior of the Old Clothes Exchange has its oyster-stall, its fountain of ginger beer, its coffee house, and alehouse, and a troop of peripatetic traders, boys principally, carrying trays. Outside the walls of the Exchange, this trade is still thicker. A Jew boy thrusts a tin of highly-glazed cakes and pastry under the peoples' noses here; and on the other side, a basket of oranges regales the same sense by its proximity. At the next step, the thoroughfare is interrupted by gaudy looking ginger beer, lemonade, raspberryade and nectar fountains; "a halfpenny a glass, a halfpenny a glass, sparkling lemonade!" shouts the vendor as you pass. The fountains and the glasses glitter in the sun, the varnish of the woodwork shines, the lemonade really does sparkle.' [2]

Obviously, it would take some time for this new and growing community to build its economic strength. Arrivals sailing in from the Continent and disembarking at Blackwall were registered, but not with the police, unlike in the rest of Europe. There were no limits or controls as such; once in London, the arrivals were home.

In Philpot Street, Judaism rubbed along next to an establishment catering boldly to a loudly vocal atheism. The noisy non-believers of the East End were curiously in tune with the debate raging in the summer of 1860 over Charles Darwin's theory of evolution. At the Commercial Hall, atheist speakers delivered thundering lectures about the inconsistencies of the Bible. In between these godless tirades, dancing girls would take to the stage to provide light relief. As the social observer Joseph Cartwright noted in his satirical poem 'Philpot Street: or The Infidels of Stepney': 'Oh if there is a God and he can hear / Come down and change this life of pain and fear!' [3]

Throughout the East End, failure to attend church was a widespread social phenomenon – at least for the Anglican church. In some streets of Old Ford and Bow Common (where Mrs Emsley owned properties), it was estimated that fewer than one in four families went to a church even occasionally. A surprising number had never set foot in one at all.

Those few who did attend were frequently non-conformist. By 1860, Whitechapel, Limehouse and Stepney could boast a wide variety of small places of worship: Methodist, Baptist, Quaker, Moravian, Apostolic and Lutheran, among many others.

Among Mrs Emsley's tenants, religious identity wasn't just about worship; it was about cultural identity. In Philpot Street, there was a meeting house for Scottish worshippers. The ever-increasing numbers of arrivals from Ireland prompted the building, in the 1850s, of new Catholic churches; handsome, grey-stoned structures in Shadwell, Whitechapel and near the docks at Poplar.

Outside of church, there was not always complete harmony between congregants and non-congregants. Around Philpot Street and further down on the Commercial Road, there were occasional outbreaks of tension between the Irish and German communities. Large numbers of Germans had arrived in the East End a little earlier in the century, settling in Shadwell and Limehouse, and frequently running bakeries. Sometimes, as one writer observed, the young German men who worked in the related refineries termed 'sugar bakeries' – hellishly hot, sometimes subterranean establishments – also lived in them, hidden away at the back in a dark 'burrow'. [4] For some reason, large numbers of fights would break out particularly between the Germans and Irish, usually after heavy consumption of drink. Pub landlords sometimes hired young German men to help keep order.

There was still a substantial silk industry in the area; the rich beauty and colour of the fabrics contrasting sharply with the increasingly frowzy streets, packed also with pigeon lofts and piggeries. These were tenants who, in a mechanised age, were still working as though they were an eighteenth-century cottage industry.

The silk weavers, many of whom still spoke the French of their Huguenot forebears, lived in properties that could double as homes and manufactories. This meant the upper storey of the house had unusually large windows in order to capture all the sunlight possible to maximise work hours. The silk looms themselves, large rectangular wooden frames in which the looms with all their delicate threads were suspended, took up much of a room. A bed might be fitted into a corner behind it. By 1860, the weavers' houses were thoroughly outdated.

The industry was in continual crisis and decline. Back in the previous century, the Spitalfields weavers had been vocal enough about falling trade to command the ears of Parliament. In 1837, one of Queen Victoria's first acts was to make the gesture of ordering twelve silk dresses from the East End weavers to help alleviate their economic woes; her example was then followed by other aristocrats. The weavers, who met in Bethnal Green pubs, cheered such help while also frequently plotting industrial action against 'masters', which could sometimes involve disabling their complex looms. At the time of Mrs Emsley's murder, the trade was appallingly precarious. In any one of those Bethnal Green houses, there could have been three or four looms being worked by various members of a family; the thrown silk, the material they worked with, was imported from China and India and bought from a middleman. The weavers worked in conditions of throat-catching dust and dirt; their children forced by lack of space to sleep under the looms. Some had songbirds to try to alleviate the tedious noise of the weaving. However, these craftspeople were being outpaced by technology. New machinery was also depressing their wages. Why pay extra when one could get the fabric made much more cheaply in one of the larger factories outside London?

In 1860, there was a further blow to the silk weavers in the signing of the Cobden-Chevalier Treaty – in essence, an Anglo-French trade agreement which allowed for the tariff-free importation of French silk. To be caught between that and the increasing mechanisation of the trade was lethal.

Not all of Mrs Emsley's tenants were mired in economic misery, though. Limehouse had seen the construction of new streets and a square of houses in the Georgian and Regency years that were, by the 1850s, well-suited to a rising class of clerical workers. Mrs Emsley had houses on Salmon Lane and Matlock Street. In contrast to the denser housing of Bethnal Green and Whitechapel, the streets here were elegant and wide. That said, shortcuts had been taken during the construction in the 1830s. The terraced houses were supposed to have been larger, but many ended up as two-storey buildings. Nonetheless, there were private and public gardens; Salmon Lane, which had been a pleasant country road leading down through market gardens down to the river just a few decades earlier, now made for a respectable, if not quite fashionable, address.

The jurors and the public at the inquest would have heard gossip about how much further Mrs Emsley's property empire extended; that it reached into the grey and green marshes that lay downriver, past Gallions Reach, into the town of Barking, which was not yet a London suburb, but which was starting to grow with ever more new-built dwellings. These would have been more attractive than many of the older dilapidated cottages in the flat countryside around. Even in the more prosperous rural corners, poverty could actually be more distressing than the squalor suffered by those in the inner city. Many rural homes, especially those built on or near marshy ground, ran with damp; the flooring oozed and neglected thatched roofs let in rain.

Mrs Emsley also had a couple of properties out in a quiet, rather remote little village called Dagenham, where there were some grand stone houses, a handsome church, and other houses, weather-boarded and clustered around a village green.

One of the more significant sectors of Mrs Emsley's property investments lay in another small town, Stratford-at-Bow. Situated close to the River Lea, and the maze of its tributaries upon which windmills still turned, this small town had grown into something quite different over the past two decades. 1840 had brought the Eastern Counties Railway, along with the rail works and goods yards that were set up on what had been muddy reed beds. By 1860, it was a vast industry with lines that stretched to Colchester, Ipswich, Bishops Stortford and Cambridge.

Yet more building was underway, to expand and improve the frequency of the train services, which were starting to carry passengers on a daily basis from their homes to their places of work in the city. For a long time, Stratford had an element of transience about it; before the advent of steam, it was a place to find excellent coaching inns to feed and water the horses and rest for the night before setting off into the country or into London. Now the element of impermanency came from a fresh population that was being housed on rapidly built roads and streets around the railway yards.

The railway company had provided accommodation for its workers in an area that quickly became known as Stratford New Town, a little to the east of the station. Many of these labourers were from Ireland. As the railway network spread across the countryside, these were the men who performed the intensive work of laying the track beds and tracks. While working in the country, they were frequently housed in the most basic communal halls, with bunks and a fire at the end of the room. The work at Stratford was less spartan and more varied, and the Irishmen who arrived in the area brought their families. Soon, the weight of numbers created a wealth of employment in local trade; around Angel Lane, there was a lively market – close to Mrs Emsley's properties on the same road.

By 1860, the area was dense with industry, and the waters of the Bow Back Rivers ran purple with dye from the works. Old water-mills were shadowed by the construction work upon a mighty and colourful baroque palace, the creation of Joseph Bazalgette, which was to house the pumps for the new sewage works that would carry waste from the centre of town all the way down to the Thames at the Beckton Marshes. This was an area rich in opportunities for landlords.

So many of the tenants that Mrs Emsley housed were having to learn how to live in this completely new way; transplanted from the natural rhythms of the country to a village that never ended, with main streets that never grew dark and working at jobs that required labour to continue deep into the night.

Those nights held other possibilities, too. The unaccustomed anonymity of the City (unlike small villages) and the labyrinth of darkened streets were, for some, a chance to seek out furtive sexual encounters of all varieties. With the docks and sailors came the brothels; but even the more respectable streets held out erotic possibilities (though naturally rather more for men than women). As much as there was misery, there was an equal determination and appetite among these new city dwellers to savour the pleasures of this nocturnal world.

The jurors who had gazed upon the battered corpse of Mrs Emsley must, like the police, have instantly jumped to conclusions about the nature of her attacker: the sort of man who could use a heavy instrument with such bestiality in the apparent flicker of an eye. The police certainly had reached for class distinctions, making special mention of her 'low' tenants on the Ratcliff Highway. The next stage of the inquest was to open up more possibilities – and also to reveal more about the curious nature of Mrs Emsley's wealth, how she dealt with it, and how her own unyielding attitude may well have provided any suspect with the trigger point he needed.

6

'Of Operations So Delicate'

❧

Barely a week after the discovery of Mrs Emsley's corpse, public houses throughout the East End were echoing with drink-fuelled debates about the killing. People discussed the murderer who still moved among them, perhaps with an edge of macabre delight. There was also the subject of the old woman's money. What would become of all her tenants – and all her riches?

The weight of pressure and expectation, and the need to keep control of potential hysteria and any hint of vigilante reprisals, was already beginning to tell on the police. It didn't help that the press was simultaneously in a state of tasteless excitement about the murder of a small child in the Wiltshire village of Road, which was being investigated by a Scotland Yard detective called Jack Whicher. This was a new age of mass media; while newspapers had been long established, the coming of the railways and telegraph meant that news could travel throughout the nation in the space of a single night. Excitable correspondents were raising public expectations of the perspicacious powers of the police.

Perhaps ten or twenty years before, the discovery of Mrs Emsley's corpse would have been a local talking point that few outside the district would come to hear of. Now, all the latest developments, even the tiniest speculative titbits, were featured in newspapers everywhere. It was a national sensation. In turn, this led to the Home Office leaning hard on the officers of K Division to deliver results.

Although they lacked the advantages of developed forensic techniques and analysis, the officers were starting to exploit a growing national network of contacts and informants. The police had to be discreet, though. They could only hint to the hungry press that they were ahead of the investigation.

A reporter from *The Times* (there were no bylines then) who had been assigned to the case was eager to relay every fresh twist.

'A rumour was current last night in the vicinity of the murder,' he reported, 'that the relatives of the deceased intend to offer some considerable reward for the apprehension and conviction of the assassin. This, or a similar step on the part of the Home Secretary, would doubtless stimulate exertion, and the more so if it were offered quickly, when the matter is fresh in the public mind.' [1]

A few days later, it was confirmed that, 'Mr Faith and Mr Whittaker, who each married a stepdaughter of the murdered woman, expressed their intention to offer a reward between them of 200*l*. The Home Secretary can scarcely do less.' [2]

The idea of a reward suggested that Mrs Emsley's stepchildren had a lingering sense of loyalty, or even affection, towards the old lady, despite the absence of blood ties. Alternatively, it might also have suggested that there was some tension in the family over what was to become of her vast estate; a cynical view might be that the offer of money to catch the murderer would have helped when it came to the matter of addressing the glaring absence of a will.

They might have wanted to demonstrate that they had more of a claim to their stepmother's property than the Crown, or indeed other potential claimants, of which they knew that there would be many.

For the sake of keeping local order, the police were keen to intimate to the public that they were not simply flailing around – there were indeed promising clues that they were pursuing. However, the message that K Division and Scotland Yard hoped to convey through the press was rather garbled.

'It is said,' continued *The Times*' report, 'there are circumstances pointing to a certain conclusion, but as to the nature of them, and the course of action being taken, the authorities occupied in the investigation are obliged for the present to manifest a necessary reserve, as well to prevent their exertions being baffled as, in the event of being on the wrong scent, to keep secret the fact that they were ever set foot in that direction lest, in a matter so delicate, suspicion should possibly alight upon an innocent person.' [3]

There was indeed great delicacy here: an implicit suggestion that a misplaced accusation could lead to mobs taking matters into their own hands.

'Those engaged in the inquiry seem sanguine of success,' added the report, 'and there is a general belief that the murderer will, before long, be in the hands of justice.' [4]

The paper noted that it was at this point that Mrs Emsley's solicitor, Mr Rose, had arranged for a temporary interment. Prior to a proper funeral, her body was 'placed first in a leaden and then an oak coffin and removed from her late residence to the Tower Hamlets cemetery.' [5]

At the time, unburied bodies were doubly sealed in this fashion because of leakages in the process of decay. Despite medical advances, many believed that disease was carried directly by foul-smelling air, so there was a special sensitivity about the disposal of the dead. Mrs Emsley could not be buried until the inquest process was concluded. Until that time, her body was placed in a repository in the large and elegant cemetery where her second husband Samuel was laid to rest in 1856.

In the meantime, there were more questions about the amount of cash kept in Mrs Emsley's house, and how much of a motive for her murder it might have been.

'It is supposed by those best acquainted with her affairs that she might have had 50*l*. or 100*l*. in the house on the Monday night on which it is presumed the murder was committed,' declared *The Times*. 'The manner in which the 48*l*. was found secreted in her coal cellar on Monday morning last, when the house was being searched, assuming it was placed there by her own hands, is a little suggestive of her penurious frame of mind, and it may be of an apprehension that the knowledge of her wealth might conduce to an attempt at robbery or violence.' [6]

The newspaper went on to describe local views of the old lady, which formed a portrait of a tyrant. She would visit houses 'collecting [rent] personally from a humble class of people, to none of whom she gave, on any pretence, more than a week's grace, and in case of non-payment had immediate recourse to a speedy process of ejectment unknown to the law'. [7]

The apparent harshness of Mrs Emsley's dealings with her tenants was clearly a theme that had been outlined to the reporter by the police and by interested neighbours and worthies in Mile End Old Town. As the East End slums were starting to attract attention from writers and observers as far away as America, there was a sense of social reform in the air. Even in the most desperate districts, paving stones slippery with urine, or soft with mounds of black ash, families huddling in rooms sometimes together with the dead bodies of the elderly and small children who had recently died, there were parish laws concerning adequate notice periods.

Quietly, the police were carefully keeping one step ahead of the newspaper reporters. They were now pursuing a line that told its own story about the emotional life of Mrs Emsley. One of the other items that could not be found anywhere within her house was one of her mourning rings.

In this sense, the intelligence network was impressive. The police had put word out to specialist jewellers in Liverpool, Manchester and Birmingham about this missing gold ring. A few days later, the team at Scotland Yard received a letter from a Birmingham jeweller called Mr Allen. He had seen such a ring, which had been engraved 'to the memory of J Jones who died 1830'.

'I beg to state I received on Friday last some rings from [sic] customer of mine,' wrote Mr Allen, 'which came to me to have the letter cut out [of the ring] and to be enamelled plain black. Not to show any letters. The ring I put in hand and have had the letters cut out and one of them . . . had the name John Jones. The letters were Roman style. You must be aware we have many such jobs . . . to take the letters out and therefore we do not think of noticing the letters . . . the ring can easily be sworn to by the jeweller who made it.'

The jewellers, he explained, always put on a special mark for identification.

'I believe the ring no 1 is the one that had the name John Jones upon it,' continued Mr Allen, 'but have sent number 2 for your inspection as possibly I might be mistaken.' [8]

The jeweller did have a plea for the officers he was helping: if the rings turned out to be unconnected with the murder case, he wanted them returned to him immediately.

Inspector Thornton was quick to inform his superiors about this exciting development.

'I beg to submit the annexed letter [sic] and rings received this morning from Mr Allen of Birmingham stating that the said rings had been sent to him by a Customer to enamel,' he wrote to the Commissioner at Scotland Yard. '[One ring] is the same description as that which was one of the rings supposed to have been stolen from Mrs Emsley . . . Mr Allen does not state who the customer is that sent it to him.' [9]

The inspector concluded that it would be best if an officer was sent to Birmingham to question Mr Allen further. A young policeman called Richard Tanner was dispatched, and submitted his report a few days later.

'I . . . saw Mr Allen who informed me that he received the rings from Mr Norton also of Birmingham,' wrote Tanner. 'This gentleman I also saw, who said the rings were sent to him by "Mr Daniels" of Liverpool to alter.' [10]

On his own initiative, Tanner had continued his journey on to Liverpool.

'I saw "Mr Daniels" who informed me he could not tell from whom he had got the rings,' continued Tanner in his report. 'He was quite sure he had them over two years in his possession. It is customary with him to take such articles in exchange allowing the value of old gold and when he clears out the old gold box, if there is any article worth altering and made saleable, he does not break it up, this was the case with the rings in question.'

There was a postscript: 'I beg to add that this day I have shown the rings in question to Mr Faith.' [11]

In the meantime, the Crown was starting to take a vehement interest in the affair. The murder – and the victim's money – was being discussed in Whitehall. It was quite clear that the machinery of government was being used to apply pressure.

'Mr Rose, in an interview he had yesterday with the Solicitor to the Treasury, informed that gentleman that in all probability, the whole of the property belonging to the deceased will revert to the Crown for want of kindred, and assuming she has died intestate, which there is every reason to believe, since a very careful search among her papers for any testamentary document has until now been wholly fruitless,' reported *The Times*. [12]

Curiously, Mrs Emsley used to joke about the lack of a will meaning that her wealth would be handed straight to Queen Victoria. However, the Crown was being too presumptive over the lack of kin, for at this point a nephew materialised. While anyone of sensibility would wish to avoid a ghoulish gold rush before an arrest for the murder, this man – a Limehouse resident – clearly saw that there was some urgency.

'A poor shoemaker named Samuel Williams ... who states that

he is the eldest son of a brother (now dead) of Mrs Emsley, has applied to be recognised as her next-of-kin.' [13]

As a shoemaker, Williams was following a family tradition, and like so many thousands of fellow shoemakers across London, was living in hollow poverty. He and his sister Elizabeth Gotz, who was living in equally modest circumstances in Whitechapel with her husband Joseph, might not at that stage have fully comprehended just how vast this inheritance was, nor how greedily the Crown was prepared to fight for it.

The Times seemed to take the establishment view. It reported that Williams had a younger brother. This was in fact the soldier in Portsmouth of whom the police had remarked on his 'bad character'. He presented himself in London to make a similar claim to the property. The newspaper noted that the siblings, 'have been unable to produce the register of marriage of their father and mother, which the elder brother says took place in a Lambeth church, but where an unsuccessful search has been made in the vestry.'

In the early nineteenth century, birth, marriage and death records were not regularised to a national system; they were the responsibility of the local parishes. It was Williams' misfortune to have either misremembered or have been misinformed about the church. All the certificates he would need did in fact exist, but not where he thought.

'So, for the present,' reported *The Times*, '. . . it is not improbable that the whole of the property left behind her, which is very considerable, may go to augment the revenues of the Crown.' [14]

There was another issue, a subject of frequent scandal and legal conflict at the time: the question of parentage. The government solicitors appeared to have unearthed an extraordinary fact: that Mrs Emsley was 'a bastard'. This in itself, if proved in court, would render her fortune forfeit; the Crown would have a huge legal claim to it. The solicitors lost no time in leaking this allegation to the press.

'Since the death of a sister, about four years ago, whose

59

legitimacy was questioned,' announced *The Times*, '[Mrs Emsley] herself is said to have denied the existence of a single blood relation.'

The solicitors had clearly been able to conduct more thorough research into her parents than the poor shoemaker.

The newspaper also recorded Mrs Emsley's own purported views on the disbursement of her worldly goods: 'The intention she expressed of disposing of her wealth to found an almshouse after her death gives colour to the notion that she regarded herself as friendless.' (15)

And while there were no fresh revelations concerning the mourning rings, *The Times* kept its readers abreast with other developments: 'It appears to be assumed as indisputable by the police authorities engaged in the effort to discover the murderer that he entered the house by the front door, that she herself admitted him, and – what is more remarkable – that the murder was committed in daylight, for there was no candle found in the room, nor any appearance of any.

'Assuming that the murder took place under those circumstances,' continued the report, 'its audacity almost exceeds its barbarity, for Grove Road, in which the deceased's house was situated, is not only itself an open thoroughfare in which there is very considerable traffic, but immediately abuts upon the Bow-road – one of the greatest arteries in the metropolis.

'The smallness of the booty, probably from 50*l.* to 100*l.* with which the murderer was able to make away with rather lessens the chance of detection for, supposing the plunder to have been considerable, and that the assassin had accomplices with whom he shared it, the difficulty of keeping a fearful secret would have been great.

'By some, it is thought for the moment that the murderer is one of a gang who are known and, if that be so, the speedy offer of a large reward, accompanied by a free pardon, to any accomplice whose hand did not actually deal the fatal blow may be expected to result in the assassin being rendered up to justice.' (16)

Police stumbles were natural; in a wider sense, they were having to negotiate a completely new landscape. Where just years before they had patrolled small communities and had been familiar with local recidivists, there were now streets teeming with thousands of people, a great many of whom were effectively anonymous and transitory. Police procedures had previously relied on superior local knowledge, but Mrs Emsley's residents numbered in their hundreds, and in wildly different districts.

'Of operations so delicate,' ran an excited inside report, 'and conducted with the view to the attainment of an important end, secrecy and discretion are of the very essence.' [17]

From this point onwards, the general public would not be privy to police thinking.

The case, rather poignantly, also attracted the attention of eccentrics. One such person, living in Edinburgh, anxiously got in touch with the newspapers. She claimed that Mrs Emsley was 'a long-lost particular friend' and 'stated that she was married to a gentleman named Tosha previous to 1815, that her father was long a factor [gamekeeper] to the Earl of Wemyes, and that her family was of the highest respectability.' [18]

A charming and innocent fantasy, but curiously very much less interesting than the truth. The life of Mrs Emsley, from her birth in 1790 as Mary Williams, was scored with hardship and spectacular reversals, the very least of which appeared to concern her legitimacy. For anyone who accused her of insensitivity towards her poorer tenants, very few, if any, knew that Mrs Emsley had herself strived to survive in those dark streets in her younger years.

Her entire life had been based within a mile radius of the church of St Dunstan's in Stepney. In the Georgian and Regency years, as the East End transformed from a district of market gardens and heaths to closely-built, filthy slums, she had witnessed the violent birth agonies of the modern city.

7

'I Deal in Old and New Things'

Mrs Emsley's footsteps frequently crossed those of the man who was to be accused of murdering her. Did either ever have the shivering sense of walking over the other's graves? Years before they met, victim and murder suspect would possibly have known each other by sight; in an area that was otherwise so transient – sailors, ship's crews, immigrant visitors – those who lived here permanently were familiar and known faces. The young Mrs Emsley very rarely ventured beyond the parish of St Dunstan's in which she was born and christened. In some ways, she was like a villager in a remote part of the country, seemingly incurious about the wider world beyond.

Perhaps this was not so unusual. At the end of the eighteenth century, east London was not quite fully urbanised. Aside from the growing docks, the land around Georgian Stepney, without buildings, was green and chalky. The local church, set back from the river by about half a mile, was still very much the focus of the community. Its spire, visible for miles, was also a focus for seamen sailing up the Thames, rounding the loop of the Isle of Dogs peninsula.

A church had stood on this site, on what was then White Horse Road (sometimes simply The Old Road) since the tenth century. It eventually became St Dunstan's, named after the saint famed for having tweaked the Devil's nose with red-hot pincers. It was rebuilt in the fifteenth century with Kentish ragstone. The bells are featured in the nursery rhyme *Oranges and Lemons* – 'When will that be? Say the bells of Stepney'.

In the late eighteenth century, the area near the church had not yet acquired notoriety for either poverty or the wild excesses of drink, drugs and sex for which it would become famed. The road that ran past the church, north through Stepney, to the sweet-scented market gardens of Bethnal Green and Hackney beyond, still had the flavour of a country lane. To the south, as the road approached the river and the reclaimed marshes, there was a heavily nautical atmosphere, not just in the rope-makers' fields, or in the ships' supply shops, but also in the pubs and inns. The Grapes, a tourist attraction today, was already a very well-established pub by the river, together with a long row of handsome houses.

A copy of the marriage certificate of Mary Williams' parents – the same certificate that her nephew Samuel Williams failed to find – does miraculously still exist.

'Marriages solemnised in the Parish of St Dunstan's Stepney in the County of Middlesex in the year 1780,' it begins. Samuel Williams, 'of this parish and hamlet of Ratcliff Batchelor [sic] and Mary Poupard of this Parish and the same hamlet were married in this church by Banns this 5th day of September, 1780.' [1]

The curate was Mr Watkins and their witnesses were Elizabeth Coleman and Robert Vaughan.

Samuel Williams senior was a shoemaker; his new wife (and this was to prove a curious and seemingly intractable glitch when it came to the matter of the murdered woman's property) was born in the

Netherlands. There is no record of when she came to England, but immigration from Europe to the east of London had been fluid for centuries.

Mary's siblings were brothers William, John and Samuel and a sister, Elizabeth. Before such things were regularised, parish records were occasionally lost. For this reason – and also because family trees drawn up decades later for legal reasons had conflicting details – the birth order is not wholly certain. But it seemed Mary was the youngest and William was the eldest.

At this time, the population of the community numbered a little over a thousand. Ratcliff hugged the shore of the river, just to the west of Limehouse; it was here that the smaller sailing boats would land at Ratcliff Stairs and take on supplies. Goods and cargo were not licensed to be dropped here, as that was already the secured business of the big docks; the quieter nature of the shipping traffic – ships' crews coming ashore to pick up food and new clothing – meant the area was not perhaps quite so raucous as the streets around Shadwell and Wapping. Added to this, a number of retired captains and master craftsmen had chosen to make their homes in Ratcliff; some living in the more elegant houses on Narrow Street, others among the fields near St Dunstan's.

Even for the more modestly waged residents, Ratcliff was pleasantly situated, and there was at least no shortage of work. There was a glass manufactory nearby, immersed in the relatively new production of panes for newly fashionable sash windows, as well as goblets and ornamental glassware for the wealthier households.

In 1794, when Mary Williams was four, the community was practically destroyed overnight by a catastrophic fire. It started, according to one account, 'at Mr Clove's establishment on Cock Hill'. [2] As many of the humble houses were timber-framed, there was nothing that could abate the fury of the inferno. Some 450 houses and 'dwellings' were burned to the ground. The disaster presaged the new age of molten industry.

There was close-built new housing, and the great docks on the Isle of Dogs drew in huge numbers of labourers. This once rural parish was ill-prepared. As Mary grew up, she would also have seen signs of increasing poverty; the first indications in the area of overcrowding and uncertain, irregular employment.

Even for those in stable households, life was becoming a new game of hazards; London in 1800 was beginning to teem with disease caused by increasingly rotten sanitation and toxic supplies of water. In quick succession, young Mary lost one of her brothers and her sister. Though the causes of their deaths were not documented, it is reasonable to assume they had, in effect, been poisoned by their surrounds. On New Year's Day 1800, Mary's mother died at just thirty-seven years old. Again, the cause of death was not given, but Mary Poupard's passing was registered at the Independent Chapel in Rose Lane.

She was buried in a rather more aesthetically pleasing spot in the graveyard of St Anne's at Limehouse, a beautiful church designed by Nicholas Hawksmoor, built between 1714 and 1727. The church and a few grand houses that abutted the churchyard were still surrounded with apple trees. Ten-year-old Mary was left with her father and two remaining brothers.

In 1801, plans to extend the scope of the nearby West India Docks were put into motion. Mary would have been witness to the substantial undertaking that was involved in the excavation of what was to become Limehouse Basin. Such intensive labour required the importation of a new labouring community. Ratcliff, which had been known since the time of the Stuarts as 'Sailortown' now had a more distinctly industrial flavour.

Gradually, the fields and the orchards to the north of this new dock, together with the gravelly rural lanes, were encroached upon to make way not just for new housing, but also new types of manufactory.

It was not altogether bleak. For the more fortunate children in the area, there were a variety of charitable institutions that provided education: the fundamentals of literacy and numeracy, plus a little Greek, Latin and rhetoric. One could either enrol as a charitable student (the parents required to pay for stationery) or for the better-off, one could pay fees. The Coopers' Company had been running a school in the area in the 1500s; it was still there in Ratcliff, but it seems that Mary was not a pupil. In later life, she did not seem to have any ability to write.

Just before Mary Williams was born, there had been the echoing booms of the French Revolution from across the Channel. The news of the overthrow of the Bourbons had been greeted by many in London with a mix of euphoria and fascination. This world appeared fresh with possibility, yet the bloodshed in France seemed unstoppable. Shortly afterwards, Britain found itself at war with France in defence of the Low Countries.

Those living in Ratcliff would have seen the consequences of these conflicts, including the ever-increasing numbers of continental refugees passing through their hamlet in search of asylum. Imports were now severely restricted and white bread had to be rationed. Many men in the area had to be watchful for agents of the Navy's sharply coordinated Impress Service. For some years, seamen had been kidnapped by press gangs, finding themselves forced into service on Royal Navy ships. In Ratcliff, the hazard was clear for all men who wished to avoid being swept up.

The wider geopolitical convulsions also had an impact on local lives and communities. This included both Mary Williams and the man who would later be accused of her murder. The conflict with France, which fast developed into a pan-European war involving Austria, Germany and Russia, had political effects throughout the British Isles. Out of anxiety over the possibility of French infiltration or invasion of Ireland, the British government tightened the act of Union, and continued to repress the rights of Catholics.

This helped to foment deepening resentment among the Irish. The war, which created food shortages everywhere, prompted ever greater numbers to migrate from Ireland to England. Many landed at Liverpool and travelled to Whitechapel, Shadwell and Stepney.

Around 1802, the man who was later to be tried for the murder of Mrs Emsley was born in County Limerick. His family would be one of the many who were forced to make that journey to London.

Despite those war years, young Mary would have been witness to wondrous changes too. She would have been quite used to other cultures and religions; Mary would have seen the sailors coming in from the Indian subcontinent and the very first of the Chinese migrants to put down roots in Shadwell.

Even as the streets around her became more claustrophobic, Mary stayed close to Ratcliff. In 1810, when she was twenty, she fell in love. Inside the cool grey stone and buttresses of St Dunstan's, she took the hand of John Jones, declared to be 'of this parish'. The ceremony was witnessed by Elizabeth Davis and David Davis. Like Mary's father, John Jones was a shoemaker. With the city's population fast growing, this seemed a secure trade. However, Ratcliff was in decline, and even with steady business, their lives were to become a struggle.

As Mary and John remained in the area, Mary's brother Samuel formed different plans, even though he too was in the shoemaking trade. In 1811, Samuel, then aged twenty-three, married Mary Richey, 'in the parish of St Mary Lambeth'. She could neither read nor write, and in place of a signature, she marked a cross on documentation that was to become, fifty years later, absolutely crucial to the surviving relatives of Mrs Emsley. [1]

By that year, there was a strong undercurrent of violence in Ratcliff, often occasioned by the screaming late-night quarrels between men and women outside the proliferating pubs on the largely unlit streets. A sense of darker danger was sharpened by the maze-like alleys around St George-in-the-East. An atrocity committed on the Ratcliff Highway in 1811 achieved a measure of macabre fame nationwide and then across the world.

Just before midnight on a winter Saturday, Timothy Marr, a tailor, linen draper, and hosier on the Ratcliff Highway, sent family serving girl Margaret Jewell on an errand to buy some oysters. They were intended as a treat for the household, which included Marr's wife Celia and his apprentice James Cowan, at the end of a long working day. The late hour might seem striking today, but Saturdays in the East End were busy with commerce deep into the night in the nineteenth century. Whitechapel would be luminous with oil lamps and splashes of red and bright blue of the women's clothing on sale.

Margaret found the oyster shop had just shut at midnight; the local baker had also closed. When she returned to the Marr house, it was darkened and she couldn't get anyone to answer the door. Puzzlement swiftly gave way to alarm; the help of a nightwatchman was sought; he and a neighbour managed to force their way into the shop. On doing so, the nightwatchman gave out a cry: 'See what murder has been committed here!' [2]

In the few minutes the serving girl had been on her errand, the entire family had been slaughtered in a frenzy: 'the carnage of the night stretched out on the floor'. [3] The premises were awash with blood. The apprentice's face had been pulverised, his brains on the wall; the Marrs had also been smashed to a pulp. Even their little baby son was found in his cradle with his throat cut. The killer had apparently left his weapon at the scene: a heavy shipwright's hammer known as a maul.

The newlywed Mary Jones, who lived and worked on Brook Street, just a short walk from the crime scene, would have not only observed, but surely would have been part of the local tumult that resulted as the news got around.

The next horror came a few days later, when the proprietors of the King's Arms, a notably respectable public house, were also found slaughtered, together with their serving woman.

The authorities closed in on a man they considered their chief suspect: an Irish sailor called John Williams. He was an acquaintance of the murdered Timothy Marr; both men had served on board the same ship.

Williams, a good-looking young man with rather startling bright, yellow-orange hair, according to those who knew him, had also been seen drinking in the Kings Arms. The case did not seem to be very much more substantial than that, yet he was arrested and held in Coldbath Fields Prison. It was clear that the local magistrates were presuming his guilt long before alibis and other lines of enquiry had been exhausted.

Before the case could come to trial, Williams was found hanged in his cell. With their suspect dead, the authorities pronounced him the killer. Williams' body was loaded on to a cart and drawn slowly along Ratcliff Highway so the locals could see that the terrifying serial killer could menace them no more. Mary and John Jones would probably have been on the route: the procession was said to have drawn about 180,000 people (though that figure must surely be an exaggeration). Williams was buried at a crossroads with a stake driven through his heart.

The evidence, which included the maul, some allegedly blood-stained trousers, and the vague words of some witnesses, was circumstantial at best. However, the police, local parish vestrymen, and indeed the Home Office, seemed anxious that there was no public doubt on the matter: the hideous murders were the work of this Irish sailor. There have since been suggestions that even though there were other suspects, the pressure was on the authorities to secure a swift and satisfactory conclusion, possibly because the alternative might have been scenes of unrest in an area which was already getting close to anarchy. In any event, there were curious echoes between the Ratcliff Highway case and, forty-nine years later, the murder of Mrs Emsley.

After the Napoleonic Wars, as the streets of Ratcliff and Limehouse became busier and more industrialised, Mary's older brother John decided to make the journey, like so many others, to America.

Emigrants would travel to Liverpool to sail to New York and Boston. At this time, there were huge numbers of poor Irish passengers, many with young families, who undertook the gruelling journey largely below deck, with weekly rations dished out by the crew so they might cook their own meals in a communal eating area. Those who were a little better off could buy themselves places in tiny cabins, offering a least a modicum of privacy.

The land for which Mary's brother set out was still, in many areas, territory to be seized, colonised and exploited. Even though it is unclear quite where in America John established himself, he was to do so with great success.

John would have certainly much greater material success than Mary and her husband could ever hope to find in Ratcliff. By the 1830s, they were still in Brook Street, the reputation of which was plummeting inexorably; it was fast becoming a rackety slum.

The chronicler Sydney Maddocks unsympathetically traced the changing nature of the streets, from the loss of some of its old crafts to the infusion of many new souls in the neighbourhood.

'The Irish came and took possession for many years of the houses which until then had been decently and tidily kept,' he wrote. 'They were a rough, hard-working, hard-drinking (if they had the wherewithal) warm-hearted, hot-headed people, who had an objection to paying rent, and loved to have a shindy among themselves, with a constable or two to fortify the mixture.' [4]

With a shade more understanding, here is a story of immigrant families struggling to find a foothold in a vast and unknowable city; finding limitations on the sort of lodgings they could secure without references (or much money); finding regular employment a more elusive prize than they might have thought when facing the bleak vista of failed harvests and agricultural poverty; and finding that drink and close family were the salves that healed the wounds caused by the daily struggle to earn pennies.

Life was scarcely any more secure for those who had spent their entire lives in the parish. According to a family tree drawn up for legal reasons sometime after Mrs Emsley's murder, it appears that she was not in fact childless; she and John had had a baby together, but the infant had died by the age of two. No exact dates were cited, not even age or sex. All the lawyers wanted to know later was that the child was definitely dead.

The courts had no interest in the shock of grief, or the years of helpless bereavement that surely followed.

In 1833, Mary suffered the further trauma of the death of her husband. Again, the records drawn up for legal reasons stated the fact baldly without stating the cause. It is possible he was one of the later victims of the cholera epidemic that had swept through the capital with particular apocalyptic ferocity in 1832, its causes remaining misunderstood for another 25 years.

Men, women and children were seized with severe diarrhoea and vomiting. Due to profound medical ignorance, most died swiftly from complications caused by severe dehydration. The cholera epidemic had begun in Sunderland the previous year, having been brought over from mainland Europe. The courts and lanes of Ratcliff were ideal for the disease; grossly insanitary, greenish-brown toxic water supplies, nowhere free from traces of human waste. The symptoms were, even by the standards of illness then, repulsive to begin with and then horrifying, as the victims lay helpless with blue skin and sunken eyes.

In the 1830s, a sewage system was non-existent in Ratcliff; a stream which was referred to locally as 'the Black Ditch' ran through Limehouse instead. This slurry cut a channel near Brook Street and emptied into the Thames by Limekiln Wharf. It was even more foul than the famously poisonous River Fleet. There was, by then, a rudimentary water supply of sorts, frequently via standpipes, provided by the East London Waterworks Company. A number of their pipes were wooden and they were drawing water from the River Lea, which was itself hardly pure. It is remarkable that so many locals survived.

As a widow in early middle age, Mary Jones was left running the increasingly struggling shoemaking business that she and John had built up. It was her living and her home.

She took in a teenage ward called Emma Cornish. The provenance of Miss Cornish was not completely clear, and it is reasonable to speculate that her own parents died in the cholera epidemic. Whatever the case, it was both a good and practical thing for Mary to have offered her a home. It meant she had an assistant, or even housemaid, to help keep everything afloat. Equally, Emma was spared the possibility of having to enter the workhouse.

In 1839, a minor theft from the shoe shop threw an intriguing light on Mary Jones' intractable nature, a forward echo of the future Mrs Emsley's granite dealings with her many tenants. She would have seen that the thief was desperate, but went ahead with the prosecution.

'Before Mr Justice Bosanquet,' ran the court report at the time. 'Jane Kendley was indicted for stealing, on the 28th of October, 1 pair of shoes, value 3s, the goods of Mary Jones.'

'The prisoner came to the shop on Monday 28th of October, about one o' clock, and asked to see a pair of shoes in the window,' testified the widow. 'I showed her a pair at 3 shillings sixpence. She said she could not give above 1s and asked for a second-hand pair. I showed her a pair of boots at one shilling 2d. She paid me 6d, saying she would call in the evening, and pay the rest. She went away – and I missed the 3s 6d pair of shoes directly. There was nobody but her in the shop . . . I have seen the shoes since at Mr Fryett's the pawnbroker. I saw the prisoner there.'

'Have you many shoes?' asked Mr Doane, cross-examining.

'Yes,' replied Mary Jones. 'I deal in old and new things. We sometimes take deposits . . . I had worn the shoes myself three or four days before, but not fitting me, I sold them. I dare say I have a hundred pairs of second-hand shoes.'

A further witness, Charles Lockyer, an employee of Mr Fryett, confirmed that Jane Kendley had been the woman who pawned the stolen shoes. It was then noted that the prisoner had previously been of good character. She was found guilty, but recommended to mercy. In the 1830s, this meant being handed the sentence of 'confined two months'. [5]

Even as Mary Jones struggled with dwindling trade, she was about to experience the sort of startling swerve of fortune found in popular novels of the time. As such things sometimes slipped into bureaucratic gaps, it is not quite possible to tell exactly when her brother John, the sibling who went to America, had died – but the effect on Mary Jones' life was enormous.

John had achieved what so many others had hoped, and made his fortune on this new frontier. Nor was all of it invested in American concerns; some was sunk into London property. So it was that the first fortune begat yet more riches.

In the late Georgian and early Victorian years, a certain class of Londoner – skilled tradesmen, builders, canny merchants – began to buy plots of land all around the periphery of what was then the centre of London. In the east, the market gardens of Hackney, the gravel fields of Old Ford, the fields of Haggerston, there was land owned by old (but cash-poor) families and by the church. This land was now up for sale. Sometimes these self-made men invested individually; sometimes they clubbed together in building tracts.

It was these men who were to shape the future of London; with the death of her brother, Mary Jones was about to join their number. As an independent woman, free of any ties, she would dive with unusual enthusiasm into the great property boom.

8

'There Were Dwellings
in Gardens'

❧

For those with regular wages, London was a kaleidoscope of possibility. Here was miraculous luminescence: theatres were beginning to use oxyhydrogen flames directed at cylinders of quicklime. The resulting stage illuminations – the limelight – could be coloured deep blue, signifying virtue and heaven, or fierce red, the hell into which supernatural villains would descend.

There were brightly lit salons, the harsh flash of jewellery; the fleshy, dripping abundance of the grander eating houses. Away from the gaslight, deep in the warm gratifying summer shadows of the revived pleasure gardens, there was the unspoken thrill of illicit sex under oriental lanterns of pale green and yellow.

Early Victorian London had a surprising sensuality made possible by growing economic strength. This was not just to do with the industrial leaps that had made mass production possible, it was also the fruit of Britain's growing colonial power.

From the marshes of Bow to the gentle fields of Homerton, land was being snapped up by newly rich developers. These men were not all local; one man who was poised to become a major property owner in the East End had emigrated from his native Yorkshire, and he would go on to marry Mary Jones.

'Mr Samuel Emsley,' recorded one newspaper, 'was of a family which sprang from Cudworth, near Barnsley. He was originally apprenticed to Mr Alletson, druggist, of Market Hill, Barnsley, and afterwards settled in London as a stay manufacturer.' [1]

By the 1830s, Samuel Emsley was an extremely successful stay manufacturer – someone who made corsets. He had chosen a shrewd time to make inroads into the ladies' underwear business. Just before the dawn of the Victorian era, the style was already for women's waists to be narrower; corseting, which had been a little looser throughout the Regency period, was now becoming much more rigid and tightly laced. Emsley had based his business in a large warehouse called the Octagon in Bethnal Green. As well as making corsets, he diversified into shoes and boots. His fast-growing wealth also made him a target for crime, rather more serious than that suffered by Mary Jones.

'Upwards of 2000*l* of property stolen,' declared the *Morning Advertiser* in February 1836, going on to detail the court proceedings that followed. 'W Steele, late a foreman in the employ of Mr Emsley, a wholesale ladies boot, shoe and clog manufacturer; and James Sims, who has also been in the employment of the prosecutor; together with two females, the mother and sister of Sims, were brought . . . for final examination.' [2]

The culprits wanted to offer the shoes and boots around different pawnbrokers, but an extraordinary amount of Emsley's stock had been removed – rather too much for the thieves to be able to shift effectively. They set fire to the surplus, and their fireplace was discovered filled with charred leather. This is the part of the crime that must have hurt Emsley the most. As if the thieving wasn't bad enough, here too was such wanton waste.

Curiously, the man who later stood accused of Mrs Emsley's

murder in 1860 not only crossed her tracks in Ratcliff; he also crossed over Samuel Emsley's on this occasion, for he happened to be the policeman who had caught Sims with his wicker basket filled with stolen goods. At the time, this young officer, attached to K Division, had a most promising career ahead of him.

Samuel Emsley was not fortunate with his employees that year. A few months later, another, almost comically similar case, came to court.

'James Waterson, Elizabeth Waterson and Samuel Osman were charged with plundering their employer,' reported the *Morning Advertiser*. [3] The irony was that this time, the theft appeared to have been carried out by a man who was a witness for the prosecution in the previous case.

These two cases threw light on to how a business such as shoemaking or corset manufacturing worked. For those making the goods, the labour at that time was at least regular, if ill-paid. A great many shoemakers worked from home, although Emsley – following the example of manufactory owners in the north, who were discovering the financial benefits of having the workers gathered together under one roof and labouring set hours under close supervision – would have had a few craftsmen and women working at the Octagon.

Emsley's first marriage, to another woman called Mary, produced two daughters. His wife died in 1841. At that time, Emsley was becoming a local eminence. He had branched out into pub ownership, at a time when that business was expanding dramatically, and he was buying up plots of land in Bethnal Green and a little further east towards Old Ford to build houses to let. The streets to the west of Bethnal Green, in the area called Old Nichol that was to become a notorious byword for slums, were already becoming noisome. There were accounts of 'dwellings in gardens' – people making their homes in lean-to sheds. [4] (In the twenty-first century, this is once more a phenomenon across London; the borough of Newham has numbers of illicit dwellings in concrete 'sheds' in back gardens.)

Such unfortunate tenants frequently found themselves in competition with pigs and cows; though the parishes were keen to put a stop to livestock being kept in residential areas, many ignored the objections. The stench in the warmer months was intensified with outpourings from local bone-boilers and cats' meat factories.

The new Bethnal Green housing held out the initial promise of a better life. 'Nearly 70 houses were built in Essex, Suffolk and Norfolk Streets between 1845 and 1854, mostly by James Lucas for Samuel Emsley,' explained *The History of the County of Middlesex.* [5]

Emsley diversified further into the dust industry. In essence, this was the early form of urban waste removal: everything from discarded meat bones to the spent cinders from household fires. Licenses were granted and this was becoming an ever bigger – and ever more urgent – business.

Great grey pale cones, taller than trees, had begun to rise above the rooftops in the East End and St Pancras. These were made up of ash and cinders, the result of hundreds of thousands of domestic coal fires and the refuse of manufacturing. This grey mulch had terrific value at a time when property was booming because it could be used in the manufacture of bricks. As it was, the King's Cross dust heap became a valuable export, disassembled and shipped to Russia. In London, the brickmakers of Hoxton and Haggerston were eager buyers of this perfectly recycled waste.

These heaps were not always as benign as they appeared. Animal and excremental waste were also deposited there. The air of decay was intense.

By the late 1840s, Emsley was very well established, operating from (and indeed living next door to) his corset-making manufactory. It was around this time that as well as buying and selling pub licenses, he had also risen to the ranks of a vestryman of the parish of St Matthew at Bethnal Green. Vestrymen were early versions of local councillors, supervising the distribution of poor relief, oversee-ing the new generation of workhouses that were being built in the parish and attending to matters such as road and pavement cleans-ing, street lighting and, of course, dust and rubbish removal. The vestrymen were required to meet every fortnight and the minutes of their meetings were scrupulously recorded by local clerks.

To become a vestryman was also a sign of some social ascension; Emsley, a working man, was entrusted with responsibility for his fellow citizens and having some measure of influence over their lives.

It is difficult to know what brought the widower Emsley into the orbit of the widow Mary Jones. There may have been shared business interests, with her late husband's shoemaking business and late brother's portfolio of residential properties, and now finding herself a rich woman with a voice and influence in Stepney and Whitechapel. There might have been local parish business either with property or licences that exerted mutual gravity. It is possible, even though women had no vote, that her views were sought on local administrative matters.

However they met, Mary Jones and Samuel Emsley married on 8 April 1843, ten years after the death of her first husband and in the parish church of St Dunstan's, where she had been christened. On the marriage certificate, it was recorded that Emsley's father was a schoolmaster. [6]

What worldly goods would Mrs Emsley, as a married woman, be required to surrender to her new husband? At the time, the law concerning women and property ownership was governed by a prin-ciple called coverture. Sharply defined in the late 1700s by the jurist William Blackstone, this described the legal precedent whereby married women had no rights to their own land, or indeed their own money. Since husband and wife were, in the eyes of the law, a unified whole, then the husband was in full control of all matters financial within the family. Whatever his wife owned was his.

Even by the 1840s, there was some social disquiet about a principle that seemed more rooted in medieval times; some cases were brought before judges from aggrieved wives essentially suing their husbands for what was rightfully theirs. Judges had a tendency to side with men. In one case, it was suggested that the husband's miserly allowances were, in a wider sense, a good thing as they suggested that he was dedicated to making sure that the family fortune was not unnecessarily depleted.

Women were not wholly powerless, though. Coverture sometimes worked the other way around. Wives who found a way to spend extravagantly and run up huge debts in their husbands' names could not be held responsible for those sums. When the various tradesmen and shopkeepers sued for repayment, it was the husband who could be liable to be sent to a debtor's prison, not the wife.

Before marriages were made, women of property frequently tried to ensure that prenuptial arrangements were set in stone. This involved getting courts to agree to special settlements when it came to the disposition of property. It seems that before her new marriage, Mary had already taken steps through her solicitor to ensure her new husband might not have any claim upon it. She had a sharp sense of having to carve out her own rights, an acute sense of the need to fight for her autonomy.

Questions of legacy and inheritance would have greatly exercised Samuel Emsley's siblings and wider family, for it was also the case that if he should predecease his new wife, she would be entitled to a third of his money and property.

Mrs Emsley's new stepchildren had little fear that her union would produce fresh offspring and dilute their own inheritances. She was now fifty-three, seven years Emsley's senior. The pair were both inclined to frugality; there was no sense, for instance, of Emsley or his wife having their own private carriage or horses. Neither seemed interested in ostentatious public display or set on being seen in the fashionable salons of the West End. Yet both had a growing East End eminence.

By 1852, Emsley started to slow down his business interests, taking the contents of his factory and putting them up for auction. His health had not been good and there is the possibility that he had a sufficiency of income and little further need of the burden of running a large manufacturing establishment. The first part of the sale was made up of '3,500 dozen white and coloured stays, and a large quantity of materials in satteens, jeans, nankeens, calicos and woollen cloths, interlinings, busks etc'. [7]

Four years later, it was all over. The announcement of Emsley's death was made in the *Morning Post* on 21 January 1856. He had died as the result of a brain haemorrhage on the 15th, aged sixty; Mrs Emsley was a widow once more.

Emsley's will ran to many close-written pages. In the first paragraph, it stated that, 'I confirm the settlement made on my marriage with my present wife in all respects,' and went on to state that, 'I bequeath all my ... furniture, printed books, plate, linen ... prints in and about my dwelling house in Norfolk Street ... or in and about any other dwelling houses I may occupy at the time of my surcease unto my dear wife Mary for her absolute use.'

The rest of the will concerned the disbursement of his properties; it is clear that Emsley had prepared well for the property boom that was now reverberating throughout the area. He had houses and land in Globe Town, and also to the north in Haggerston; property gathered around the site of the gasworks near Cambridge Heath, and plots of land in streets that were still at the planning stage. Emsley also owned chunks of wasteland abutting the route of the Eastern Counties Railway, over which he had fought legal battles over the years.

Some of the estate went to relatives who were still living in Barnsley and other northern towns. The Emsleys held close to one another. Although it cannot be stated with great certainty just how tightly Mrs Emsley remained clasped into the bosom of the clan, it was later to emerge that two of Samuel's brothers, Edward and Thomas, had met socially with Mary after his death and enquired with seeming lightness about what she planned for her own estate.

With the Emsley family no doubt wondering about the division of Mrs Emsley's assets following her own death, the police were about to make some decisive moves.

9

'I'll Serve the
Old Bitch Out'

∽

One of the more popular stage melodramas that frequently featured on the playbills of theatres at the time was *The Miser of Shoreditch*. Set in the sixteenth century, it involved virtuous star-crossed lovers, an energetic and shameless villain, knife fights in moonlit forest glades, a comical sidekick, a hero wrongly accused of murder, a spectacular inferno and, at the centre of this drama, an elderly miser called Jasper Scrimpe. His obsession with hoarding gold was presented as one of the key mysteries: how could a man's soul become so deformed?

As the character himself declares, 'I had learnt the all-important secret, and as I hugged and gloated o'er my precious treasure, I shouted aloud "I have the world, the world at my command – for I have gold! Gold! Gold! Ha, ha, ha!"' [1]

Misers were also a source of fascination to Charles Dickens' newly enriched John Boffin in *Our Mutual Friend*, published in 1864. In the novel, Boffin (who had inherited lucrative dust heaps) demanded that Silas Wegg read him true chronicles of the lives of such men and their eventual fates. This literary taste was neither fictional nor niche; in the real world, contemporary social observers noted that stories of misers had a particular hold on the popular reading imagination.

The public view of Mrs Emsley was not wholly dissimilar: reports of local gossip included East End women who thought she was an object of shame for going about in such old clothes when she could very easily afford the finest dresses.

Even now her murder was to be monetised. The police, although energetically pretending to the press that they were far ahead with their investigations, were actually almost paralysed. There was the increasingly uncomfortable sense of a ruthless killer still on the loose in those streets, and a sharper approach was needed.

They found it in money. In the last week of that dark August, leaflets were handed out on the streets: '£300 reward', they declared. 'Murder. Whereas Mary Emsley, widow, has been brutally murdered at 9, Grove-road, Mile End-road . . . £100 reward will be paid by Her Majesty's Government to any person giving such information as shall lead to the apprehension and conviction of the guilty person or persons; and the Secretary of State for the Home Department will advise the grant of Her Majesty's gracious pardon to any accomplice not being the actual murderer, who shall give such information as shall lead to the same result.

'A further reward of £200 will also be paid by Mr Ratcliff, solicitor, Dean Colet-house, Stepney, to any person who shall give information as above. A mourning ring to the memory of J Jones, who died 1830; a dark coloured pocket-book, containing an acceptance of £25; also a check [sic] on the Bank of England for £10 are missing. Information to be given to Inspector Thornton or Sergeant Tanner . . . or to Inspector Kerresey, Bow Police-station.' [2]

The reward was the equivalent of some £35,000 in today's money, but any straight comparison is difficult to make because it would have gone so very much further. It was a colossal sum. There would have been many residents of Whitechapel, Shadwell and Limehouse who would have imagined having that amount of money; discussions in the pubs about how such a reward would lift a family from all care for a great deal of time.

The police were interested in the mystery of Mrs Emsley's missing cheque; it had been paid to her by Mr Carryer, proprietor of an 'operative chymists' and it was for the rental of the shop. The newspapers also reported that 'a little book in which she made entries of her rents as she collected them, is also missing'.

Inspector Thornton and Sergeant Tanner were informed when the first of many prospective reward hunters materialised. The most notable, reported *The Times* were 'three men, having the appearance of German Jews . . . [who] described the appearance and occupation of some persons of bad character, any one of whom they thought capable of committing such a crime, and suggested that they should be watched.' [3]

This was obviously not enough to merit any kind of reward or, for that matter, any kind of attention. However, the information being fed to reporters was now taking on a distinctly racial dimension. Newspapers reported 'two strange-looking men' who had, some days before the murder, been witnessed by an opposite neighbour 'to enter the house of the deceased'. This had served as a reminder of another occasion when 'a man having the appearance of a Jew hawker intruded himself into the house, and importuned [Mrs Emsley] so much to buy some of his wares that she became alarmed, and went to the back door, and, by way of feint, called "Thomas", upon which he took his departure.' [4]

This domestic invasion had clearly made a strong impression on Mrs Emsley's neighbour; it also made quite an impression on the police. This was the invocation of the Jew as a faintly unsettling Other; supremely unconcerned about imposing himself upon an old lady and only fleeing at the suggestion of a male servant being summoned.

Another report suggested that 'three or four Frenchmen' had been 'lurking about' the vicinity of Mrs Emsley's house and that they were escaped convicts. It was alleged they were selling slippers door-to-door, claiming they were of 'French manufacture'. Once admitted to their victims' homes, they conducted violent burglaries. These Frenchmen were now alleged to be 'well-dressed', as though they had recently profited from crime; it was also suggested that when Mrs Emsley's corpse was examined, her slippers appeared to be brand new. [5] This sort of garish speculation said a lot about public-house prejudices, as well as fear of foreign infiltration.

An editorial in *The Times* widened out the theme of unease, detecting in Mrs Emsley's murder a metaphor for London itself – a city 'in its dotage', 'falling into that state in which old misers are murdered and nobody knows about it for several days'. The leader added darkly, 'it has been said that there are as many Roman Catholics in London as there are at Rome; it may now be added that there are as many deserts and ruins.' [6]

The line in *The Times* about the numbers of Roman Catholics in London was to do with tensions in Ireland and the steady growth of violent resistance to British rule. The murder at Stepney would later be found to have a number of strange echoes with the Fenian movement and authoritarian responses to it.

Meanwhile, on the morning of 24 August, there was another tragedy at 9 Grove Road. PC Watson had moved into the house, acting as a full-time security guard for the property. He chose to move his family in with him. There is nothing recorded about why Watson should have wanted his wife and four-year-old son to join him in such a notorious house; they would have had perfectly comfortable dwellings of their own. This was still an age when darkness presented dread-inducing thoughts, however. A property in which an old lady had been savagely murdered, her blood soaked into the floorboards, might well have made a most unattractive supernatural prospect to be alone in throughout the small hours, even for a worldly policeman.

On that morning, Watson's son was upstairs in one of the back rooms, fiddling with the open window. He climbed on to the ledge that overlooked the back garden some thirty feet below. Perhaps something caught the little boy's eye, or he may have been distracted by another noise in the house. Whatever the cause, he fell and died. There is no record about whether the grieving family was replaced in the house by any other policemen; it is difficult to imagine any of his colleagues would have been keen on the idea. The horrible accidental death of the child only served to inflame local interest in the case. Even just a fortnight after the murder, it was being used as a byword.

In a case of serious assault (as we now call it, grievous bodily harm) involving two local middle-aged men outside the 'Edinburgh Waverley' tearooms in Limehouse, a police court heard that they got into a violent fight; one was beaten so badly his jaw was fractured and three of his teeth 'were loosened'. Before the punch-up had begun, one man told the other he was going to 'serve him' in the way that 'old Mrs Emsley had been served'. [7]

Against this backdrop, the inquest into Mrs Emsley's murder continued. 'There was again a considerable attendance of the inhabitants of the neighbourhood,' one newspaper noted drily of the crowds gathering outside the Railway Hotel. [8]

In a sign that the step-family was taking a more careful financial view of the entire case, two solicitors were now present. One was the faithful Mr Rose, representing Mrs Emsley's estate. It was noted by interested reporters that he was also 'of the trustees under her marriage settlement' – in other words, one of the figures there to ensure that the property empire was not simply appropriated by others. Also in attendance was Mr Ratcliff, the Emsley family solicitor, there to look after their interests.

There might have been those on the jury, and some among the general public, who wondered quietly if the widow's trusts might have been at the root of this affair and whether the killer might have been either a member of her step-family, or indeed one of the men who helped her maintain that increasing property wealth.

A woman who lived across the road from Mrs Emsley was called to the stand. On the widow's last day, Caroline Barnes had seen her 'making her bed in the first floor front room. I saw nothing else remarkable during the day.'

However, the next morning, she saw something electrifyingly odd, in the circumstances: 'About twenty minutes to ten o'clock,' she said, 'I saw some one moving paper-hangings in the upper part of her house. I did not see who it was, but I concluded it was Mrs Emsley.'

By that time Mrs Emsley was judged to have been dead.

'[I] took more notice of the paper than the person,' continued the neighbour. 'I could not say whether the person was a man or a woman. I was standing at the time by the scullery window in my own house, which commands a view of the top room of the deceased's house.

'Mrs Emsley's bedroom window was not open,' Mrs Barnes added. 'I saw the window of the front room at the top of the house opened on the Tuesday morning. I mean I saw it moved up by a hand. I did not take sufficient notice to be able to say whether it was the hand of a man or a woman. I saw the window open and the paper-hangings move.

'At the same time, I observed a slight piece of paper with a red pattern hanging down outside the window.'

Had the murderer spent the night in the house? That piece of paper – was the red pattern the old woman's blood? Mrs Barnes added that she saw someone go up to the front door and knock that Tuesday morning, 'shortly after ten'. The door was not answered. Whoever was moving the paper-hangings was not inclined to go to the door. These were the details that haunted Arthur Conan Doyle some forty years later, as he brooded over the case.

Further unsettling evidence came from a boy called William

Smith, who worked for Mr Lindsall, a linen-draper based on the Mile End Road. Lindsall wanted to give Mrs Emsley a bill, and early on the Tuesday morning, young William took it to Grove Road. Somewhere between half-past eight and nine o'clock on the Tuesday morning, he walked up the path, knocked on the door and heard nothing from within the house.

William told the jurors that he, 'looked through the keyhole of the front door and noticed that the back door was open', for he could 'see right through the house into the garden behind and the trees and shrubs distinctly'.

However, he 'heard nobody and saw nobody in the house'.

Greengrocer Archibald Mann, whose pitch was at the corner of Grove Road, recalled seeing Mrs Emsley on the Monday evening, and also recalled seeing a man who 'worked for her' whose name he did not know; they appeared to be engaged in some business involving a new stove that the man was pulling on a cart.

Another neighbour, Richard Farnyhough, was called before the coroner and added his own slightly unsettling memory of the night that Mrs Emsley was thought to have been murdered.

'I remember my dog barking,' he testified. 'I heard it more than once. The first time was . . . from midnight to about 4 a.m.

'The dog does not usually bark so much,' Farnyhough explained, adding that he did not actually get up to investigate, but lay in bed thinking about burglars and violent robbery.

'I had been at the London and Westminster Bank that day, and received some money,' he said. He had put the money in a trunk and stashed it under his bed. Even in a relatively tranquil street, the fear of night-time intrusion was strong.

Farnyhough also gave an outline of his relationship with Mrs Emsley, and a talk they had several days before her murder, which vividly revealed her sharp and sardonic sense of humour. The wallpaper – clearly an overwhelming obsession for her – had become a point of conversation.

'She offered the paper to me at prime cost,' said Farnyhough. He demurred, though mentioned to her that he also had a house in Shropshire which he rented out and that he might write to the tenant to see if he wanted the house freshly papered.

'How long has he been in the house?' asked Mrs Emsley, according to Farnyhough.

'Eight or ten years,' Farnyhough said he told her.

'Don't you write,' was Mrs Emsley's reply. 'For it will be introducing a bad practice and he will be wanting the house papered again.'

This recollection evoked a laugh from the jurors and spectators.

'I took her advice and did not write,' continued Farnyhough. 'And I felt much obliged to her, for the tenant has since papered the house at his own expense!'

At this, there was an explosion of laughter in the stuffy backroom.

There was further laughter when Mr Farnyhough mentioned his servant, an 'Irish girl' called Bridget MacDonald, who claimed she did not hear the dog barking, but who was also reluctant to be called to the inquest as a witness.

'She told me she would not "swear" for anybody,' said Farnyhough. 'She is a Catholic, and I dare say the priests have some influence over her, and she said to me, "Sure, and why should I swear at all?"'

He impersonated Bridget's accent, which the jurors greatly relished. Farnyhough also earned a laugh when he described the people who came knocking at Mrs Emsley's door on the Tuesday: 'I am sorry to say they were not of the first class, nor yet of the second.'

Local attitudes to Mrs Emsley, and a possible wider motive for her murder, seemed to be presented by one of her employees, a man called William Rowland, who introduced himself to the coroner as a former warrant officer who had been formerly based at Worship Street police station. Rowland lived in one of Mrs Emsley's houses at 25 Barnsley Street. He collected some of the rents and effected some of the repairs across her wide property empire. Rowland reiterated the care the old lady took after dark if ever anyone came to the house; how she would peer out of her window until she could be sure who she was talking to. On the day of her murder, Mrs Emsley went out to collect some rents herself in Barnsley Street.

'She had a dispute with one of her tenants,' said Rowland, 'a shoemaker called Smith. He had assaulted her and torn her basket, and she appeared to be very much excited.'

This was a reminder to the inquest of Mrs Emsley's eccentricity, vulnerability and also what seemed like a curious streak of malice, or at the very least contrariness. Mrs Emsley employed people to collect rents, so why did she deliberately choose to face the hostility of any tenants who were perhaps in great difficulties?

'Did you hear the man threaten her?' asked the coroner.

'I did,' replied Rowland. 'He said, "I'll serve the old bitch out".'

Rowland had more to say about Smith: 'He is a lame man with a crutch. They had a dispute about some arrears of rent. She seemed very much excited indeed, and I settled the quarrel. She said to me, "This man wanted to rob me; I have got a note here."'

He explained that he assumed Mrs Emsley meant she was carrying a fifty-pound note. The reason for this colossal sum in cash was that she was on her way to settle the balance for all the wallpaper she had recently bought.

'It was not an unusual thing for her to quarrel with her tenants,' said Rowland. 'She was usually very peremptory in demanding her rent. I have heard some of the tenants make use of bad language to her, but never positively threaten her. She has told me that they threatened her, but I never heard them do so.'

This not only opened up the range of potential suspects – could the old lady have been attacked by one of her enraged tenants? – but also appeared to swing a discomforting light on to the 'shoemaker Smith'. Several days later, the man in question, George

Smith, felt forced to write a rather pained letter to the editor of *The Times*. Disputatious he may have been, but he was also a *Times* reader.

'In that report [of the inquest], the evidence of a Mr Rowland is given,' he wrote, giving his address as 16 Barnsley Street. 'And as I am the person alluded to named as Smith and as that report as it now stands is calculated to do my character and business a very serious injury, I trust, Sir, that with your usual kindness, you will give the origin of the difference between Mrs Emsley and myself, the truth of which Mr Rowland well knows.'

Smith went on to supply the explanation himself: 'As the report now appears, it would be thought I attempted to rob her of 50*l*. The real state of the case is this: Mrs Emsley called as usual for her rent, and I paid her, deducting 1s for repairs done to the house, which she instructed me to have done, saying at the time, I could get it done cheaper than she could. A dispute arose between us, and in an excited manner, she took my receipt book away, saying I owed her 2*l*. Knowing the balance in her favour was only 2s, I went after her to recover it, and took hold of her basket to see if it was there.

'On my way home,' he added, 'I met a policeman, to whom I stated the circumstances; he advised me to go to the police court. I went home, and while shaving myself for the express purpose, Mr Rowland came into my house and expressed his willingness to settle the matter between us. He did so, and my rent book shows my full payment up to that date.

'I trust, Sir, as the statement is so vague as it now stands, that you will allow me space in your journal as early as possible to protect myself from further bearing the stigma the statement is likely to engender.' [9]

The letter received due prominence. What Smith did not deny was the intemperate and ungallant language used to an old lady. Mrs Emsley clearly had the power to provoke even respectable *Times* readers.

Aside from the curiosity of an elderly woman antagonising even the better sort of tenants, Smith had little idea of another layer of vulnerability: Mrs Emsley was illiterate.

The fact was at last made plain to the jurors, and the man who acted as her amanuensis was called.

Joseph Biggs of '25, Pollard's-row, Bethnal-green-road', was a man beyond his middle years who described himself as 'a minister of the [Catholic] Apostolic Church'. He was, he told the assembled company, 'on very intimate terms with the deceased – no-one more so.'

'I wrote her letters for her, and her receipts,' Biggs testified, 'and have done so, I think, for the last four years.'

Ever since the death, in fact, of Samuel Emsley.

'I saw her frequently, sometimes twice a week,' continued Biggs. 'She used to call at my house, and I returned her visits. Almost every Sunday evening I called upon her, and sometimes on Tuesdays. On Tuesdays, she used to call at my house, and I used to see her home.'

His clear suggestion was that this was an association that ran rather deeper than paperwork. The solicitors acting for the Emsley family would have been keenly sniffing the air for any possibility that the minister might have been angling for some of the deceased's property.

'If she wanted to go out any day,' said Biggs, '[Tuesday] was the most convenient one, and I was in the habit of going out with her. I last saw her alive on the Sunday evening before the murder. I called on her at about eight o'clock and left about ten. About a week before that, I wrote to Mr Cook by her request, stating that she had some paper-hangings to sell.

'Mr Cook replied, making an appointment to call on her on the Tuesday and an arrangement was made between her and me to meet him that day at eleven o'clock at her house.'

As it transpired, that was the morning after her murder.

'I did not keep my appointment,' revealed Biggs. 'And for this reason: my son wanted an early dinner and I thought it better to remain at home and dine with him, and then go to Mrs Emsley's as early as I could after that. I got there at about half past one. I knocked several times at her door but could gain no admission.'

He assumed that he was so late that she had given up on him and gone out.

Did not her absence and the subsequent silence bother him, asked a juror.

'It did a little,' replied Biggs. 'I wondered she had not been, but lately her business had taken her much about Ratcliff and I was not greatly surprised at not seeing her.'

Biggs told another juror, in answer to a question, that she had frequently entrusted 'plate and valuables' with him.

The coroner wanted to know did Biggs, 'hold any paper, in the nature of a will or otherwise, in which she disposes of her property?'

'Not any,' he responded. Nor, he added, did he know of any. The solicitors for the family would, again, have been on full alert at this point.

'I have reason to believe it was her full intention to make a will,' said Biggs, 'but I have no cause for thinking she had made any.'

Nor, he went on, did he really know about the full extent of her wealth and property holdings.

'I saw her on the Sunday evening prior to her death,' he explained. 'I wrote a receipt for her that evening on the inside of an envelope. She had a book in which I used to enter her rents, when due and when paid. But that book did not refer to the whole of her property.

'I used to prepare her receipts at my own house except under special circumstances. I cannot say how many houses the book has reference to. It is in the custody of Mr Rose, the solicitor, to whom I handed it when I heard of the death of Mrs Emsley.'

One juror was keen to hear more about Mrs Emsley's wealth:

did Biggs, with that invaluable book of all her properties and rents, really not know how much she had?

'I never calculated the amount of her weekly rents, although I had the book in my possession,' he replied. 'I only made the entries. I am afraid to say how much she received on the Monday [the day of her murder] lest I make a mistake. She used to say sometimes how much she had collected but they were mere passing words, of which I took no notice.'

The sly juror could not contain himself.

'How much do you suppose?' he enquired. 'You can surely give us some idea, being, as you were, so much in her confidence?'

Biggs hesitated, then responded.

'I am afraid to say lest I should say wrong,' he said. 'What she received on the Monday was from her trust property, of which she could not dispose. She used also on the Mondays to collect rents in Angel Court, or Angel Lane, Ratcliff, where she had some property.'

Angel Court was a grim, filth-encrusted proposition, but this was where Mrs Emsley had spent her youth and formative years when the area was happier. What other impulse could have made her wish to go back there repeatedly?

The jury was also keen to probe Biggs' relationship with the elderly woman.

'Are you a widower?' Biggs was asked. He responded that he was.

'If it is not irrelevant,' continued the juror, 'may I ask were you on intimate terms with any of Mrs Emsley's family?'

'No,' said Biggs, 'I did not know any of them.'

The juror pushed the point: 'Did you ever propose marriage to Mrs Emsley?'

There had clearly been local gossip and the framing of the question had a dash of mischief about it, but Biggs was sworn to answer, and he did.

'Yes, from the commencement,' he said, 'in these words: "The will of the Lord be done".'

At this, there was a loud guffaw from among the spectators.

Biggs, with full dignity, added: 'All the intercourse between us on that subject began and ended by my saying "The Lord's will be done".'

This subsequent remark was greeted with a vulgar roar of laughter throughout the backroom. This was not the last time that Biggs, and his romantic overtures towards his very rich friend, would be scrutinised in public.

What of the relative strangers drawn to Mrs Emsley's door by her efforts to sell all that surplus wallpaper? One such anxious figure presented himself at the inquest, having read of the murder and clearly wishing to ensure he did not become a suspect. James Wright, of 5 Saville Place, Mile End Road, testified that he had been to see Mrs Emsley on the Saturday before her death. His visit was in the evening; he was let in by the charwoman Elizabeth George and Mrs Emsley invited him upstairs to look over the paper-hangings.

'Having looked these over,' said Wright, they went downstairs, 'into the parlour and had a chat for about half an hour.'

Wright saw, 'a man sitting on the stairs between the passage and the back door leading into the garden'. This man 'had a book in his hand', and as he and Mrs Emsley were passing, the old woman said to the man, 'Go into the garden, and see if you cannot find some weeds to pull up.'

The witness said that he had never seen this man before.

The coroner was, at this point, apparently a little distance ahead of the police and his inquest seemed set on identifying those who had been seen around Mrs Emsley in her final hours. Around this time, there had been some wider debate about the way that coroners and police seemed frequently to be in competition over investigations. On this occasion, instead of enquiring further into whom the man on the stairs was, Humphreys thought it politic to adjourn for a few days to allow officers of the K Division to pursue their own leads. He told the jury that they, 'were assembled with the view not only of ascertaining the cause of death but also, if possible, who was the person by whom the death was occasioned'.

When the inquest reconvened, it was time to investigate the old lady's eccentric habits a little further. Elizabeth George, the char-woman, of 8 Tugwell Street in Lamb's Fields, was called. She provided a portrait of what must have seemed to many like uncanny isolation; at a time when even middle-class households were gener-ally bustling with people, Mrs Emsley's lonely routines must have sounded jarringly strange.

'I was in the habit of going to work at the deceased's house once a week on Saturdays,' Mrs George told the assembled local worthies. 'She kept no servant and I was the only person who assisted her in the housework. The deceased slept in the first floor front room. She always made her own bed. Sometimes it would not be made until the evening, just before she went to bed. I was there last Saturday fortnight – the Saturday before the murder. I never saw her sleep in any other room than the front first floor. I knew her habits well.

'It was not her practice,' she continued, 'to receive any person she did not know after dusk. In the evening, it was her habit, if there was a knock at the door, before she opened it, to look out from the window to see who the person was.'

'She might sometimes have admitted strangers after dusk,' added Mrs George, 'if they came to buy anything. She had some paper-hangings she wished to sell, but I never knew her sell any-thing else. A man, whom I did not know, came about the paper on the last Saturday I was there. He called about six o'clock in the evening and stayed until seven. He went upstairs into the different rooms in which the paper was kept. He did not take any of it away with him – but I thought I heard Mrs Emsley say that he was to come again. She appeared to know him but I did not. The talk went on upstairs.'

After further questioning, it seemed that it wasn't just the three of them in the house at the time. There was also a man whom Mrs Emsley had engaged just a few months beforehand as a general workman on all her rented properties.

'Mullins was there at the same time,' said Mrs George, 'waiting to be paid. He was waiting in the back yard, and I think the man [the visitor] must have seen him there. I do not know whether Mullins knew him.'

Who was this visitor? Mrs George could not be certain that he was actually there to buy wallpaper, and he certainly left with none. The jury was left with the curious image of these men loitering in a rich lady's house past the hour when she would have been comfortable with them; 'the workman Mullins' waiting out in the backyard, and who may also have been the man referred to in the earlier hearing, sitting on the stairs, reading a book and being scolded by Mrs Emsley to go and pull some weeds instead. In addition, there was this man who may or may not have been interested in wallpaper, moving around in the rooms upstairs as the charwoman listened below.

The next witness somehow intensified that odd sense of impropriety, of domestic unease. Elizabeth Pashley, of 16 Grove Road, lived directly opposite Mrs Emsley and had clearly taken an interest in her regular comings and goings. Also, it seemed, she was among the very last to have seen her alive.

Mrs Pashley testified that she saw Mrs Emsley, 'about seven o'clock on the evening of Monday 13th August, sitting at the window' – the night on which medical evidence suggested that she had been murdered.

The neighbour, 'saw the house at twelve the same night, and noticed that the front parlour shutters were not closed'.

The report continued: 'Thinking that circumstance unusual, she [Elizabeth Pashley] mentioned it to her mamma. She observed the next morning that the house was in the same condition with respect to the shutters. She never saw them closed after that, nor the blinds moved, nor did she ever see the deceased after seven o' clock on the Monday evening.'

There was another disquieting detail: this most assiduously observant neighbour 'saw nobody go to the house that evening'. Added to this, 'she heard no-one knocking to gain admission'.

Whoever had got into the darkening house in that summer twilight had, it was implied, done so by stealth.

Another neighbour in Grove Road, Elizabeth Muggeridge, had also noted the disposition of Mrs Emsley's shutters; even the fact that one of the window curtains seemed to be drawn back a little further than usual. That odd impression of a still and silent night was re-enforced; given the stupendous violence that had been wrought in that house, there seemed to be no sense of it in the hours before or after it.

Mrs Emsley was clearly not a monster to all of her tenants: the testimony of Martha Sophia Chapman instead gave the impression of a humorously warm and occasionally rather vulnerable old lady. Martha Chapman lived at 11 Windsor Terrace on Canal Road, around the corner from Mrs Emsley, and she happened to pay rent to her. Martha saw Mrs Emsley on that final Monday evening, at some time, she said, between six and eight – 'certainly later than six', she told the court.

It appeared that Mrs Emsley sometimes dropped in on Martha on Monday evenings on her way home (which would have been after she had been collecting rents elsewhere). The Chapmans – Martha's husband was a compositor working for a firm called Skipper and East – were, on most occasions, congenial company for Mrs Emsley. On that final Monday evening, Mrs Chapman, standing at her garden gate, saw Mrs Emsley walking up the road, away from the bustling rush of horse traffic.

She invited her landlady in for a cup of tea, but Mrs Emsley had told her that, 'no, she was very tired and wished to get home'.

'She then went away,' the report continued, 'and the witness had not seen her since. The deceased was alone and when Mrs Emsley left [Martha Chapman], she went in the direction of her own house.'

Mr Humphreys had been wide-ranging in his witness calls; he managed to summon forth the Mr Cook that Joseph Biggs had written to. On 10 August, said Mr Cook, a builder of Park Road in Peckham, he had received a note from Mrs Emsley asking him to come and have a look at the wallpaper that she was so absurdly keen to sell. This wasn't, it has to be said, some abstract offer: Mr Cook and Mrs Emsley had apparently known each other for some two years. Their mutual interest was obvious; the building, acquisition and letting out of ever more property, spreading east and also south of the river Thames. Mrs Emsley had bought some plots of land and John Cook obtained a lease from her in order to build on them.

Cook had sent her a reply stating that he would be happy to call on Tuesday 14th to inspect the 'paper-hangings'. He kept his own appointment, knocking on her door at half-past ten, then, with no answer, going off for a walk and trying again at intervals. He gave up and went away. The court was invited to assume that certainly by the Tuesday morning, Mrs Emsley's lifeless corpse was in that upstairs room.

While adjourning, Mr Humphreys produced a galvanised response from all those in the room. For it seemed that there had been in the last couple of days a momentous development in the police investigation: one so great that it was simply impossible for the inquest to continue until he could 'justify' presenting the new evidence in public. The jury was thus primed to return the following week. In the meantime, the news that came from the investigating detectives created a sensation throughout London and the land.

10

'Good God, this is
a Foul Plot!'

❧

The unusually wet weather had made the going hard on London's pavements and roads. Despite the efforts of crossing-sweepers – destitute children or elderly people making an effort with brooms to keep the mulch of dust and dung heaped up on the sides, in the hope of receiving tips – the rain gave the city an uncomfortably viscous quality. Although there were frequent omnibus services operating on fixed routes, many city dwellers still walked. The soil of the streets would cling to shoes and boots as tenaciously as any walk across a sodden field.

On the evening of Saturday 25 August, a man walked from his family's lodgings in Chelsea – then one of the newer suburbs in the west, with its rural past still in living memory – to the district of Westminster.

In 1860, the final section of construction work was underway on the new Palace of Westminster. It was completely rebuilt after the medieval palace had been destroyed by fire some two decades earlier. Despite its gothic elegance, combined with the earlier splendour of

Westminster Abbey, the surrounding streets had become notorious for their pockets of poverty. Living close by was one of the men investigating the murder of Mrs Emsley.

Inspector Thornton's wife answered the door to the man called James Mullins on that early Saturday evening. Mullins was tall, with reddish salt-and-pepper hair, was about fifty-eight years old, reasonably smart in fustian and corduroy jacket and trousers, with waistcoat and kerchief. He had been working for Mrs Emsley in various capacities for almost a year – the labourer with a book in his hands. Now he appeared to be in a state of some excitement, claiming he had information concerning her killing. Mrs Thornton told Mullins that her husband was out and that he should instead call on Sergeant Tanner. Mullins thanked her politely and did so.

Tanner lived in Wood Street, where James Mullins found him. He claimed to have been observing the movements of Mrs Emsley's rent-collecting agent Walter Thomas Emm, who lived in Bethnal Green in a well-kept cottage on the edge of a patch of land known as 'Emsley's Brickfields' – part of Samuel Emsley's construction business. A brickfield in that time was an area of what appeared to be semi-wasteland, semi-industrial concern, with pools of water where the earth had been dug out and patches of greenery, some cultivated, depending on how active the manufactory was. As well as the small kiln, with its taller chimney, rose-red with heat and ready for firing the earth, there would be neat piles of manufactured bricks arranged in great cubes.

Mullins told Tanner that he had set up watch there, and on that Saturday morning, at around eight o'clock, he claimed he had watched as Emm left his cottage, ventured into the brickfield and went into a shed about fifty yards from the house. Emm 'had a small parcel in his hand' when he entered this rickety construction. Mullins told the sergeant he had waited in his vantage spot and watched as Emm re-emerged from the shed about ten minutes later, without the parcel, and looked around carefully as if to be sure he was not being watched.

Sergeant Tanner listened to this curious story with obvious interest.

'What do you suppose the parcel contained?' he asked Mullins.

'I do not know,' replied Mullins, 'but I will show you where the shed is.' [1]

At this, Tanner suggested that the two of them should go to meet Inspector Thornton at his Scotland Yard office the following morning.

First thing on Sunday morning, as the city echoed to the urgent clamour of church bells, James Mullins marched up Whitehall and turned into Scotland Yard. In the main building he was met by Sergeant Tanner and Inspector Thornton. Both officers must have wondered from the start about Mullins' striking self-possession when dealing with them, and when outlining his own amateur methods; it is not quite clear when the labourer disclosed his own, rather surprising, professional history.

This was at a time when such a thing as police procedure was sometimes still a matter of extemporisation. Rather than simply obtaining the address of Emm's cottage and the brickfield and getting on with it themselves, Tanner and Thornton took Mullins with them (an easy journey via horse-drawn cab on the Sabbath-quiet streets). What then followed seemed both messy and oddly comical, yet it was also to prove crucial in the trial that was to come later.

It was about half-past eleven when the three men reached the edges of Emsley's Brickfields. Throughout the course of this journey, Mullins had told the policemen he had suspected for some days that Emm was responsible for the murder of Mrs Emsley. Upon arrival at the site, where they were joined by Sergeant Thomas, Mullins pointed out the shed in which he claimed Emm had deposited that mysterious parcel.

'You know, I am very clever in these matters,' Mullins informed Thomas. 'I have been working hard day and night to discover the murderer.' [2]

He told the others he had suspected Emm as he was in the business of collecting rent for Mrs Emsley, and whenever Emm had presented himself at her front door she had never hesitated to let him in.

The brickfields were surrounded by a wooden fence, in which there was a gap the policemen clambered through. After Mullins had pointed to the shed, Thomas approached it. As he did so, Emm emerged from his cottage. Mullins held himself back behind the wooden fence, partly obscured. The policemen told him they did not want Emm to see him.

As Emm went about his business, he was approached by the policemen. He knew them by sight as they had been familiar figures in the local streets. Having introduced himself and his official capacity properly, Sergeant Tanner asked Emm if, 'he had not been in this field at half-past eight on Saturday morning'. Emm replied that he had not. He had in fact been in bed at that time as he had been 'very ill'; he had not left the house until about an hour and a half later. Emm told the policeman that, 'he could send to his wife who would make the same statement'. (3)

Thornton sent Tanner to see Mrs Emm before she had a chance to consult with her husband; in the meantime, he instructed Thomas to conduct a search of the shed. Mrs Emm replied as quickly to the questioning as her husband; he had been unusually late in bed on the Saturday morning and did not leave the house before 10am. Tanner, having taken the notes, returned to Thornton as Thomas inspected the contents of the outhouse.

The court was later told that he found that 'it was full of lumber, bricks, mortar and rubbish.' (4) As Emm and his wife stood outside their cottage with Thornton, the two other policemen were beckoned back over to the fence by the side of the brickfield by the still-concealed Mullins, who now appeared to be bristling with impatience. As they went to him, Mullins told them: 'You have not half searched the place. Mrs Emsley had a box at the time she was murdered. Come, and I will show you where it is put.'

Bemused Sergeant Thomas told Mullins: 'The place is full of lumber. I do not think there is anything more there.' This appeared to agitate Mullins further; he told the policeman he would go to the shed with him. Thomas barred his way: 'Emm does not know that you are the informer and we do not wish at present that he should know'. [5]

Mullins did not appear remotely concerned about whether Emm knew or not that he had called the police; he swerved past and set off across the brickfield to the shed, forcing the policemen to follow him. Thornton and the Emms watched as Mullins told Thomas: 'Look now! Go into the place.' Thomas did so, followed by Mullins. According to the report, he then said: 'Pull down that damned slab at the side of the wall. Pull down those bricks.' Thomas pulled at the stone slab in question. After some effort, he groped behind it and found a paper parcel.

Sergeant Thomas emerged from the shed and, at this, Mullins withdrew a little. Inspector Thornton took the parcel – 'tied up with shoemaker's wax end', plus also what looked like petticoat string – and opened it with Walter Emm looking on. Thornton found 'two lenses, portions of a telescope, and other trifling articles'. There were also four teaspoons, and a 'German silver tablespoon', not of any startling value – but apparently recognisable as having come from Mrs Emsley's house. [6]

There was more within the wrappings. As the inspector now fished out a cheque, Emm immediately recognised it and cried out: 'Good heavens! It is Pickering's cheque paid to the old lady on the day of the murder. I did not know it was there. Good God, this is a foul plot!' [7]

As the now seriously agitated Emm looked on, the policeman asked Mullins to come forward properly – there was scarcely any point in his hiding in the background any further.

'Have you found anything?' asked Mullins.

The inspector nodded, and said yes, he had 'found something'.

'Have you found any damned money?' demanded Mullins.

'I could not say now,' answered the inspector. [8]

In the course of an otherwise chaotic investigatory manoeuvre, Inspector Thornton made what he considered a significant observation, which he kept carefully to himself. The wax-end string that had been used to tie up this odd parcel matched the string that Mullins was using as laces in his boots.

The air of extemporisation continued as this small gathering in Emsley's Brickfields gazed upon the parcel and each other: the three policemen, Walter Emm and his wife (with their children looking on from the cottage); and James Mullins. On what appeared to be pure gut instinct, Inspector Thornton made his decision. He asked Emm to accompany him to the Arbour Square police station in Stepney.

Thornton then turned to Mullins and asked him to do the same.

Emm appeared to be terrified. As Thornton allowed him to go indoors briefly to wash, accompanied by Thomas, the sergeant watched as Emm broke down crying, unable to move or speak through his sobs. We can only guess at the pale expression of horror on his wife's face as her husband, convulsed, was finally led away. We can only summon a picture of his sons and daughter, staring in distress and confusion. For Emm's family, that Sunday morning must have seemed the most extraordinary visitation of catastrophe.

Mullins' response was rather more succinct. According to Inspector Thornton's later evidence, he exclaimed: 'Is this how I am to be served after giving this information?'

Then he subsided into silence as Thornton asked him to accompany them. 'He walked there by the side of Sergeant Tanner,' recalled the inspector. [9]

Mullins might have calmed himself in order to focus on the enormous reward. Being asked to attend a station was not the same as an arrest. Indeed, with the parcel disclosed – the property of the murdered lady apparently found irrefutably in Emm's shed – Mullins might well have thought that the day was about to bring a most satisfactory conclusion.

At the station, Emm was formally charged and told he would be tried for 'being concerned in the murder of Mrs Emsley'.

The station had a dock, much as courtrooms have today. Following the charging of Emm, Inspector Thornton turned to Mullins and instructed him to take his place in that dock. Mullins was then presented with exactly the same charge: 'being concerned in the murder of Mrs Emsley'.

'The two prisoners were much affected,' stated a report in the *Evening Standard*, 'and the man Mullins was evidently labouring under great excitement.'

The men were told that they were to be brought the next day before a Mr Selfe at the Thames Police Court. Until then, they were both detained in 'separate cells' with a 'police constable'. [10]

As they were taken away, Inspector Thornton pursued his earlier instinct. With a couple of colleagues, he got a cab to drive them up to Barnsley Street, where Mullins had weekday lodgings in the shadow of the railway viaduct. Their intention was to carry out a thorough investigation of all his belongings and work tools.

Thornton was also inspired to send a man over to Chelsea to investigate the rented family dwellings of Mullins' wife Catherine, where Mullins stayed at the weekends. That meant a search not merely of rooms, but also an investigation of the dust hole – the area outside the lodgings where spent ashes from household fires were dumped. Thornton was thinking of the bloody footprints and of the boots that created them.

Meanwhile, the curious scene at Emsley's Brickfields had been witnessed by passers-by and the news spread quickly through the streets.

The next morning, a huge and vociferous crowd had gathered outside the Thames Police Court. Partly, it would have been due to the sheer excitement of the drama and the chance to look at two men who might very well be killers. There might also have been some relief, a sense that a ruthless murderer so pitiless that he would strike down a helpless elderly lady was no longer at liberty.

Throughout the short hearing, official attitudes towards Emm seemed quite different to those shown to Mullins. It was noted by Mr Young, the lawyer appointed for Emm, that the court should most certainly grant bail to the shoemaker. Young told Mr Selfe that Emm, 'was a most respectable man' and 'had been in one situation for eighteen years'. That situation had been his service to the Emsley family. More than this: Emm had a friend in Holborn, a Mr Gordon, who was happy to stand surety for the bail money.

Bail was not granted to Mullins; he was to remain in custody. In the court, the investigating officers now presented fresh evidence. Inspector Thornton, called as a witness, 'produced a hammer' which was 'found at Mullins' lodging'.

The hammer, Thornton stated, was an instrument 'that Mullins was always in the habit of carrying about with him'. He added that Mullins, 'is by trade a plasterer and it was such an instrument as was used by those in that trade'.

It was his view, Thornton continued, 'that it was with such an instrument that the deceased, Mrs Emsley, was struck. On the left side of her forehead was a deep cut, about an inch and a half in length – one end of the hammer was about that length,' he added, 'and had a sharp end.'

The search of Mullins' lodging room had also thrown up a discovery on the mantel shelf – 'a piece of tape' (or ribbon) the court was told, 'which is of the same pattern and description as that around the parcel alluded to'.

That same day, with the sensation now having spread throughout the East End, the inquest met for the penultimate time at the Railway Hotel.

'The whole neighbourhood was in a state of excitement consequent upon the apprehension of Mullins and Emm on suspicion of being concerned in the murder,' reported *The Times*. 'The inquest room was crowded and a number of people stood in a group in front of the deceased's house, hard by.' [11]

The arresting officers were called to give their evidence. Sergeant Tanner was reported to have caused 'sensation' in the inquest room when he revealed that Mullins had told him on Saturday, prior to the Brickfields visit, that, 'I will behave well to you if it all comes off right.' In other words, this seemed to be a straightforward offer of a bribe to a police constable; a suggestion that the enormous reward could be shared.

Tanner told the court that he replied to Mullins: 'You know I have reduced your statement to writing and you can call on me to produce it any time. No advantage will be taken of your information. I hope you think we are above that.' [12]

Inspector Thornton was next, and equally keen to impress upon the inquest the vital clue of the hammer. He reiterated that Mullins never went anywhere without it.

The official eagerness to have ensnared the murderer had led to a kind of hurried procedural free-for-all. On top of this, even though he was allowed bail, Emm was still under the darkest shadow of suspicion. There were questions he had to answer.

Mullins and Emm now faced being swept into the violent maelstrom of a legal system that had little patience for the niceties of proper adversarial trials. It was a legal system that seemed very much more a game of chance than that of today. The wildly differing backgrounds of the men added an element of piquancy. Walter Thomas Emm and James Mullins, though both labouring men, stood at opposite poles in the fast-developing churn of urban industrial society. Their fates were being shaped by this.

11

I Was Not in Her Debt

✛

Even for those who were seemingly secure, the abyss was all too close. A slip, a mistake, or worse, a single turn of events outside one's control could send the entire structure of one's life into the darkness. In many of the most popular melodramas at that time, the hero would find himself wrongly accused, imprisoned and waiting for execution. Audiences thrilled to these highly colourful stories because they echoed a deeper fear about the possible abuses of justice.

Walter Thomas Emm, forty-five years old, married with three children, was standing at the edge of that precipice.

This proud man had, unusually for a shoemaker, reached a hard-won plateau of economic security from being the general assistant to the Emsley family since 1842. At a time when holidays for the working classes were rare, Emm and his family had started to enjoy the opportunities opened up by the new railway lines, with pleasure excursions to seaside resorts.

At what price had that stability come? Understandably, in many of the streets where she owned property, Mrs Emsley was a figure of hate not too far removed from the bailiff. Rent-collectors were no less hated though; and Emm, as one such middle-man, would have been – at very best – an ambiguous figure to many tenants. He was an agent with the power to have a backsliding family evicted; a man to whom desperate appeals would be made, for just a little more time, for just a scintilla of compassion in the face of unexpected unemployment, bereavement, or illness.

No matter how well-thought-of he seemed to be, there was a cold granite aspect to Emm's nature. His job would have been impossible without it.

Did he actually nurture secret and violent resentment to the old lady? Was Mullins' gambit with the parcel in the brickfields inspired not by insane greed, but based on a genuine hunch that Emm was not as mild as he seemed?

The indeterminacy of Emm's social position was intriguing. By the mid-1800s, there was a rising lower-middle class composed chiefly of clerks and shopkeepers. Then there was the expanding urbanised working class: men and women, forced out of agricultural work and exiled from the countryside by improved machinery, now seeking their livings in the larger towns. Emm was somehow neither working class nor lower-middle, yet he and his family managed to carve a little respectability out of unpromising and uncertain foundations.

As a shoemaker, he had been working in the orbit of Samuel Emsley and then his wife. London's shoemakers had, in the earlier part of the century, been a voluble element in the radical new movement of trade unions. It had been shoemaker Thomas Hardy who, at the end of the eighteenth century, had issued a demand that there should be votes for all.

Bethnal Green was at the centre of London's shoemaking industry in the first half of the nineteenth century, with workshops and warehouses along the length of the Hackney Road.

The sheer scale of Samuel Emsley's warehouse is an indicator of how fast the city's population was growing; the demand for shoes was huge. Unfortunately for men such as Emm, there was also a huge amount of competition from the shoemakers of Northampton, who had established that town as the national centre for the trade over the previous 200 years. In 1841, the town alone had 1,821 shoemakers, and with it the strong reputation of having secured the contracts to provide footwear for the military. Less established London shoemakers had to fight harder to get their quality produce sold.

The idea of the London labouring classes growing angrier was constantly in the minds of those who moved in fashionable and political society. In the 1830s and 1840s, hostesses in the exquisite salons of Mayfair and St James's were anxious about the hostile potential of these masses in the East End. The Great Reform Act of 1832 had, from the point of view of the vast majority of working men, not reformed a single thing. For the working classes, any semblance of security that had come through the goodwill of concerned landlords and small, interdependent communities, was fast vanishing into the maw of the cities. One anonymous family sinking into destitution and near starvation looked much the same as any other.

The 1830s had also brought the much-hated Poor Law, overseen by a new species of government inspector, as well as local worthies. Rather than alleviate the distress of the unemployed with straight-forward financial assistance, the idea instead was to direct them to workhouses.

Walter Thomas Emm lived his life surrounded by workhouses. Every time he walked past one, he must have speculated that, like many other unfortunate shoemakers, he might one day end up as an inmate. The workhouses were administered by committees (sometimes drawn from local vestrymen). In *Oliver Twist*, published in 1839, Charles Dickens sent the unforgettable image out to the wider world that the diet in these institutions consisted solely of gruel. An oatmeal dish made either with milk or water and thinner than porridge, gruel was certainly part of the rota of dishes, but it was by no means all.

The minutes of the Mile End Old Town Workhouse from 1860, for instance, show the 'Guardians of the Poor' – the administrators – debating putting some groceries out to local tender, thus supplying the house with 'meat, cheese, butter, potatoes', 'scotch barley, split peas', 'legs and shins of good beef' and 'necks of mutton for the sick'. [3] Meat was rare on the menu rota; but otherwise there was more than just oatmeal. The truth was that in the London workhouses, no matter how forbidding and austere, few actually went hungry.

Obviously there was a darker side away from the fiction of Dickens; otherwise, hundreds of malnourished and ill parishioners would have been queuing for admittance. Broadly, the very business of setting foot in the workhouse brought utter humiliation and the stripping away of individuality. Husbands were separated from wives, children from parents. Vulnerable inmates were forced together with violent drunks.

The work could be grim. The workhouse at Mile End Old Town advertised for 'about 50 tons of the very best Guernsey granite spills for breakings ... to be delivered into the stone yard of the workhouse'. [4] While children and teenagers were taught useful skills such as shoemaking and sewing, the older inmates were given occupations of crushing futility.

Much in the way now that many of those committed to prison have acute psychiatric problems, so too did workhouses become a form of horribly deficient default care for the most vulnerable people. The Mile End workhouse committee of 1860 did at least regard their care as needing a specially advertised position. One announcement in a local newspaper required 'a man aged between 25 and 50 years of age to take charge of the HARMLESS LUNATICS in the imbecile ward on the male side of the workhouse'. [5] The position offered a salary of twenty pounds a year.

A gatekeeper was wanted too. This wasn't prison, as the inmates could leave if they chose, but the gates were closed at a certain hour. 'Required:' ran another advertisement, 'strong, active and intelligent single man between 25 and 45 years of age. Salary £25 with board, lodging and washing. Applications in the candidate's own handwriting. No-one need apply whose character for sobriety and honesty will not bear the strongest investigation.' [6]

This final stipulation – strikingly strong for the post of gatekeeper – was an indication of past abuses. These would have been the subject of intense local chatter in the public houses; Emm would have been grimly aware of the possibilities of degradation that such places had to offer.

There was a seamy side too. Some workhouses attracted a notorious reputation for sexual predators; middle-class male adventurers pretending to be destitute in order to gain access to the male dormitories for the night so they could opportunistically seek out paid sexual contact with young men.

Then there was a distinctly gothic element which gave the institutions a particular frisson of horror: in the 1830s, paupers who died within those walls would have their corpses sold to teaching hospitals for the purposes of dissection. Having lost all their material goods, even in death the destitute were also to lose the one thing which had been incontrovertibly their own.

But the Mile End workhouse could also be a valuable sanctuary in cases of total disaster. In 1860, there was a teaching post advertised at the house, which very firmly stated that the candidate should have a proven history of kindness towards children. The desire to educate was genuine.

For many years, the East End had been suffused with talk of reform. There would have been shoemakers such as Emm who had aligned themselves with the Chartist movement. This was the closest that Britain came to a popular uprising in the earliest years of Victoria's reign. The Chartists, like the Owenite movement before them, wanted universal male suffrage, the opening of elections to much broader fields of candidates, and the payment of salaries to anyone elected as Members of Parliament so the working man could participate properly in the work of government.

The movement came and went in waves; it reached a seeming high point in the days before a vast rally, intended to pass a multi-million signature petition to Parliament, took place in London in March 1848. Could revolution, the tinder spark floating from Europe, have been a possibility that day across the Thames on Kennington Common, where the Chartists had gathered?

Emm and his wife would have been acutely aware of the Chartist demonstration. It is highly unlikely that Emm would have gone anywhere near it; nothing in his conduct suggested any outward desire to upturn the status quo. More than that, a man hoping to hold on to a secure situation would never have ventured into a potentially violent and radical demonstration where he might very easily be seen by acquaintances or friends of his employer.

Conversely, his situation also now helps to illuminate a new class of city dweller who, by the mid-1800s, was able to enjoy not just the spectacle of the metropolis rising around them, but also to dive into many of its pleasures, both sensory and cultural.

For those living in Globe Town, there was a regular omnibus service into the centre of the city. Many routes had been taken over by the London General Omnibus Company and featured vehicles with standardised green and gold livery. The carriages would be drawn by two horses; there was seating for eight in the cab downstairs, plus additional spaces, reached by means of a narrow twisting staircase, upstairs on the uncovered roof. For the Emms, the most convenient route was that which ran from Stratford to Mile End to Whitechapel into the increasingly gaudy lighting of the West End.

In 1860, a prototype form of electrical lighting was being tried out, and witnessed with wonder, on Hungerford Bridge near Charing Cross as 'mercury discharge lamps' were hung along its length. In the thick darkness of a sooty London night, the electrified mercury within them gave off a curious green/blue light, creating a faintly uncanny effect that was utterly hypnotic to those who came to see it. [7]

Elsewhere, the main shopping streets of the West End, with their large windows illuminated with bright gaslight, filled with fashions of rich red, green, indigo and startling canary yellow. Families such as the Emms had no need to spend any money in these quarters; the spectacle was dazzling enough. Windows for shops for gentlemen of fashion contained fantastical peacock visions. Into these premises would swarm the 'dashing young parties' attracted by 'the pea-green, the orange, and the rose-pink gloves; the crimson braces, the kaleidoscopic shirt studs, the shirts embroidered with dahlias, death's heads, race-horses, sun-flowers and ballet girls'. [8]

Meanwhile, with the introduction of limelight, the stage had become an ever more dazzling spectacle. There was an inexhaustible range of entertainment. At Astley's Amphitheatre, there were vast productions involving live horses. In 1860, one such epic was *The Emperor's Decree*, set in Russia and featuring a variety of battle recreations on horseback. There was an abundance of light comedy to be enjoyed elsewhere, with farces involving cross-dressing and drunkenness. Other theatres offered dramas concerned with startlingly topical issues, such as poverty and Irish immigration.

Close to the Emms' home, genteel culture came in the form of the Eastern English Opera House, which gave popular performances of a wide variety of arias. There was sophisticated drama and Shakespeare to be found in Aldgate and on the fringes of the Minories in theatres such as The New Royal Pavilion.

The cottage that Walter Emm and his family lived in on the edge of the brickfields might perhaps have seemed austere at first glance, but it was comfortable. It had been one of the properties owned by Samuel Emsley, and it was his widow who collected the rent.

However, Emm was a class above the sort of tenant who was required to pay weekly: he had the superior arrangement of paying annually.

As he told the police, this meant in his view that he 'owed no debt' to Mrs Emsley; he saw that in technical terms, any question of rental money did not have to be considered until the sum was actually due. This removed one of the possible motives that he could have had for murdering her: the intolerable burden of trying to find the sums to pay her. (Though it was later to emerge that his financial dealings with the old lady were a shade more complicated than he at first presented them to be.) In terms of trust and respectability, this annual rental agreement put him on the same level as the middle- and lower-middle-class clerks who inhabited the far grander houses in and around the nearby Tredegar Square.

The Emm family had been there many years. At the brickfields, there was at least a semblance of open space (one report reckoned it to 'be about seven acres'). Walter Emm was indulgent towards his sons Edwin, aged sixteen, and ten-year-old Walter, whom he allowed to keep pigs ('a dozen black pigs', according to one report), in a patch to the sides of the brickfields. In many other parts of the borough, people keeping livestock were being reported to the Inspector of Nuisances.

The brickfields that abutted the large cottage were also showing signs of urban innovation. Some of the land behind had been dug up into pale brown trenches of soft clay, ready to receive iron pipes. The Metropolitan and District Board of Works was bringing a fresh, regular water supply into the area (this work being replicated all over London).

The brickfields also had one other advantage over many nearby streets. What might now be regarded as a chilly and undignified discomfort – a lavatorial facility consisting of a rudimentary wooden outhouse with wooden furnishings and a brick-lined pit beneath – would have been tolerable when located far enough from the main dwelling and when it did not have to be shared with a number of other families.

The Emm cottage, if tumbledown, would still have featured the principal items of Victorian domestic comfort. The furnishings would have been robust and well made. There would have been books, many more than just a Bible.

Of course, people needed light to read by. Domestic gaslight had come to the East End in the early 1850s – the laying of pipes by rival suppliers in Stepney and Ratcliff led to pitched battles between labourers, and indeed a couple of fatalities during these fights. By 1860, gaslight in private houses was still the province of the slightly better off. It is reasonable to assume that Emm and his family spent their evenings under the flickering glow of candles and oil. It is also probable that the three children were themselves literate (they would certainly prove to be winningly articulate in court), receiving a proper education, even some ten years before the Education Act would guarantee it. There was a range of schools nearby, from private establishments to the so-called Ragged Schools, which had been established as charities for the children of the very poor.

It was around this time that even the poorer homes were becoming slightly better equipped when it came to cooking. Emm would have studied the pictorial advertisements in the *East London Observer* for new sorts of kitchen ranges and stoves that were coming on the market.

In the midst of all of this were some less welcome changes. The open land of the brickfield had been 'recently purchased' by Mr Whittaker and Mr Faith, the stepsons-in-law of Mrs Emsley. There were also several small huts some distance from the Emm house that were said to be inhabited by 'squatters' [9]. Emm was instructed to make them move on, for Whittaker and Faith were keen to start building on the vacant soil. There was room here for several new residential roads and terraces of good housing.

The one serious nuisance for many households, especially in the summer months, was street dust (as opposed to the cinders and ashes being collected up for bricks). The constant horse-drawn traffic on the Bethnal Green Road, the Globe Road and the Mile End Road, threw up a daily sandstorm of dust and grit which, with open windows in the summer, would have infiltrated Emm's cottage. Great numbers of people complained that London air gave them a heaviness in the lungs. 'Chymists' such as those who paid that final rent cheque to Mrs Emsley, were selling products such as an 'Asthmatic Soothing Elixir – Contains No Opium'.

There was also growing radicalism, which found voice in the nearby Victoria Park. As one American observer wrote: 'There are two or three acres of open land, unenclosed, upon which the people gather for any kind of meetings and we could ... see several different crowds or assemblages. The people were the workmen of London, that we could see plainly enough by their brawny arms, work-worn hands, and care-worn faces. The mechanics of London are, to our eye, a sad looking set of men.' [10]

Meanwhile, a huge engineering project was underway beneath Victoria Park that summer; the district's vestrymen, by now seeming a rather antediluvian form of local authority in the face of this great tide of modernisation, and soon to be replaced by a unified city-wide administration – fretted about 'the sewerage efforts being executed by the Metropolitan Board of Works'. Sir Joseph Bazalgette's great system, construction of which had begun in 1858, was a masterpiece of tunnelling, and also fearsomely complex in terms of construction. The brick-lined northern high-level sewer, running from Kentish Town down to Hackney, met the sewer that ran from Oxford Street eastwards. The junction of these two great tunnels (these having been fed by hundreds of smaller tunnels) was at the south of Victoria Park. From there, the main outfall tunnel, aided by a baroque palace of a pumping station at Bromley-by-Bow, took the waste of central and north London down through Plaistow, Beckton, and out into the Thames.

The sense, in Mile End Old Town, of a city of perpetual commerce, of ceaseless traffic on roads and pavement at all hours, even on Sundays, was intense. In 1860, there were many instances of what was known as 'Sabbath-breaking'; shops open for the sale of food and drink; labourers attending to jobs as though it was a weekday.

All of this was a source of horror for the area's more religiously-inclined middle classes. By 1860, there was a concurrent effort to limit drinking. The Temperance movement had been gathering pace throughout the 1850s. Alcohol was denounced as the source of most sin, and it was the working classes who were perceived as being most in danger. In the north, it was the activists of the Chartist movement who had been leading the way in persuading labouring men to renounce alcohol since the 1830s. In east London, with its deeply ingrained drinking culture, which was brought by the sailors and the docks, it was harder to distract men either with the virtues of self-education or health-promoting country walks. That said, by this stage the city was a long way from the vivid gin-sodden nightmares of the eighteenth century. Other than a few notorious taverns in Shadwell, those who held pub licences in 1860 understood that they had to make their establishments seem to have a certain atmosphere of comfortable and unthreatening merriment.

Nevertheless, the multiplying numbers of public houses, increasingly with handsome bars and clever use of glass, mirrors and gaslight to create a dazzling simulacrum of smartness and grandeur, were a powerful lure to men and women alike. Each corner of Victoria Park gained large and impressive new public houses, placed strategically to catch dressed-up weekend promenaders, as well as weekday local custom. The architecture was deliberately suggestive of the grander middle-class homes.

The Emms were encircled by breweries and distillers; not just the mighty Truman, Hanbury and Buxton institution that was growing across both sides of Brick Lane, but more modest concerns such as the St George Brewery in Whitechapel, which advertised among its wholesale prices nine gallons of double stout for '14s 6d'.

This was the city of Walter Thomas Emm; bright, fast and restless; impatient with the fusty traditions of an established church that was more associated with the countryside and with the landed aristocracy than anyone who lived and moved through the crowded streets. With the security of regular wages, this was also a city of terrific opportunity. Emm might have expected his well-turned-out, well-spoken and pleasantly behaved children to do better than him, to perhaps think about positions as clerks or schoolteachers.

There were also a great many families who found the economic tides and currents much more difficult to swim against, who could be pulled by necessity into minor crime that was punished with disproportionate severity – families who somehow could never quite get a steady foothold in this pitiless city. One such family was headed by James Mullins.

12

The Gravitation
of the Blood

For the moment, Emm was uneasily at liberty on bail. By contrast, James Mullins was in a cell in the Clerkenwell House of Detention, a prison on the edges of the City of London and close to the noxious River Fleet. It was a house of pestilence; disease frequently roared from cell to cell, and many had been carried out as corpses before their trials. Mullins' manner as he sat in that cell was, for the most part, observed as being 'quiet'.

The legal system of the metropolis still resembled that of village assizes, so it was that Mullins was required to be present at the ongoing inquest into Mrs Emsley's death before he himself stood trial. The coroner's inquiries were almost at an end, but the rumour had circulated through the streets that Mullins was to be brought to the Railway Hotel on 17 September.

'The services of a strong body of the divisional police were called in requisition to maintain order and guard the avenues to the court,' reported *The Times*. The crowds were to be disappointed, as Mullins remained in his cell. However, Emm, the man he had accused, was there. Emm's treatment from the onlookers suggested that the wider public had settled upon the questions of innocence and guilt. He 'appeared to be an object of sympathy to the audience', ran one report. [1]

'From day to day during the last week, hundreds of people have been to see [Emm's] cottage and the little out-house or "lean-to",' [2] continued the news item. These sightseers had been particularly keen to catch a glimpse of the flagstone under which Mullins had said the parcel would be found. This interest was a curious combination: the local response, similar to that of a village, and the broader lure exerted by the colour of the newspaper reports. The means by which news entered the bloodstream of the city had changed.

Yet the apparent spontaneous sympathy for Emm, the public perception of this man as the wronged innocent in this tragic affair, was also a narrative rooted in the popular theatre. The public seemed to have chosen their hero. They had also, it seemed, settled upon their evil villain.

Mullins stayed in the prison that day. The reason for his absence from the inquest was a brief wrangle between the coroner and the Home Office, arguing over the legality of a prisoner being examined, or even seeing particular items of evidence, before he formally came to trial. Meanwhile, one of the jury members had heard through local gossip that the alleged murder weapon – a hammer – had been found. The juryman, 'should like to understand how, where and under what circumstances it was discovered, for rumours were abroad in connexion with it'.

The coroner was firm: the detective officers would answer questions on the hammer the next day. Moreover, 'the rumour to which reference was made did not rest on any statement put in evidence before the jury, nor did it turn on the accuracy, which was unquestioned, of the representatives of the public press who had reported the proceedings,' he declared. 'On the contrary, [the rumour] seemed to have been recklessly put into circulation by someone outside the court acting under no sense of responsibility.'

There was more, something that would cast a shadow of guilt over the whole Mullins family.

A lurid newspaper report had focused on Mullins' teenage daughter Mary, who was a domestic servant. Mary 'was living in a situation at a house in Chelsea. Her master, after reading the reports of the proceedings at the inquest ... sent for the young woman, told her that as she was the daughter of Mullins, a returned convict, and charged with the murder, he could not retain her any longer in his service.

'He, therefore, requested that she would at once leave the house,' the account continued. 'She went to the lower part of the house with the object, as it was supposed, of collecting any articles which belonged to her. She remained there a considerable time and the master sent down a little girl to ascertain the cause of the delay, and upon going into the kitchen she found Mullins' daughter raising a slab of the floor.

'She told the little girl she had dropped a shilling through a crevice in the floor, requested her not to tell her mistress of what she had done and as an inducement to her not to do so, gave her half the supposed loss. The stone was quickly replaced and the girl left the house.' [(3)]

What could have been the purpose of this mysterious story? Why relate an anecdote about a servant girl being summarily dismissed because of who her father was? The lifted kitchen stone was left as a mark of suspicion – a place, perhaps, to hide stolen property.

'Whether the lost shilling was found,' the article went on, 'or whether any other article of value was discovered beneath the stone is not at present known.

'It is said that both Mullins and his wife were in the habit of frequently visiting their daughter. The daughter was formerly convicted of robbery, the father was convicted and sentenced to four years' imprisonment for robbery, and it does not appear that any very extensive catalogue of good actions are set down to the account of the wife of the accused.' [4]

The implication was plain: what could one expect from a family such as that? In later years, newspapers were under furiously strict legal rules forbidding reporting on any suspect's previous convictions before trial, and they were most certainly not allowed to make nudging hints about the alleged bad character of an entire family. This information was clearly being supplied to the newspapers by the police. In addition, the police had chosen to withhold another aspect of Mullins' past that would surely have cast him in quite a different light to the public.

The weather the next morning was foul. Grove Road was dark under sluggish clouds, the dull weight of approaching autumn pressing down on slate-grey canal waters and the browning oak leaves in Victoria Park; it did nothing to dampen the electrical atmosphere outside the Railway Hotel.

The jurymen had been gathered for the last time and there were scenes outside of 'extraordinary popular excitement'. It was widely known that, at last, the public would have a chance to see Mullins.

'Some hundreds of people stood in the road in front of the hotel for nearly two hours regardless of a drenching rain,' reported *The Times*. 'So deep and vindictive is the popular feeling towards the prisoner that apprehensions were entertained in some quarters that his appearance in so tumultuous a crowd might lead to a riot and strong precautionary measures were therefore taken to maintain the public peace and, if need were, to protect him from personal insult or violence. [5]

'The state of things was calculated to excite alarm,' noted *The Times*, as though this indeed had been a popular melodrama. 'As the time wore on the multitude kept constantly augmenting and the excitement grew in proportion.' [6]

The clamour was so great that the jury had some difficulty getting into the hotel. Among those pushing their way through the crowds and police were, once again, Mrs Emsley's solicitor and her stepsons-in-law, Faith and Whittaker. Walter Emm was 'in attendance with his bail'.

'About ten o'clock, the prisoner Mullins arrived in a cab in charge of Mr Howie, the superintendent of the divisional police,' recounted *The Times*. 'As the cab approached, the crowd made an ugly rush towards the entrance of the hotel, and he [Mullins] alighted amid a scene of uproar. He was instantly surrounded by a formidable body of police officers and escorted into the house, hooted and derided by the multitude outside.' [7]

Mullins was taken to an upper room as the jury and witnesses awaited the arrival of the coroner. As soon as John Humphreys was in the building, Mullins was taken downstairs 'and placed at the end of the table round which the jury sat and immediately in front of the coroner. There he stood during the whole of the subsequent proceedings . . . his manner was quiet and self-possessed and he betrayed no feeling except such as was indicated by a constant compression of the lips and the pale hue of his features.'

The journalists noted his 'thin sandy hair', his 'slight baldness' and the fact he was 'slightly above the middle height'.

By this stage, Mullins had a solicitor: Hubert Wood of Coleman Street Buildings in Moorgate. Wood immediately rose to complain that he had not 'been allowed a private interview with his client'. The coroner told him he was perfectly free to speak to the prisoner in the presence of the custodial officers. Then, one by one, new and old witnesses were called, this time to face Mullins as they gave their evidence.

Returning to the inquest was Joseph Biggs, the self-styled apostolic minister who had served as Mrs Emsley's amanuensis. The jury was reminded that he had proposed marriage to her many times and that they were on 'intimate terms'. There was still some comical suspicion among jury and onlookers that Biggs' emphasis on their closeness was part of an early bid to lay claim on some of the old widow's wealth. He was there to identify items that had been found in the parcel in Emm's outhouse. Among them were the two telescopic lenses.

'I think I saw them once in Mrs Emsley's possession,' said Biggs. 'I have no doubt in my own mind that I did, though there are no marks about them by which I could positively swear to them.'

Also recalled was Mrs Emsley's weekly charlady Elizabeth George. She was called upon to identify two rather ordinary spoons which had also formed part of the parcel, and, more importantly, to identify Mullins as having been present in Mrs Emsley's house on the Saturday afternoon before her death.

'Had you often seen him there?' a juror asked.

'No,' replied Mrs George.

'Did you hear any conversation?' asked the coroner, about that Saturday.

'I heard the deceased talk to him about whitewashing some kitchen ceilings,' said Mrs George. 'He came at six o'clock and stayed till about seven. He was paid 6s for work he had done for her. I heard no conversation between the deceased and him about anything else other than whitewashing.'

The coroner and the jurors were, without quite articulating it, clearly trying to reach towards some kind of motive. If the conversation between Mrs Emsley and James Mullins that Saturday evening had been filled with hot words, then a sense of anger might explain the later violence.

The next stage of the proceedings was more pointed. Dr Gill, the medic who had first examined Mrs Emsley's corpse on 17 August, was also recalled. The coroner showed him Mullins' hammer and asked if the head wounds suffered by the old lady could have been inflicted 'with an instrument of this kind?'

'Decidedly,' answered Dr Gill. 'The wound over the eyebrow corresponds in length with the sharp end of the hammer. The contused wounds at the back of the head might have been occasioned by the butt-end of it.'

The coroner asked if the doctor had any reason to believe that the wounds were made with an instrument 'sharp in its edges, not round?'

'Decidedly,' said Dr Gill.

Hubert Wood, the defending solicitor for Mullins, declined to ask the doctor any questions of his own.

There had been a strong current of excitement among the crowds outside at the arrival of the man they deemed to be the innocent victim in this lurid drama. Walter Thomas Emm was next to stand in that stuffy backroom to face questioning, and was happy to give the coroner his own account of that extraordinary weekend when the police turned up at the brickfields. Then came more questions.

Was Emm in financial thrall to the widow?

'I have had a great many business transactions with Mrs Emsley,' said Emm. 'I was not indebted to her at all. I had some building contracts with her.'

Yet was he not also paying rent to her? Emm made a fine distinction.

'I was not paying her off by so much a week,' he explained. 'I was paying her by the year. I do not consider I owe anything until the time for payment comes. When I owe a debt, and have got time to pay it in, I do not consider I am indebted until the time arrives.'

Journalists briefed by the police had found that Emm's financial relationship with the old lady was not quite as straightforward as it was presented at the inquest. There was, according to the *Observer*, 'an agreement drawn up between Mrs Emsley on the one part and himself on the other, whereby the first-named agrees to sell, and the other agrees to buy, certain tenements therein specified, for the sum of £100, to be paid by quarterly or other payments, and upon which already more than one-half has been paid, as shown by the acknowledgements of the deceased woman'. [8]

In other words, Emm was not merely managing property and collecting rent; he was working towards becoming a landlord himself. The outstanding debt he had to Mrs Emsley was actually a business investment, not just a means of keeping a roof over his head.

However, even in this there was an example of Mrs Emsley's 'extreme meanness', according to *The Observer*. The report noted that, 'the receipt stamp, acknowledging some of these payments, on the leaf of a small memorandum book, was not written upon or defaced, in order that it might be cut off from the top of the page, and affixed at the bottom when the page was full, thus making one stamp available for payments extending over many months, but at the same time rendering perfectly invalid all the previous payments.' [9]

The inquest was also not told how Emm took on some of the tougher rent-collecting propositions, too alarming even for Mrs Emsley. She had recently bought a number of houses in a 'Chancery sale' – houses that had been lost to their owners through law cases – and as such, inherited a large number of tenants with these homes. Due to grinding legal machinery, no one had been collecting rent from these tenants; a state of affairs the tenants quite obviously grew comfortable with.

Mrs Emsley had made an initial visit to her new houses to let the tenants know they would now be paying rent to her. As a result, she 'was threatened with personal violence' by the tenants if she should even so much as make the request again. Emm was then sent in to deal with the recalcitrant tenants, and it was some of these properties, among others, that he had been in the process of buying from the old lady.

The coroner asked if Emm knew James Mullins.

'I know Mullins,' he replied.

The two men were a matter of feet away from each other, separated only by a table.

'Since the death of Mrs Emsley,' continued Emm, 'I have never seen him in the brickfield, except on the morning of Sunday week, when the officers were present.'

At this, Emm was allowed to withdraw and the next witness to be called was his sixteen-year-old daughter Susannah. The coroner asked for her account of the weekend when the fateful package was found; he smelled deceit and he wanted to get to the heart of it.

In a dramatic turn of events, Susanna told the court she had seen Mullins in the brickfields near the outhouse the day before he arrived with the police, on the Saturday.

'That was about half-past two in the afternoon,' she said. 'He was looking down on the ground as if he was in search of something. I saw him about a quarter of an hour but afterwards I did not take any notice of him, for I went about my work.'

Did he perhaps have anything in his hands?

'He had nothing with him that I saw,' replied Susanna. 'I told several people that I had seen him – an aunt of mine, among others.'

Where was she when she was watching Mullins' movements?

'I was in my father's house when I saw Mullins,' Susanna explained. 'He was three parts over the field, or about twenty yards or so from our house.'

Wood was permitted cross-examination. He wanted to know more about the shed. How many other people, he asked Miss Emm, could have gone in and out of it during the course of that weekend? Susanna, possibly misunderstanding the question, told the coroner and jurors she did not go to the shed with anyone on the Sunday.

Was there, asked Wood, any kind of fastening on this shed door?

'The shed door stands open,' said Susanna. 'It is broken and won't shut.'

She was pressed further on the point by Wood, who was clearly trying to show that anyone might be able to slip in there to hide a package. However, Susanna remained adamant: 'There is only one door to the shed.'

In other words, she was saying, it would not be easy to enter it unnoticed from the Emm family cottage.

Now it was the turn of the youngest member of the Emm

family. Ten-year-old Walter was summoned into this intimidating room full of grave-looking grown-ups. The news report described him at once as 'an intelligent boy'.

His testimony was even more galvanising. After identifying Mullins across the room, the boy declared: 'I saw him in front of the house on the brickfield on the Friday before my father was arrested.'

The boy was asked what he saw Mullins doing.

'It was in the afternoon,' replied Walter. 'He was lying on the grass with a handkerchief to his eyes, at the back of the school wall. I saw him there about half an hour. I had gone out to look after my pigs. I told my sister when I went in that I had seen him.'

It was a curious, unsettling image; a man lying in a brickfield motionless, with his eyes covered. What could Mullins have meant by it?

'I saw him again on the following day after dinner,' continued the boy. 'He came towards a heap of sand in the field, where they were putting down some drainpipes, and then went back again. I was there in the field over against the fence, minding my pigs.'

The coroner wanted to be sure that the boy was certain it was Mullins he had seen and not someone else.

'I was so near Mullins as to be able to know it was Mullins,' replied Walter. 'I knew him before, because I went down to Stratford with my father to see him and his son.'

After being questioned by Hubert Wood, Walter added that he 'saw Mullins in the brickfield one or two weeks before the Friday'.

Having heard all this, the coroner called for the court to be cleared of spectators as he and the jury deliberated on what they had heard. None of the evidence that day had been to do with the body of Mrs Emsley; instead, the inquest had turned decisively into a pursuit of the truth about the mysterious package. At this stage, its contents – the optics, spoon, even the ribbon – struck witnesses as being intensely familiar. What was the meaning of them? Were they the grand total of an opportunistic theft following the murder?

There was obviously the very puzzling question of why, if the package had been put together by Emm, he had decided first of all to steal such relatively worthless items and then, furthermore, to hoard them in a place where anyone might eventually happen across them.

The inquest was now focusing on another idea: not only that Mullins had planted this evidence in order to incriminate Emm, but that the mere fact of having stolen such items from Mrs Emsley's home made him the killer.

The coroner and jury returned after half an hour and announced they would reconvene at a later date. In the meantime, Mullins should be taken back to the Thames Police Court in Stepney for further deliberations on his detention. As Mullins' custodians escorted him out of the Railway Hotel into the street, a riot almost broke out.

This was an ever-present fear of the police: that local people, inflamed with rumour, alcohol and vigilante adrenaline, would launch a roaring attack. Outside the hotel, there was a tightly packed crowd. For both the prisoner and the men guarding him, the effort to move through this claustrophobic corridor of shouting, swaying men, must have been harrowing.

'A cab was drawn up to the door of the tavern,' ran a report, '. . . upon which an almost indescribable scene of tumult occurred. The crowd had remained in the open road in the rain during the whole of the investigation inside to hear the result and to see Mullins. A narrow pathway, thickly lined by policemen on both sides, was kept from the door to the cab; the warder first took a run, and was then followed by the prisoner and Superintendent Howie; and all three having got inside, it was driven off amid the yells of the mob, who ran by the side of it for some distance.' [10]

The crowd had no doubts in the matter: Mullins was the savage murderer. As he was sitting in that cab between his two custodians, Mullins would probably have experienced the primal fear of being the target of an unthinking mob. Curiously, this was a particular fear with which he was already well acquainted, as we shall see later.

The architecture of the hearing did not seem to allow for a protestation of innocence; Mullins had not been given an opportunity to speak. Despite the presence of his defending solicitor, the hearing had gone in one direction only and left him looking stained and sinister. Now, all in a single day, he was being driven to the Thames Police Court to hear the more forensic case being prepared against him. Did Mullins have an explanation for his extraordinary behaviour in the brickfields? If he did, was anyone willing to listen to it?

13

'A Gentle Talk with You in Any Other Place'

❧

The hansom cab arrived unmolested at the Thames Police Court ten minutes later, some distance ahead of the shouting crowds. In a separate cab was Walter Thomas Emm, still nominally a suspect. Swiftly, both Emm and Mullins were formally charged with 'wilful murder'.

As the court swiftly filled with a number of Emm's friends, Mullins stood quite alone.

'When the prisoners were placed in the dock,' ran the newspaper report, 'the court was crowded to excess. Emm had previously surrendered with his surety. Mullins had to be led out of the cell behind the court by Roche, the jailer, and it was some time before the police were able to force a passage through the crowd.' [1]

The lawyers assembled: Mr Wontner, representing 'the relatives of the deceased'; Emm's defence was Charles Young; Hubert Wood had arrived from Mile End to represent Mullins.

This was not yet the trial, more a pre-hearing, and the magistrate, Mr Selfe, rather strikingly, had to be given a full update of what had happened at the inquest. Wontner then stated that only two witnesses would be called to the dock, as time was yet needed to supply 'the proof of the murder', as he put it. The public had no doubts, but there was more work to be done. In fact, the police had quietly been assembling more evidence – or, as Mullins' defence might have seen it, marshalling more circumstantial facts around their firmly-held theory that he was the killer.

Many years afterwards, Arthur Conan Doyle was particularly struck by the sheer velocity of the case and the way it was constructed.

'The case was prejudged by the public before ever the prisoner had appeared in the dock,' he wrote, 'and the evidence which the police had prepared against him was not such as to cause them to change their opinion.' [2]

The purpose of this hearing was to demonstrate why Mullins had to be held in custody; that the author of that scene of bloody carnage was too dangerous to be allowed his liberty. Even though Emm had not yet been discharged, there was now little sense that he was associated with the crime. The focus was completely on Mullins, the court now being invited to regard him as a psychopathic murderer.

So it was that the accused man now watched the witnesses in these more formal legal surroundings. Up to the dock stepped John Faith, Mrs Emsley's stepson-in-law, followed by Dr Gill, who again relayed in greater detail than before how he found Mrs Emsley's corpse; 'the broken skull, the membranes of the brain', the maggots, the 'state of pulp'.

Wontner now stepped forward in the courtroom and produced a plasterer's hammer for all in the court to see. It had, he said, 'been found in the dwelling of the prisoner Mullins'.

'He asked Dr Gill if such an instrument as that was likely to cause the wounds he described?'

'It is my opinion,' replied Dr Gill, 'that an instrument like that did occasion the wound.'

'Have you measured the sharp end of that instrument?' asked Wontner.

'I have,' replied the doctor, 'and it corresponds with the length of the wound above the left eyebrow.'

'Look at the other end of the hammer,' said Wontner. 'Would that produce the circular wound you have spoken of?'

'I have no doubt,' responded Dr Gill, 'the skull has been fractured by such an instrument as this. The circular wound has been produced by repeated blows, and forced into the brain, and I judge this by the extreme crispness of the edges.'

Now the magistrate had a question: 'Was that injury done by one blow, Mr Gill?'

'No, sir, not by one blow,' explained the doctor. 'The opening is too large to have been inflicted by one blow. It was done with some heavy instrument, as the wound was starred in all directions.'

'It now only remains for me to state that I shall be prepared with further evidence on a future occasion,' said Wontner.

While Emm was once more allowed to walk out of court, surrounded with family and wellwishers and his bail fund of £200 guaranteed by his friend Henry Gordon, Mullins was transferred back to the House of Detention.

A few days later, on 26 September, the prisoner was brought back to the dock.

'Mullins appeared to be ill, care-worn and agitated when he was placed in the felons' dock,' described a report. 'He paid great attention to the evidence and was in frequent communication with Mr Wood, his solicitor, throughout the day.'

By contrast, the newspaper noted, Emm, also recalled to court, 'was in good health and spirits'. [3]

There was little wonder. Wontner told the magistrate that having listened to all the evidence, and having had further communications with other parties, 'there was no foundation for the charges that had been made against him by Mullins.' Wonter ventured his view that Emm was 'entirely innocent'.

'Is Emm in court?' asked the magistrate, rhetorically.

'He is, sir,' said Emm's solicitor, Mr Young, 'and he attends upon his bail.'

Young beckoned Emm forward. Now looking at Emm directly, the magistrate addressed him.

'It has been intimated to me by the gentleman who conducts the prosecution that there is no ground for detaining you any longer in custody,' declared the magistrate. 'You are, therefore, discharged, there being now no imputation upon you as to any implication in the murder of Mrs Emsley.'

This development appeared to cause Mullins acute discomfort.

'He was evidently not prepared for the acquittal of Emm,' ran one report, 'and watched him with intense anxiety as he moved through the court to the clerk's room.'

'It is necessary,' said Wontner, 'that I should enter into minute details of all the circumstances concerned with this horrible murder . . . It was well-known not only to the prisoner, but many persons in the neighbourhood [that] the unfortunate old lady [was possessed of considerable property].'

'There was no doubt,' he continued, 'that a knowledge of these facts led the person, whoever he may be, to commit the murder. It was also well-known that she was unattended by any domestic servant and that she resided alone in the house. It will appear in the course of this inquiry that the deceased watched with considerable scrutiny every person who called upon her, and that she refused admission altogether to any person who was a stranger to her.'

The chief question in this preliminary inquiry, according to Wontner, was this: was the prisoner the person who committed the murder?

The solicitor then pointed to what appeared to be the biggest irony of this most shocking crime: the fact that the very first concrete lead the police managed to get hold of, some three weeks later, was the testimony of James Mullins about the parcel hidden in Walter Thomas Emm's shed. It was thanks to 'some intervention of providence', as Wontner put it, that something in Mullins' manner made him, rather than the shoemaker, an immediate suspect. In addition, the incriminating parcel was tied up with a piece of wax end 'similar' to that found on Mullins' mantelshelf when the police searched his lodging.

Wontner quoted a witness, one of Mrs Emsley's tenants, who had had dealings with Mullins on the day of the murder. The witness testified that Mullins, 'had been engaged in his occupation as a plasterer' in the witness' rented rooms, but that 'he had left the job unfinished, promising to return the following morning'. Mullins apparently did not do so; in fact, he rematerialised 'about the middle of the next day'.

What then followed seemed a leap: 'He did not account for where he had been,' said Wontner, 'and the only inference to be drawn was that he was at the old lady's.'

Wontner went on to quote another witness, a man who claimed to have seen Mullins in the first light of dawn on the Tuesday morning, hours after Mrs Emsley was thought to have been murdered. This witness, James Mitchell, saw Mullins at five o'clock in the morning on Stepney Green while he himself, 'was going to his employment at the docks'. Mullins, according to Mitchell, 'appeared pale and in an excited state'.

Next came a curious, but uncannily acute, observation. Mitchell had, 'gazed on Mullins intently and stated that he judged from his manner that he thought him an officer in plain clothes'. The echoes of Mullins' past were now starting to reverberate around him. The sensation must have been unnerving for the man in the dock.

Mitchell told Wontner that after he had heard about the murder, he got in touch with the police. It was while Mullins was being held in the last few days that the witness was taken to the Clerkenwell House of Detention, where he went into every cell. On entering Mullins', he recognised him instantly. Again, this was something of a leap: why would recognising a man he had passed on Stepney Green necessarily point to anything at all, let alone a suggestion of guilt?

Wontner wanted to bring up two other 'circumstances' which would 'prove the prisoner's connexion with the murder'. These new items of evidence seemed on the face of it rather more serious. First was 'a silver pencil case which was known to have been in the possession of the deceased, and which had some spots of blood on it, and had been sold by Mullins' wife to a person in Chelsea'.

Second was that 'at the house where the prisoner lived with his wife and family' – quite separate from his Bethnal Green lodging, these were rented rooms on the border of Chelsea – 'a Blucher boot was found by Inspector Thornton in a dusthole there. This,' *The Times* quoted Wontner as saying, 'had large nails in the sole of it, each of which corresponded to nail marks' which had been noted in the blood upon Mrs Emsley's landing.

A few moments later, in a startling piece of gory judicial theatre, Inspector Thornton and Sergeant Dillon, who had been called to illustrate the point about the boot print, came into the courtroom bearing a length of wood wrapped in oil-cloth, which they unwrapped. Thornton announced that 'the bloody footmark had been cut out of the floor'. With this, he held up the blood-soaked wood that had been sawed out of the landing outside the murder room, with the footprint marked in it, for the magistrate to see.

Following this, Mrs Emsley's putative suitor Joseph Biggs took to the stand and was shown the lenses found in the parcel. Could he confirm they had belonged to her? Biggs believed them 'to be the property of the deceased. She exhibited them to him three weeks or a month before her death.'

The silver pencil case was also positively identified by Biggs: he had for some time been entrusted with it, before returning it to Mrs Emsley. It was 'a very peculiar pencil case'. Biggs was asked if Mrs Emsley could write.

'I never knew the deceased to write,' he replied. 'I used to write her letters and receipts. She had an account at the London and Westminster Bank some time ago, but not of late. She had drawn all her money out of the bank to make purchases.'

These were not minor purchases and the sums were not footling. Mrs Emsley was buying up more property and more plots of land in the east for houses to be built on.

That silver pencil case appeared to be crucial. Dr Gill was recalled and said that he was satisfied 'in his own mind' that there were spots of blood upon it. They were, he explained, spots of human blood.

Next to be called was Thomas Pryor, landlord of the Royal Oak in Keppel Street. Pryor had bought the pencil case from Mullins' wife, Catherine.

'On the following Sunday,' *The Times* reported, 'in light of what he had read in the newspapers, he was induced to send for the police and the pencil case was given up to Inspector Thornton.'

It was now Inspector Thornton's opportunity to produce the hobnailed blucher boot which had been found in the dust-hole at 12 Little Orford Street, the Chelsea residence of the Mullins family, where James Mullins generally resided at weekends. This boot, averred the inspector, had been seen being 'flung out of the back window of the room occupied by the prisoner and his family'.

A new witness was called, the one Wontner had referred to earlier in his opening remarks. Michael Gaffney, a cooper and tenant of Mrs Emsley lived in Queen's Row, Bethnal Green. On Monday 13 August, said Gaffney, Mullins 'inspected some work' in 'his dwelling' (a plastering and papering job) and then said that he would call back the next morning to attend to it. Gaffney expected Mullins 'early on the following morning, but he never came until one o'clock in the afternoon'. This was the afternoon after the old lady was supposed to have been murdered. When he did arrive, recalled Gaffney, Mullins 'appeared in a very excited state' and put some wallpaper up 'topsy-turvy'.

'Mullins did not go on with his work as he ought to have done,' added Gaffney. William Rowland – a fellow 'paper-hanger', who also did work and collected rents for Mrs Emsley – came around to lend a hand to Mullins. The work went on until Friday. Gaffney recalled how on that day Rowland mentioned that he had heard an old lady had been murdered in Grove Road, and he wondered whether it was Mrs Emsley.

'I have heard something about it myself,' Gaffney remembered Mullins saying. Rowland went out on an errand; on his return, he exclaimed, 'I'm blowed if it is not true about the old lady!' He and Mullins apparently stopped their work and retired to a local pub to discuss the matter.

Rowland, twenty-five years old, was not just a general handyman; he had also been a warrant officer at the Worship Street Police Court. Like Emm and Mullins, Rowland was trusted by Mrs Emsley to collect money for her, and like his colleagues, he was a frequent visitor to 9 Grove Road. At the inquest in the Railway Arms a few days before, Rowland had given the impression of being a go-between, settling arguments with Mrs Emsley's more disputatious tenants. He was one of the few people who would have had unquestioned access to the old lady. Rowland would also have worked closely with Emm. After he was called to the stand, Rowland threw what might have seemed deliberately lurid light upon the behaviour of Mullins.

He testified that he last saw Mrs Emsley on that Monday 13 August just after lunchtime to give her two pounds in collected rents. That week, recalled Rowland, he and Mullins had a few conversations about the quantity of wallpaper Mrs Emsley had bought. He also remembered that on the Friday, when he told Mullins that the murder victim was indeed Mrs Emsley, it was Mullins who said, 'let us have something to drink'.

'He seemed very much alarmed and terrified,' said Rowland. He recalled that, as they drank rum in The Queen's Head on the

Cambridge Heath Road, Mullins' hand 'trembled very much and he shook violently'.

Rowland next ran into Mullins a few days afterwards (and a short while before he was arrested) and remarked to him that he had heard no new developments in the murder investigation. He then told Mullins, with what sounded like an edge of threat: 'I have strong suspicions of the man, and I have him in my eye now. I will never lose sight of him until the perpetrator of this diabolical murder is discovered.'

'Did he make any remark?' asked Wontner.

'He said, "I also suspect a man, and am watching him now",' replied Rowland. 'He then became anxious to leave me and wanted to go away.'

Observers of Mullins in the court that day reported that his manner veered between thoughtful calm and 'extreme agitation'.

The police's case, in some senses, seemed improvised. In its anxiety to secure a conviction, K Division appeared to approach the question of evidence with a certain hurriedness. In grabbing at these confiscated lengths of ribbon, boot, and hammer, they appeared to be marshalling circumstantial items to fit a theory that had been formed in an instant in that brickfield. The hammer, if it had been a weapon, had no trace of blood upon it, and there was nothing to suggest that the discarded boot – also free of blood, and which by itself had limited significance – actually belonged to Mullins.

When the hearing was adjourned, and Mullins was waiting under guard in an adjoining room to be conveyed back to his cell, he tried to make light of the evidence, telling his solicitor that he was sure it would be 'upset'. He was shaken, though.

'I am surprised Emm is discharged,' said Mullins. 'Depend upon it, he knows all about it.'

Mullins' young daughter Mary wanted to see her father, and she was allowed into the anteroom, the pair of them watched closely by Sergeant Tanner. At one point, Mullins pointed at Tanner and said to his daughter: 'Beware of that man; don't speak to him; don't look at him. If you meet him in the street, cross to the other side of the way.'

The horse-drawn van arrived to take him back to his prison and it travelled via the police station at Worship Street in Shoreditch to pick up some other prisoners. The van was cellular – divided into small compartments separated by bars – and Mullins was securely locked in. However, in its stately progress through the streets of the East End, it had attracted the same roaring crowd that had assembled to catch a glimpse of Mullins at the Thames Police Court.

As the van stopped at Worship Street the crowd caught up with it.

'A costermonger got up upon the steps of the vehicle,' reported the *Manchester Guardian*, 'and called out: "Mullins, you ------ rascal, you will be hanged, and I shall see you swinging".' As the newspaper noted, 'if Mullins had not been securely locked in a compartment . . . he would have been dragged out and torn to pieces by the mob.' [4]

The following morning, the crowds at the Thames Police Court were out in even greater force. The van carrying Mullins arrived just after eleven o'clock and the spectators 'groaned and yelled loudly as the gates of the courtyard closed'. Mullins then had around two hours to wait before he was formally arraigned before the magistrate, John Selfe. He appeared 'in much better health and spirits' than the previous hearing and 'quite unmoved throughout the long examination'. Indeed, he frequently consulted with his solicitor and 'occasionally took notes of the proceedings'. [5]

Mr Wontner, representing the Emsley family, now announced to the court that he intended to complete the evidence and 'trace the movements of the prisoner up to the commission of the murder'. He claimed he would be able to demonstrate that Mullins 'was the party at the house' on the night of the murder, that he could produce evidence which would trace Mullins up to eight o'clock on the night of the murder, and that he would call a witness who could show that he saw Mullins 'going in a direction towards the house of the deceased'.

The question was, continued Wontner, could Mullins himself 'give an account where he was, after he was last seen about eight o'clock on the night of the murder and between that time and five o'clock on the following morning when he was seen on Stepney Green?' Added to this, explained Wontner, the court would be hearing more about the discovery of a boot outside Mullins' dwellings in Chelsea.

Wontner declared that there was a witness who found the sole of this boot so worn out that there was an opening in it, and in that opening had been found human hair. That had given rise to the theory that, 'in his opinion . . . a rather violent theory . . . that the finding of this human hair in the boot had some connexion with the murder, and that as the deceased was lying on the ground that this hair had become entangled in the boot.'

Perhaps, added Wontner, 'that was a theory too violent to assume; for it was well known that as the prisoner was a plasterer, the finding of this hair was only significant of his trade, as it was a common practice to mix hair with mortar, and it might be possible that this might have got into his boot otherwise than in the peculiar manner supposed, as it was well-known that the refuse found at a barber's shop was used by plasterers'.

Dr Gill was recalled, confirmed that he had examined the boot and there was indeed human hair 'adhering to it, between the welt and the sole'. With this, he handed the magistrate a folded piece of paper containing three of the hairs in question.

Human hair aside, still no one had established beyond doubt that the boot actually did belong to Mullins. Was his own solicitor cautioning calm? Was Mullins himself looking on so quietly because of rising confidence?

A new witness was called. Fifteen-year-old James Clarke told the court he lived with his father at 10 Temple Terrace in Bethnal

Green. Clarke said he knew Mullins and saw him on Monday 13 August at his father's house. Mullins was there to carry out maintenance. He began work at 'two o'clock in the afternoon and finished at four. The job was quite complete then.' This account was corroborated by shoemaker Isaac Tyrell. He lived a few doors down and was also having work done by Mullins, who was 'engaged in pointing tiles in the front kitchen and also knocking down the ceiling'. He used a 'sharp-pointed hammer' – a plasterer's hammer.

At this, Sergeant Thomas came forward in the court and produced Mullins' hammer, which had been 'found in his lodgings'. Tyrell looked at it and said that, yes, it 'was such a hammer as that'.

Tyrell took the instrument in his hand, felt along the edge of it and told the court that the hammer he saw in Mullins' hand 'appeared to be rather sharper at the edge than it is now'. The work on the ceiling went on until nearly six o'clock that evening.

'Mullins did not finish the job and was to have come the next day to complete it,' said Tyrell, but he saw nothing of Mullins on the Tuesday. Instead, Mullins came back to complete the work on Wednesday.

Of the hours closer to the murder, another fresh witness – John Raymond, a tailor of Hoxton Square in Shoreditch – told the court that he had been on Grove Road that night, 'outside a public house, waiting to go into a urinal, which was then occupied by a man. When that man came out of the urinal, he [Raymond] took his place.'

The person who left that urinal, said Raymond, was Mullins. He had 'a distinct view of his countenance as he left the retiring place'. Mullins, he said, 'went around the corner of the public house and down the Grove Road in the direction of Mrs Emsley's house'.

Raymond added that he saw Mullins again, 'this morning in a room in this court', as proof that he had no difficulty picking him out from among others. He was adamant, on questioning, that Mullins was the man he had seen leaving 'the retiring place'.

The next man to take the stand was dock labourer James Mitchell of Eden Place in Hoxton. He relayed his story, more luridly now, of a pre-dawn encounter with Mullins on Stepney Green on the morning of 14 August, declaring that he was struck 'with the extraordinary agitation of the man'.

'His eyeballs appeared as if they were coming out of his head, his lips quivered, his whole frame trembled violently, and his knees knocked under him,' Mitchell recounted. He told the court that as he approached Mullins on the street, Mullins 'tried to avoid him and passed inside of him'. Then Mullins 'made a bit of a stagger backwards'. Mitchell was obliged to step to one side; he also 'took his hands out of his pockets'. The suggestion was that he felt the need to ready himself for possible aggression.

There was another outbreak of confusion. Mitchell added that he had been walking south towards the docks while Mullins had been walking north towards the Mile End Road, back in the general direction of Grove Road, which was about a mile away. The magistrate stopped Mitchell for a moment. If, he said, 'it was intended to be set up that the prisoner had just come from the Grove Road when the witness met him, he must have taken a very circuitous route'.

The solicitor stepped in with a possible explanation: 'A very circuitous route, sir. The object in calling this witness is to show the extraordinary excitement and manner of the prisoner early in the morning of the day after the murder was committed.'

Now it was time for light to be shone on Mullins' living arrangements in Bethnal Green – the lodgings set aside for his working week. Caroline Grimson, described simply as 'a single woman', lived in the same lodging house in Barnsley Street and had been there since February. Mullins, she said, lived 'in a back room downstairs'. Conditions seemed a little less ideal than some of the properties that Mullins maintained for Mrs Emsley.

'There were no proper fastenings to the front door,' explained

Miss Grimson. It did mean, however, that 'lodgers could go in and out of the house when they liked'. She remembered seeing Mullins there on the Wednesday 15 August. Miss Grimson revealed that 'in the room which the prisoner [Mullins] occupied, he sometimes allowed a poor woman and some children to live. The children slept there. The oldest child was eight years old.'

This was how people in the foulest rookeries lived: strangers sleeping in the same room. The suggestion of it would have sent a frisson of fascinated revulsion through many of the court onlookers. It raised an instant unspoken question: why did Mullins allow this woman and her children to share his space? Was 'the poor woman' a prostitute, given that the children slept there and she didn't? The court was not interested; the atrocious, squalid impression was left in the air.

Sergeant Thomas was recalled to the stand to discuss the police raid. He said that on 18 August he found a key in the bedroom of the murdered Mrs Emsley, and showed the key to the court.

'It locks and unlocks the door of the room in the house in Barnsley Street where the prisoner lodged,' Thomas explained. When the sergeant took Mullins into custody, he noted that the suspect 'had not the key of his lodging in Barnsley Street about him'. Thomas told the court that he had had to break into the lodgings.

Thomas also described how a search had been made of the dwellings in Chelsea. There, a 'plated teaspoon' was found. 'It corresponded with one of the three spoons found in the parcel in the shed attached to the dwelling of the man Emm who was given into custody . . . on the prisoner's information,' revealed Thomas. The initials on each of the teaspoons were 'WP'.

The magistrate wanted to clarify where the key to Mullins' Bethnal Green lodgings had been found.

'On the first floor, in the deceased's bedroom,' confirmed Sergeant Thomas.

How might Mullins' relationship with Mrs Emsley be best summarised? To answer, Elizabeth Fuke, one of Mrs Emsley's tenants, was called. Mrs Fuke was 'a married woman' who lived at Jane Street on Commercial Road East. She recalled that around 1 August, Mullins was engaged to do some plastering work 'at the expense of Mrs Emsley'. Mullins, she said, 'did not bring sufficient materials for the work, and he complained that Mrs Emsley was very mean'.

Mrs Fuke said that she'd asked Mullins how much mortar he wanted; Mullins replied 'sixpenny worth', which Mrs Fuke gave him. She said that Mullins told her that Mrs Emsley was 'a miserable old wretch, and would not give him sufficient materials to do his work, or half-pay him for what he had done and it was a great pity such a miserable old wretch should be allowed to live'.

The witness told the court about another conversation concerning Mrs Emsley, where she said Mullins told her, 'I will give you some idea about this miserable old wretch. She sat down this morning to a breakfast I would not take. She would not allow herself a farthing to buy any milk.' Apparently Mullins' passion began to subside at this point, as Mrs Fuke told the court that he said, 'you have no need to take any notice of what I have said to Mrs Emsley'.

Walter Thomas Emm, no longer a suspect, was called as a witness. Emm said he last saw Mrs Emsley alive at around two o'clock on the day of her murder. This happened to be on Barnsley Street (as well as the Mullins' lodging house, she owned almost every other property on the street). They made an arrangement to meet again on Wednesday 15 August, as it was usually on a Wednesday that they would set out along the Bow Road to Stratford New Town to collect the rents from her many houses there.

Were there any witnesses who could confirm his movements on the day and night of Mrs Emsley's murder?

'About six o'clock,' replied Emm, 'I went with Rowland as far as Bethnal Green workhouse, which he can prove. Plenty of witnesses can prove where I was from seven to eight o'clock.'

Then there was a moment of electricity. Before leaving the stand, Emm defiantly turned to Mullins, who was staring at him impassively, and said: 'Has Mullins any questions to ask me?'

Wontner leaped in, telling Emm he must not put questions to the prisoner; but Mullins wanted to answer him.

'I will have a gentleman who will have a gentle talk with you in any other place,' he said.

After this flash of enmity, Wontner had some questions about the relationship between Emm and Mullins.

'Has Mullins ever been to your house in the brickfields?' he asked.

'Very often, sir,' replied Emm. 'He has had tea with me there.'

'When did you first become acquainted with him?' continued Wontner.

'About the middle of February last,' responded Emm. 'Mrs Emsley brought him to me. That was the first time I knew him. He has four or five times had tea with me. If he wanted a shilling or two, he always had it, as he knows he had.'

The evidence over, it was time to sum up.

'Prisoner at the bar,' said the magistrate, 'having heard the evidence against you, do you wish to say anything?'

'No, sir,' replied Mullins. 'I will leave it all to my solicitor.'

'Stop!' said the magistrate. 'Hear me. You are not bound to say anything, but what you do say will be written down, and may be given in evidence against you hereafter.'

Mullins' voice, according to reports, was now very much fainter. Still, he replied: 'I will leave it all to my solicitor.'

This was the moment that Mullins' impassive façade collapsed. He became 'greatly agitated, and looked appealingly towards [his solicitor] Mr Hubert Wood'.

The strategy of maintaining his silence until the main trial, however sensible it may have seemed in theory, giving as it did time to build a careful case for the defence, must have torn too hard at his nerves. Mullins knew exactly where he would be going next, and the magistrate pronounced it.

'James Mullins,' he began, 'you are committed to Newgate to take your trial for the wilful murder of Mary Emsley.'

Mullins was taken out of the court, and placed inside the police van. As it left, the gathered crowd outside 'yelled and groaned loudly'. Perhaps if they had known something more of Mullins' past, those people might have hesitated. The case was rather more perplexing and complex than the police were suggesting.

The murder victim, Mary Emsley, of Mile End Old Town, as portrayed by *The Strand* magazine. The image is that of severe respectability; but her neighbours remembered that despite her wealth, her clothes were old, her habits 'eccentric' and 'miserly' — and she had a taste for pineapple rum.

As well as writing about Sherlock Holmes, and a variety of other stories, Sir Arthur Conan Doyle was intrigued by any real-life case where he sensed a possible miscarriage of justice. He might also have been drawn to examine this 1860 murder because of its macabre and seemingly inexplicable elements; a reflection of Holmes's labyrinthine investigations.

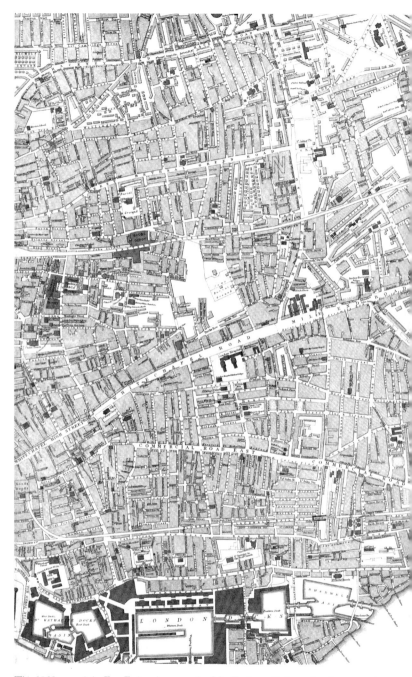

This 1863 map of the East End – the streets that Mrs Emsley walked to collect her rents – is a portr
of poverty and wealth side by side. The narrow streets were filled with poor, insecure tenants whilst the
factories and docks were fuelling London's economic boom. And the map could not keep up: what it does
show in the empty spaces are the land-plots sold to create many more streets of terraced houses.

MILE END GATE.
REMOVED OCTOBER 31ST 1866.

DRAWN BY C READ 155 WELL ST HACKNEY N.

Despite the slum dwellings and the squalor, Stepney and Mile End were filled with colour and commerce in 1860. Coffee houses (some toying with the new idea of self-service) and tea rooms competed, and stalls offered fried fish, hot wine and raspberryade. There were also theatre and even opera performances.

The artist Gustav Doré portrayed London as a city of darkness; here, the illustration is of Seven Dials although it could quite easily have been Ratcliff in the East End in 1860, where Mrs Emsley owned houses. Doré depicted the street's impoverished shoemakers desperately trying to make a sale, overcrowded and rotten dwellings, and children wandering ragged.

"MAMMON'S RENTS"!!

House-Jobber. "NOW, THEN, MY MAN; WEEK'S HUP! CAN'T 'AVE A 'OME WITHOUT PAYIN' FOR IT, YER KNOW!"

[*See the "Bitter Cry of Outcast London."*]

Rent collectors were seen as brutally oppressive, as this famous cartoon by Joseph Swain from *Punch* magazine demonstrates. In Charles Dickens's *Little Dorrit*, collector Pancks is a chilling moral blank. Mrs Emsley's agents would have presented an equally grim prospect to tenants hit by calamity. The old woman herself evicted people if they missed a week's rent.

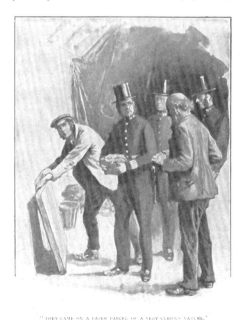

" THEY CAME ON A PAPER PARCEL OF A VERY CURIOUS NATURE."

This illustration from *The Strand* shows the moment the murder investigation was galvanised when one of Mrs Emsley's employees — in hope of the vast cash reward — led the police to an odd parcel of seemingly random items stolen from the old lady.

One of the suspects had himself been a policeman, joining some decades earlier with Robert Peel's pioneering Metropolitan Police Service. By 1850, as pictured, the uniform had evolved a little and the job was seen as offering career advancement opportunities for intelligent working class men. However, working class communities in the East End broadly loathed them.

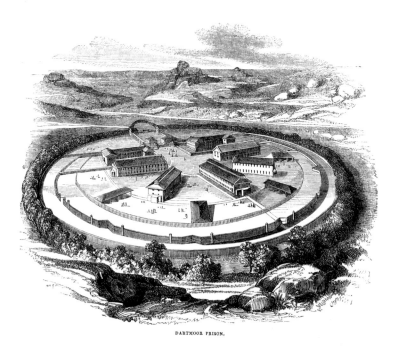

DARTMOOR PRISON.

One of the old lady's employees had previously been sentenced to penal servitude in the much-feared Dartmoor prison. Yet in the 1850s, this jail in the open wilds was seen as a healthier prospect than any in London, especially for those with chest problems.

The Central Criminal Court, where the case was heard, presented a theatrical spectacle for onlookers. Well-lit so that every facial expression of the accused could be observed closely, with a 'sounding board' above their head so that their every utterance could be caught, the person accused of Mary Emsley's murder found themselves the centre of an elaborate legal drama. This image shows a trial from 1883 set up in a similar manner.

In November 1860, the death sentence was pronounced upon the accused, as illustrated here by *The Strand*; but even as he was donning the black cap, the judge, Lord Pollock, seemed to sense that something was amiss, and that the whole story had not been heard.

Newgate prison, pictured here in the late nineteenth century, inspired fear; it also saw a sub-genre of literature called 'the Newgate novel' which featured the exploits of criminal anti-heroes. Dickens's Fagin met his gothic doom within these walls, and the person convicted of Mrs Emsley's murder spent their last night in a roomy cell watched by officers, writing by oil-light.

The New Gallows in the Old Bailey.

Public hangings – seen here outside Newgate prison in the late eighteenth century – were still taking place as late as 1860. On 21 November 1860, at 8am, the individual convicted of Mary Emsley's murder was taken outside the prison gates to the scaffold in front of an estimated 30,000 rowdy London onlookers. Middle class spectators hired overlooking rooms and watched through opera glasses.

14

The Man who Might
have Been

❧

Those officers working on the Emsley case may have heard rumours of James Mullins from older colleagues. This thin, angular man with reddish peppery hair and reading spectacles, reduced to doing labouring jobs for an old woman, had once been one of their most promising pioneers.

Indeed, the man who stood in the dock could conceivably have become a senior superintendent at Scotland Yard – perhaps even a commissioner. If Inspector Thornton had listened extensively to gossip, he would also have known that, despite an incredibly auspicious beginning to his career, together with fast promotion, Mullins had acquired for himself a bad name. There had been trouble after he had been sent undercover to Ireland; and he was acutely sensitive to perceived insults and inclined to come into conflict with colleagues.

When Mullins was a young man in the early 1830s, he was among the brightest prospects of a band of around 3,000 recruits who had been appointed by Robert Peel and the Home Office to form the new Metropolitan Police Service.

Before 1829, London was policed by parish, like the rest of the country. In Stepney and Mile End, there would have been one special constable, one nightwatchman and a parish beadle. These figures were under the supervision of the local magistrate, hailing either from a grand or at least very rich local family. In other words, as the city grew, responsibility for keeping order and bringing criminals to justice was much as it would have been in the smallest rural village. In London, there was also a reserve force of volunteers and militia, there to be called if riots or large-scale civil disobedience broke out.

By the 1830s, London also had what would now be considered as semi-private police forces at work: men specifically appointed by the aldermen of the City of London, for instance, or keeping watch over the rich cargoes at the West India Docks.

The first recruits for Peel's new Metropolitan Police Service were chosen both for toughness (from the very beginning, these uniformed men, armed with sticks, were wildly unpopular with the labouring classes, who felt certain they would swaggeringly abuse their authority and throw their weight around), as well as a certain native quick-wittedness. There were a number of Irish recruits in the first wave of Metropolitan policemen, and conflicts with the wider public began at once.

Mullins had Irish parents, but 'spoke with an English accent'. Although his earlier career is not recorded, he joined K Division when he was about twenty-eight. The most important aspect of this new force was the fact that it carried no firearms: the policemen were not militia men who could fire upon protesting crowds. They had wooden truncheons, rattles and notebooks. The work was dangerous. While London was not generally a city of mass disorder, there were occasional surges. A mob marched on the Duke of Wellington's home at Hyde Park in 1831; an unexpected riot on Gray's Inn Road in 1832 led to one policeman being stabbed to death.

A city could be, by its nature, anti-authoritarian, teeming with individuals, adamant about expressing political and religious belief and freedoms. The police in those early days were called to many outbreaks of disorder in churches. Militant Protestants caused uproar by disrupting services they clearly considered dangerously papist, and the police were called upon to restore some measure of peace upon fighting congregations.

To make up for their lack of weaponry, this first generation of policemen received rigorous and semi-military training. On joining the force, Mullins would have presented himself to a surgeon for a fitness medical. Then there would have been a rudimentary literacy test. After this, the physical training would have begun. Mullins would have been required to report to a drill ground at the Wellington Barracks just off Birdcage Walk near Westminster. For the following few weeks, he would be sleeping there, too. During this period of preparation, pay would have been at the low rate of ten shillings a week.

Each class consisted of about thirty men. Mullins and his companions would have been required to parade 'for several hours each day, six days a week'. There was 'close-order drill' and also 'sabre practice'. Sabres were not part of the policeman's uniform – the idea was more about instilling a sense of disciplined combat and control. The unfamiliar sword exercise would have given Mullins a physically toned quality, perhaps even a greater sense of general confidence. Unlike some of his fellow recruits, he was never a great mass of brawn and muscle. The sabre practice would also have given him and his fellows a means of fusing physical and mental focus.

During those first weeks at the barracks, there would have been instruction concerning all the duties of a police officer. Mullins would have been required to memorise a handbook concerning all the regulations, and for his first six months as a full-time policeman, his superiors would have pulled him aside at random times to test him on the subject.

The training over, Mullins would have been assigned to shadow a more experienced policeman somewhere in the centre of town. The high fashion of Piccadilly lay very close to poor alleys and courts to the back of Regent Street and also, further up, to the city's most notoriously poverty-stricken area of St Giles. On his first few patrols, Mullins would have seen extreme contrasts: at night, the windows of the shops glowing in pale oil-light with rich purples, greens, yellows and reds; in the streets beyond them, all colour subsumed by the black soot and grey mud, the windowless houses dark, the ragged people drinking maniacally to dull their pain. Mullins would have witnessed real depravity: older women corralling young girls aged no more than nine or ten for the purposes of prostitution.

After Mullins' induction, he was transferred to K Division in the East End. Some crimes in the 1830s were baroque; in 1832, for instance, police were required to investigate a macabre outbreak of the body-snatching of dead children from a Poplar churchyard. This was at the time when cadavers were being sold secretly to rogue surgeons (the most famous of the corpse stealers were Burke and Hare in Edinburgh). There were also numerous cases of bigamy around the docks; husbands returned home from long spells overseas only to find their wives had remarried, with resulting repercussions of violence.

There were absent husbands to be dealt with as well, plus men who would not take responsibility for the children they had fathered. In 1833, one such case concerned a young woman and man who had broken into a warehouse where, as the reports later described, 'familiarities took place'. The familiarities resulted in pregnancy and it was for the police to bring the errant boy before the local court.

The streets that Mullins would be supervising were, even by the early 1830s, overcrowded and rough. To the north of the docks near Tower Hill lay the slums of Rosemary Lane, where eighteenth-century courts were filled with families fighting to make a living at the lowest end of the scale by selling dog excrement for tiny sums to the leather tanneries south of the river (it was used in the tanning process).

Many of the poorest were Irish immigrants. Perhaps Mullins' superiors might have thought he would be able to strike up a relationship of trust with them. (Conversely, some twenty years later, senior officers were reluctant to send Irish constables to patrol Irish areas for fear they would either be too close to those being policed or that their uniformed presence would inflame old resentments.) In broader terms, the new policemen were violently unpopular in the East End. In 1834, a hatmaker called Thomas Morris gave voice to his vinegary view that the police were 'the lower order of Irish ... These men are red-hot Irishmen, just imported, who run out and strike every person they meet.' [1] Conversely, it is possible that some of the Irish slum residents might have viewed a uniformed Irishman, an agent of the British state, as a traitor to his own people.

The police were primarily conceived of as helping to prevent crime rather than bringing perpetrators to justice afterwards. The presence of men such as Mullins on the streets was supposed to act as a deterrent to any potential offenders: a reminder that the city was under control.

Serious violent crimes, together with more commonplace outbreaks of street fights, petty assaults, attempted robberies and attempts to pass off forged coins (a very frequent crime), were logged assiduously, with reports sent on a daily basis back to Scotland Yard. Equally, orders issued from the Yard would be delivered to each station at the start of each day. Before this, at half-past six in the morning, there was fifteen minutes of drill. The younger constables were inspected by more senior officers not just to ensure that uniform and notebook were present and correct, but also to make sure that the men were perfectly sober.

One of the greater temptations, both on day and night patrols, was for officers to accept offers of hospitality from tavern owners. This was most especially an issue on wintry night patrols, when spirits were considered an excellent way of keeping the chill at bay. Excessive consumption not only created an appalling public impression, but also caused episodes of embarrassment. In one West End ward in the 1830s, there was some local alarm caused by a vast and rather bloody fight outside an inn in the small hours. Locals rushed in to the police station to summon help, only to find the constables fast asleep, smelling of alcohol.

In a rigidly hierarchical and class-bound society, the needs of the growing city meant that the act of joining the police allowed working-class men the opportunity to take a big step towards a more elevated position. The principle of promotion had been set down at the very beginning by Peel. Rising in the ranks would be the result not of cosy patronage, but quite plainly by 'activity, intelligence and good conduct'. [2]

It was a case of property being stolen from a very rich man that brought young PC Mullins of K Division (his number was K66) fully to the admiring attention of his superiors at Scotland Yard, and later, in the Home Office. In February 1836, Mullins was on the trail of warehouse plunderers in Bethnal Green. The warehouse was owned by a young corset-making entrepreneur from Barnsley called Samuel Emsley, who would, seven years later, marry Mary Jones. Mullins had been monitoring James Sims on a cold Saturday night and apprehended him in Lamb's Fields with a wicker hamper filled with stolen goods. Mullins followed the trail from there.

Samuel Emsley was reportedly so pleased with the officer's efforts that he gave him a ring as a thank-you gift, which was accepted gratefully. More than that, Emsley went to the police office in Arbour Square – the very building in which Mullins would later be accused of murder – specifically to give warm testimony to Mullins' superiors and to recommend that the skilled policeman be promoted.

Perhaps it was Emsley who swung it, or perhaps Mullins' senior officers were perfectly aware of his intelligence and effectiveness without any prompting from others: he got his promotion. The young policeman had not only found for himself a secure position that would guarantee both an income plus specially designated dwellings, he had also crucially found a very large measure of acceptance. Mullins was needed and appreciated.

Though the newly promoted sergeant's East-End beat was lively, in some curious ways – possibly because of the proximity to open spaces and the river – the area was not quite so harrowing a prospect as, for instance, the claustrophobic rookeries of Clerkenwell, gathered around the open sewer of the River Fleet ditch.

In policing terms, the age of mob violence and rioting was also receding, despite the constant neurotic fears of the city authorities.

However, there was a growing discomfort in Whitehall at the numbers of Irish people arriving in Liverpool, Manchester and London; more specifically, about a sense that there was a contagion of sedition coming over from Ireland with them. British rule in Ireland, from the administrative offices of Dublin to the network of Anglo-Irish aristocratic landowners, had long been brutal and unhappy. The vast rural population (Ireland's population then was some eight million people, as opposed to today's four million) were frequently resentful about their powerlessness in the face of indifferent and sometimes cruel landlords.

In the years before the nightmare famine that would scour and scar the entire island of Ireland, there were, in the small villages, groups of men who gathered together in secret societies. The fear in Whitehall, in this new age of steel, coal and vast manufactories, was that the agricultural labourers sailing to England and flocking to the big cities to find work would bring with them these secrets and conspiracies against the Crown. Chartists were one thing, but what sort of subversive and damaging action could these new arrivals take if they bent themselves to it? More than this, the money that could be made in the cities could then be sent back to the secret societies in Ireland, to be used to foment uprisings against landowners.

Sergeant Mullins had joined the Metropolitan Police Service because his cleverness, literacy, and a degree of physical courage were properly appreciated. Now, in this paranoid political climate, Scotland Yard and Whitehall started to appraise this smart young man in quite a new way. Robert Peel had set down from the start that his policemen were not to be used as spies. But some time later – after Mullins received another proud promotion, and a transfer to Ireland and its new police force – a spy is exactly what the Home Secretary wanted him to become.

15

The Spy with the
Stolen Soul

❧

James Mullins became a spy in an age when spies were not popular folk heroes. It was only with the later Edwardian fictions of William Le Queux and John Buchan that espionage became a matter of adventuring with clean morals. In the Victorian age, as in all previous eras, spies were not the sort of people found in any kind of polite society; the very idea of spying was rooted in dishonesty and deception. So unpopular was the principle of undercover surveillance that when the Metropolitan Police Service was founded, its first commissioners wanted it to be known that its constables were there for all the public to see: these men would never be used as infiltrators or agents provocateurs. Quietly, that changed due to a spreading sense of instability in Ireland.

Robert Peel had spent a lot of time thinking about Ireland's policing. After the initial success of the new London service, with its different divisions finding their rhythms and working methods with some speed, the decision was taken to set up a mirroring structure in Ireland.

Three cities – Dublin, Londonderry and Belfast – would have their own policemen, and as in London, they would have the same hierarchies of sergeants, inspectors, superintendents and commissioners. Also like the Metropolitan Police Service, they would not, generally, be armed; instead, they would carry truncheons or batons. However, there were provisions made to allow Irish forces the recourse to firearms. Unlike their London counterparts, the constables would be required to live in barracks – some military habits were difficult to foreswear.

From the start, efforts were made to fit in with the religious sensibilities of each community policed. Catholic villages would get the services of Catholic constables, while villages to the north would be assigned Protestant officers. Sectarian tensions were there from the very start, though. In August 1836, there was uproar in the village of Foxford when a constable called Nixon was alleged to have placed an orange lily in the window of the local police barracks: the flower symbolising the increasingly militant Orange Order, a Protestant grouping. As Catholic pamphlets throughout the community thunderously declared that this proved that the new force was intended as a tool of oppression, Nixon was removed from his duties. Colonel Shaw Kennedy, the chief commissioner of the Constabulary of Ireland, investigated and found no such proof; despite local fury, Nixon was restored to full duties and wages.

In the years and decades before the famine of the 1840s, resentment and anger were roiling through Ireland's countryside. It was literate, educated men who were running secret societies dedicated to preserving the interests of Catholic communities against the hated landowners and British government. Members of these proto-Fenian societies became known as Ribbonmen, as previous generations of such groups had worn ribbons or laces as a means of identification.

Even though the members were Catholic, the Ribbonmen were not religious in motivation; their interests lay in republicanism and revolution. Their imaginations had been captured by the possibilities of the French Revolution, and the inherent conservatism of priests and bishops were of no use to them.

Given that the activities of the Ribbonmen were completely counterbalanced by the roaring of Protestant Orangemen in some areas, there might at least have been an acknowledgement from the British government that both would have to be monitored very carefully. However, politicians in London regarded the Ribbonmen as deeply sinister in their potential – a threat to stability that had to be neutralised. Landowners in the countryside who evicted tenants found themselves under attack from insurrectionary men with stolen firearms. Those who worked for the landlords had their windows smashed, large mobs surrounding their houses threatening to burn them down. The Ribbonmen were effective in their secrecy, melting into local village communities; as such, their more lurid actions caught the attention of the London press.

Reports came in of great phalanxes of men marching across the green land as though in military step, armed with muskets, bayonets and even swords. None could quell the republican spirit of the Ribbonmen.

Across the Irish Sea in Manchester, some declared themselves nervous of the sheer numbers of Ribbonmen that were now in the city.

'I have been battling with that society for the last nineteen years in this locality,' the Reverend D Hearne told the *Manchester Guardian*. 'I know no worse enemies of Ireland than the Ribbonmen. They are, I am told, very strong in Liverpool, under the name 'Hibernian Societies', 'Friendly Brothers' etc ... I believe the ribbon infatuation in Ireland to be principally kept up by supplies from this country.' [1]

It was in Manchester, in the early 1840s, that a plan of espionage was devised; the plan that would subsume the life of James Mullins, by now settled in Ireland himself, with an Irish wife and small children, and promoted to the rank of inspector.

The Home Office got in touch with the Roman Catholic Archbishop of Dublin, Daniel Murray. Murray was implacably opposed to the Ribbonmen and had gone as far as to obtain a papal bull excommunicating entire local lodges. The ribbon societies, in all their robust republicanism, were not much moved by such airy penalties. They had to be thwarted by rather more solid means.

A priest in the countryside near Dublin succeeded in eliciting from one unwitting Ribbonman a trove of intelligence regarding plans and future meetings. This intelligence, which included names of prominent members, was passed back to the Lord Lieutenant in Dublin. In turn, he reported to the Home Secretary, Sir James Graham. There was already monitoring of Ribbon lodges in Liverpool, Manchester and London, and now the government was able to begin the secret interception of correspondence passing between England and Ireland.

'The letters of suspected persons in a postmaster's district were ordered to be forwarded back to the General Post Office,' it was reported. 'In a short period, a number of letters were sent marked to Dublin by a postmistress in the north of Ireland, by which means the authorities learned that a meeting of delegates from all parts of the United Kingdom was to be held to alter the signs and the passwords of the society.' [2]

Among the ranks of the Ribbonmen on the mainland, there was one particular delegate who was living in Manchester. He received a letter from Ireland – again, monitored – inviting him to that meeting. With this, the Manchester police quietly moved in. The man in question was detained before he could set sail. Meanwhile, having travelled from Dublin to Manchester, Inspector James Mullins began a close study of the delegate held in custody: not only of his appearance, but also any mannerisms and habits he had, plus the details of his working life.

This was because Mullins was about to steal the man's identity.

The next phase of the operation must have required not only

careful planning, but also carefully composed nerves, especially for a father with young children to think about. Mullins, now with a borrowed name and life, set sail from Liverpool and headed northwest to a busy town called Ballinamore, which is now in County Leitrim, near the River Shannon. Ballinamore had, in previous years, filled with families from the east of Ireland who had been dispossessed by their landlords. There was a great variety of skilled tradesmen, as well as agricultural workers. The combination of grievance and education made the area fertile territory for the Ribbonmen. If Mullins' mission was successful, men would be sent to the gallows; equally, if he were to be discovered, he would have been treated by the Ribbonmen as the most atrocious sort of traitor and there would be no mercy. On arrival, as one report went, Mullins 'delivered his credentials and was heartily welcomed'. [3]

Mullins the spy was now being greeted by delegates as an old friend. He played his well-funded part well: he 'spent money lavishly', which meant drink and food for his companions, but he must surely have been very tense – Ribbonmen had shown no compunction about extreme violence. Even though the plain-clothes constabulary knew where Mullins was, they themselves were hidden at a little distance. Effectively, Inspector Mullins was on his own.

The night before the main meeting, Mullins accepted an invitation from one of the other delegates to spend the night in his public house in the small village of Ballyconnell, a few miles north. Mullins accepted, but when the men got there, they found that 'all the beds were occupied'. The landlord asked his wife to sleep in their daughters' room, while he and Mullins took the master bedroom. They tarried a while; indeed, the two men drank 'long and deep' and 'vowed eternal friendship'. [4] Mullins must have carefully probed for names.

On arriving back in Ballinamore the next morning, the pair were immediately pitched into a throng of delegates gathering in the main street. Mullins' new friend eagerly introduced him to the others as the delegate from Manchester. The two men found themselves gravitating towards an inn, inside which even more delegates were mingling. It must have taken some effort on Mullins' part to maintain not only an appearance of composure, but also a broader heartiness towards his new friend and the other Ribbonmen jostling around him.

However, before any proceedings began, one young Ribbonman, having watched Mullins closely in that clamouring bar, was suspicious. So much so that he decided to approach him.

This young man was, according to the report, 'more cute than the rest', meaning that he was acute and sharply intelligent. He found an opportunity to draw Mullins to one side and asked him a few innocuous questions, to which Mullins gave innocuous answers. Mullins had fallen straight into the trap. The questions were coded; Mullins was supposed to have answered with set cryptic responses, but didn't give a single correct answer. The young man, evidently as good an actor as the inspector before him, quietly withdrew, letting Mullins return to the general conversation and hubbub.

The young man pulled a couple of his close friends out of the bar and told them it was clear that the man claiming to be one of their number was nothing of the sort, and had clearly never been a Ribbonman. They had to decide there and then how they were going to deal with the spy. The decision was taken to kill him: the fastest and most effective course.

The young man and his associates went back into the bar and found Mullins sitting at a table with some others. He was invited to step out for a moment into the backyard. Mullins' instincts told him exactly how much danger he was in. He rose from the table and made his way towards the back door of the bar. He opened it, but then turned around, claiming he had left his hat behind. Stepping back into the bar, Mullins tried to get out another way, but the room was packed tight. With his intended assassins closing on him, Mullins got close to the front door and shouted with some force: 'Police!'

There must have been at the very least some confusion; possibly a moment of panic. The room certainly would have been alive with consternation, of people moving disjointedly. After a minute or so of chaos, several plain-clothes police entered the bar, armed with guns. As they held the stunned drinkers in that room, their uniformed colleagues arrived shortly afterwards with fixed bayonets. The public bar was surrounded and stragglers rounded up.

'Only one, who fought desperately, and displayed great courage and presence of mind, effected his escape,' reported the *Manchester Guardian*. 'The rest were indicted for simply meeting to unlawfully conspire.' [5]

Mullins had had a narrow escape, and the assignment was ultimately a failure. As his cover had been blown, so too had any opportunity for him to penetrate deeper into the organisation, perhaps spending weeks or months in this new undercover role. As it was, no new intelligence of any great value had been obtained, no blueprint of the society's further plans. More than this, the Ribbonmen who had been rounded up were implacably silent. No matter what methods were used, the authorities would not learn anything of any use. Indeed, the rippling consequence of the entire operation was to drive the Ribbonmen into deeper layers of secrecy.

Inspector Mullins, back in Dublin with his young family, now found himself in daily fear for his life. The Ribbonmen knew who he was and what he had done. Here was a son of Ireland actively working to betray his countrymen and lead them to their violent executions. Mullins understood very well that anyone could find an opportunity to murder him – and his loved ones. His work also put huge pressure on his marriage.

Mullins' Tipperary wife Catherine was, in her heart, with the Ribbonmen. There were times in the aftermath of the operation when she begged her husband to secretly turn his affiliations and swear allegiance to the Ribbonmen and continue working in the Constabulary of Ireland as a double agent, feeding intelligence to the rebels and working within the organisation to bring it down. She was loyal to Ireland: why wasn't he?

Catherine became a neurotic, distracted figure; in time, she refused to sleep in the same bed, or even the same room, as her husband. The reason she gave had a chillingly atavistic quality: she claimed that in the darkness of the night, her husband was being haunted by an evil spirit. Clearly the spectre was punishing him for his wicked priorities.

The strain was too great and it was impossible to remain in Ireland. Mullins applied to be transferred back to London. The idea was that with the resumption of police duties in the capital, the Mullins family might revert to a degree of normality. Ironically, it was this move that was to set him against colleagues in Scotland Yard and start his precipitous fall. Mullins would be shocked by just how far it was possible to drop.

16

'His Conduct was
Very Bad'

❧

After the sea air of Dublin, the bitter, greasy fog of London must have been difficult to readjust to. The city to which Mullins and his family returned was now glowing hotter with the furnaces of industry and was drawing immigrants from all over. When he was last there, Mullins had seemed assured of a strong and satisfying future with the police; now, all that seemed to have changed and he could not understand why.

In Ireland, he had been an inspector; on returning to K Division, Mullins was told that he was once more a sergeant. This was possibly for budgetary reasons; perhaps the division could not afford one more inspector. However, the demotion was more than just a blow to his pride.

He was back in the East End, where the docks were now being served by an elegant and unusual new expression of industrial progress: an innovative railway, sweeping along a four-mile viaduct, powered not by steam locomotives, but by steam-hauling machines that pulled the trains along on cables, themselves miles-long in length and held on giant drums. Mullins found that his demoted duties would be focused on and around what was called the London and Blackwall Railway.

It was a line intended mainly for passengers embarking and disembarking steamships downriver; instead of the grindingly slow sail to and from London Bridge on the gridlocked Thames, one could now leave a ship at Blackwall and transfer to the train. The service included carriages painted in rich blue and gold livery, divided into first and second class, running every fifteen minutes into the heart of the city. On the face of it, it was a more agreeable proposition for a policeman than breaking up drunken fights, dealing with harrowing outbreaks of domestic brutality, or even investigating internal cases of police malfeasance, of which there were a growing number. Mullins, although demoted, still had a degree of responsibility; there were also several ordinary constables assigned to the line, posted at the stations along the route, who were under his control.

Mullins and his family had lodgings provided near Fenchurch Street station. They shared a house with two other men, a constable called Dempsey and a guard on the railway called Rutherford. It was not long before tensions in the house began to rise. Rutherford conceived an ill-will not only towards Mullins, but also to his wife and children. Eventually, Rutherford lodged a complaint with his superiors at the railway about 'the dirty habits' of the Mullins family and their general 'disorderly conduct'. [1] He wanted them evicted.

It is difficult not to detect a tang of anti-Irish feeling in this outburst; indeed, in the popular press and journals of the time, portraits of Irish people were nakedly bigoted. The stereotyped Irishman was depicted either as vaguely simian with an elongated jaw and an infernal temper stoked up with excessive drink, or as a childlike simpleton with an attachment to fairy stories. Even sympathetic newspaper coverage (in 1843, there was a harrowing report of a family in Shadwell where the poor father, an unemployed coal whipper, was left looking after two disabled boys in a squat, newspapers stuffed into windows and only one chair in the entire room) tended towards generalised pity for the unsophisticated Irish people who could not cope with London life.

The understandably sensitive Mullins received the intelligence of his neighbour's 'dirty habits' accusation with boiling anger. Given that the security of the roof over his family's head was being threatened, it would have been surprising if Mullins had not been furious. He told his colleagues that he was going 'to have a word or two' with Rutherford, but he appeared to have rather more in mind than a simple row. Mullins wanted to confront Rutherford in front of his own colleagues on the London and Blackwall Railway.

One Wednesday afternoon, Rutherford boarded the train he was guarding out of Fenchurch Street. Sergeant Mullins also got on board. The system of the railway, sweeping across that viaduct, had a further unique feature. As well as being hauled along on a vast cable, certain carriages could be detached at stations along the route. Thus, if one was sitting in the carriage marked Limehouse, that was its destination. Each carriage opened up at the end to allow the guard to carry out the decoupling. Thanks to metal pins in the main haulage cable, the detached carriage would stay in its allotted station and only the front carriages would proceed the full length of the line, joining up with the stationary cars on the return journey.

As the train was gliding past St Anne's Church at Limehouse, Mullins realised he was in the wrong carriage, one that would be decoupled. As the train was slowing before West India Dock, he opened the carriage door facing the front and stood on the open platform facing the front cars. What happened next is not entirely clear.

Mullins was intending to step across between carriages, but instead fell down into a slowly widening gap and on to the tracks. The accident and resulting injury was horrific. Some part of the train hit Mullins' leg. According to one account, the wheel of the carriage that Rutherford was in 'went over his knee'. When help arrived, Mullins was 'insensible'. [2] At that time, smashed bone and

171

heavy loss of blood could very easily have been fatal. Somehow, Mullins was kept alive as he was transported two miles back up the line to the London Hospital at Whitechapel.

Mullins stayed there for the next three months, but the gruesome incident did not appear to win him any great sympathy; instead, he gained a reputation for being quarrelsome. When he recovered, Mullins was returned to the London and Blackwall Railway. It cannot have been easy for him to go back, and indeed there was more violence to come.

Late one night, in the small hours, the officers at the Shadwell police substation were startled when Sergeant Mullins burst in, his clothes torn, 'apparently exhausted'. There were signs that he had been beaten. Dazed, Mullins told his colleagues that after the last train had run, he had been walking down the line along the section of the great brick viaduct that crossed the canal and ran parallel to the Commercial Road. It was from this vantage point that Mullins said he was able to see three burglars attempting a break-in at the back of a property on Brunswick Terrace in Stepney. Mullins said that he went down the stairs at Stepney station and, making his way around to the property, surprised the burglars in the act. He said he tried to arrest them, but it was hopeless: he was overpowered. After 'beating him in a brutal manner', they then 'disabled' him. (3)

The injuries were such that his continued employment as a policeman seemed impossible. Even then, among Mullins' hostile colleagues, there was a sense that the whole thing was a fabrication and that the sergeant had staged the beating in order to gain official sympathy from his superiors at Scotland Yard and be pensioned off. The fact that such a rumour had any traction said much about Mullins' colleagues. His story, it was later said, was 'not contradicted by those who knew it to be a fabrication because they were glad to relieve the force of Mullins at any price'. (4)

He was superannuated, and his pension was to be thirty-five pounds a year. This was hardly a generous sum, the equivalent of roughly £1,700 today. The accommodation would no longer continue, either. Mullins and his family were faced with the prospect of trying to find some form of secure work and housing. He was no longer young, and there were still people arriving on London's streets from all over the world. Thankfully, a new full-time position was suggested to Mullins by a Sergeant Carpenter of K Division. The job was supervising the security of the huge goods yard of the South Eastern Railway at its Bricklayers Arms terminus half a mile south of Tower Bridge in Bermondsey.

The family moved south of the river, where the atmosphere was every bit as rough as the East End. A little distance from the weather-boarded dwellings of Rotherhithe, near the Surrey Docks, was a newly constructed district of small terraced houses with alleys running through the back. Near these, Bricklayers Arms station was a speculative London terminus for trains run by the South Eastern Railway. Almost from the start, this station, named after a local pub and given a grand classical entrance that was quite at odds with the poor and frowsy nature of the Old Kent Road, focused less on passengers and instead became a huge goods depot, with custom-built brick sheds and warehouses.

As with labour at the docks, commerce would not sleep. Deliveries would come by night as well as day. Also like the docks, the opportunity for theft gave the authorities constant anxiety. Mullins was there as a sort of private policeman, carefully supervising goods being unloaded and reloaded from railway wagons and sent on. The station and line were extraordinarily busy; the surrounding residential terraces continually echoed with the shriek of steam and the metallic clanks of shunting.

The work was steady, and combined with his pension, should have given Mullins if not a reasonable living, then certainly a degree of stability.

So the criminal prosecution, when it came in December 1853, was startling. It made newspaper headlines: 'Scandalous and

Wholesale Plunder by a Railway Officer'. Both Mullins and his wife Catherine stood accused of theft. In the early days of the railways, pilfering of freight was widespread across the country, but the reason for the attention on this particular case was the trusted provenance of the accused: a former policeman on a decent wage.

The complainants were a Norwich-based silk and woollen manufacturing concern called Bollingbrook, for whom a consignment of check wool and poplin was supposed to have been forwarded to a Mr Dibley of Dorking; and a man based in the Kent town of Sandwich, who had sent a package of valuable drawing instruments via the railway to be delivered to an address on the City Road.

In both the cases, nothing had been received at the other end.

The court in Lambeth heard about the meticulous procedures that went with all such deliveries. Charles Gull, who worked for the Eastern Counties Railway, via which the textiles had been sent from Norwich, testified that he had sent the parcel on to a clerk at Bricklayers Arms called William Jackson. Jackson in turn confirmed he had signed chits and receipts, and had duly sent the parcel on to the correct slot in the warehouse. From this point, a Mr Murphy, the warehouse clerk, confirmed he had entered the parcel in his book and that only happened when it was loaded on to the correct railway truck.

Despite all these stages of its journey being carefully documented, the parcel never arrived in Dorking. Following suspicions in the goods yard, the trail of the missing goods led swiftly to James and Catherine Mullins. Both stood impassively in court as, with hideous irony, Sergeant Carpenter, who had alerted Mullins to the job in the first place, was next to take the stand.

'I went to the house of the prisoners, number twelve Patters Place, Bermondsey,' said the sergeant. 'I had previously left the male prisoner in custody at the Bricklayers Arms station.'

Carpenter did not make it clear what had sparked the initial suspicion that Mullins might be the thief; obviously, none of the missing goods were on his person or indeed within the grounds of the yard, but he was quick to set out for Mullins' home.

'I saw the female prisoner at the house and told her that her husband was in difficulties and that I was to search the house,' he told the court. 'She said that she knew he was in trouble and that she had heard from him. I then searched the house and found several pieces of the stuff called wool-check, of three several patterns, and these, on comparing with the patterns of a part of the lost property, I found exactly to match.

'I told the female prisoner that the goods . . . had been stolen from a parcel sent from Norwich to Dorking and that the pieces found in her house exactly corresponded with them,' Sergeant Carpenter continued. 'She said she knew nothing about them and could give no account of where she got the pieces of stuff. In the same room, I found a purse containing several duplicates, two of which were for pieces of print pawned.

'I asked her what these duplicates referred to and she said "they belong to myself". I also found a gown made of stuff of the same kind as one of the patterns of goods stolen from the Norwich parcel. She replied that it was nothing of the sort, as she could show where she bought it.'

Sergeant Carpenter told the magistrate that after examining Mullins' house, he then visited pubs and pawnshops that sold stolen goods and found clothes that had been made up with the materials.

The court heard that Mullins had claimed the material had been bought at Petticoat Lane Market. There might have been a slender chance that it was true, but rather more difficult to explain, it seemed, were the missing drawing instruments originally destined for the City Road, which were also found in the Mullins home.

Mullins had also indulged in other transgressions, it emerged. Colleagues at the railway yard had witnessed him 'sucking the monkey' – a colourful expression referring to the practice of tapping an ale barrel and 'sucking from its contents through a large quill'. [5]

This detail appeared to have been the tipping point for the presiding magistrate. Mrs Mullins was found innocent of attempting to sell on stolen goods, but there seemed to be no doubt of Mr Mullins' guilt as a petty thief. The punishment was far from petty: the former police sergeant was sentenced to six years of penal servitude.

For a man in early middle age with three young children, this was a shattering prospect; not merely the idea of incarceration combined with serious physical labour, but also the economic catastrophe. Until the two boys and the little girl were old enough, it was Catherine who would have to provide for them.

There was further immediate cruelty to face. For reasons undocumented, a place was not found for Mullins in a London gaol. It was possibly due to overcrowding – while London's population had been expanding, prison building had not. Mullins was first transferred to Leicester, which was simply too far from London for Catherine to visit him with the children.

However, for reasons again undocumented, the authorities decided to transfer him again to Dartmoor Prison in Devon. It is reasonable to assume in this instance that Mullins was proving uncontrollable (or 'incurable', as one prison officer later termed his behaviour) and to speculate that in kicking out against his sentence, his conduct was so extreme, and disobedience of the presiding officers so implacable, that the only option was to move him somewhere with a growing reputation for dealing with the hardest cases.

Much later, in the wake of the murder of Mrs Emsley and its consequences, one anonymous prison officer was prompted to write to a newspaper with his recollections of that transfer, and of Mullins' behaviour: 'His conduct was very bad and required constant watching by the officers. He was removed to Dartmoor with another convict.'

The actual journey, alleged the prison officer, provided Mullins with an opportunity for an outbreak of calculated violence.

'His attack on me was while crossing Dartmoor Hills,' recalled the officer. 'On account of the difficult road to Dartmoor prison, it was usual to let the convicts walk up one or two of the steepest hills. On this occasion while walking, they contrived to pick up a large stone each, and when about getting into the cab, Mullins aimed a desperate blow at me with his stone, with the intention to take my life, and so to effect their escape.

'Immediately Mullins struck me, he made a snatch at my pocket where the keys of the [leg] irons were, but fortunately, the blow not having the desired effect as anticipated, I was enabled to trip up his heels, and with the assistance of the cabman, I succeeded in securing them.'

The officer felt some bitterness towards the putative escapee: 'The blow struck me on the left cheek,' he wrote, 'which it almost broke, and I carry the mark to this day.' (6)

This unsigned letter to a newspaper ought to be treated with all due care – the anonymous officer might not even have identified the correct man. If all this was absolutely as he said, was it actually the case that Mullins had attempted to kill him, or simply to stun him with the stone prior to stealing the keys and making good his opportunistic escape? Such interpretations of Mullins' character were later to prove crucial.

Whatever happened on those moors, the escape attempt had failed and Mullins was inside Dartmoor Prison. Originally built at the start of the nineteenth century, the gaol had been intended for prisoners of war. In 1850, with the site pretty much empty, it was turned over for civilian use. There were still sentences of transportation to Australia, but they were diminishing, and were largely in lieu of the death penalty. From 1853, anyone sentenced to anything under fourteen years could now expect to serve the time out in a domestic institution. It was from this point that government plans were laid for more prison building. Dartmoor Prison carried with it a sense of the wild gothic: Newgate on the savage moors.

At first sight, it must assuredly have filled convicts with horror. One might escape from the prison, but to what? No sanctuary would be afforded in the nearby villages and a single night on the moor under the merciless ice of a winter sky would kill as surely as cyanide. Added to this, initial impressions of the prison – a circular compound ringed with a high stone wall, and within, like spokes on a wheel, stone-built blocks pointing towards the centre – would have been equally comfortless.

Despite all this, Mullins would have soon found that, in some ways, the Dartmoor authorities were leaning towards fashionable ideas of rehabilitation. Curiously, in official circles, Dartmoor was actually seen for a time as being a much more benevolent option than any institution in London or any of the larger cities. Sitting in the lee of a low hill and looking out over wind-scoured, sheep-flecked heathery wilderness, the prison was actually felt to have a healthier air about it than any other. Some men were sent here precisely because they had chest and breathing problems and were felt to stand a better chance of thriving out in the open than living in the fetid confines of an inner-city gaol.

In addition, the regime at Dartmoor was not deliberately brutal at the time when Mullins arrived; it only grew harsher as the century went on and the later Victorians of the 1870s placed heavier emphasis on the idea of punishment, with floggings and stone-breaking, as opposed to reformation.

Reforming ideals aside, the prison Mullins knew as his world for those six years could still be dark and brutal. Clearly the guards were capable of cruelty, as indeed were great numbers of the men over which they were keeping watch. A blacksmith who had been imprisoned there at the same time as Mullins later complained at a public meeting in Holborn that not only were there 'brutalities', but also 'the rankling sense of injustice rendered the reformation of the inmates impossible'. [7]

It was perhaps because of Mullins' continued insistence on his innocence that he was not granted a 'ticket of leave' halfway into his sentence. This was an early form of parole: the original idea had been that men who had been held in prison hulks on water could, if their behaviour had been exemplary, earn their freedom with strict conditions such as curfews, official checks on financial dealings, prohibitions on meeting with certain associates, and even a complete ban on alcohol.

It is not difficult to imagine the mental state of Mullins in that freezing stone prison. He might have felt the pitiful police pension he had received was an insult, one he used to justify the Bricklayers Arms thefts to himself. Whatever the truth, it is easy to see how such a man, who was once in the employ of the Home Office, might have been unable to resist feeling increasing resentment at the way that he had been treated by the state since the espionage disaster in Ireland. Any possibility of a respectable future seemed elusive.

Mullins was released in the darkness of December 1859. Emerging from the gates of Dartmoor, he would have had enough money saved from the small payments made for his prison occupations to secure a ticket back to London.

After six years, Mullins made his way back to his wife and three children. His eldest son had been trying to make a career as a sailor; his youngest daughter was in service to a family near Belgravia. The family lodgings were in a boarding house in a backstreet of Chelsea. Mullins remembered a name from his past who might just offer up an opportunity for proper rewarding work: a family who might be more willing than most to overlook his penal servitude because of his previous invaluable help almost thirty years beforehand.

The man Mullins had in mind was Samuel Emsley. Surely Mr Emsley would not turn away such a faithful servant? Of course, Mullins had no way of knowing that Emsley had died in 1856, as he was halfway through his Dartmoor term.

Mullins would have made his way back to the old Octagon warehouse where Samuel Emsley had conducted all his business.

On arrival, he would have found the premises under different management; possibly he would have been directed to see Faith or Whittaker, Emsley's sons-in-law who lived locally and who still had strong business interests in the Emsley estate. From there, Mullins might have been directed towards the widow he had never before met: the second wife of Emsley, a woman in command of her own personal property empire.

As 1860 dawned, Mary Emsley was buying up property at an increasing rate, including a couple of speculations south of the river. She needed help not only in collecting rents, but also in maintaining these houses.

There is no account of the first meeting between the bespectacled and articulate Mullins and Mrs Emsley, but she was no snob and it is perfectly reasonable to assume she responded well to his intelligence and his willingness to work – alongside Walter Emm and William Rowland – as a form of property manager.

And just months later, her blood was dashed across the walls of her lumber room. But before James Mullins was to begin the fight for his life at the Old Bailey, it was finally time for the old woman to be laid to rest in the ground.

17

The Dark Twisting Paths

~❧~

It rained hard on the day of Mary Emsley's funeral. Under the dripping trees of the Tower Hamlets Cemetery, the gravel and clay was soft; the old woman's grave was a little distance away from the rather grander sepulchre under which her husband Samuel lay. The mourners would have had to watch their steps on the slippery grass and mud as they made their way to the graveside. The woods and the pathways of this cemetery were little more than half a mile away from her house, just on the other side of the Mile End Road. It had been opened in 1841, one of the seven vast new Victorian cemeteries designed to cope with the surging city population and its consequent rising number of dead.

It would perhaps have been more fitting if Mrs Emsley had been laid to rest in the churchyard of St Dunstan's, where she had been christened in 1790, but there was no room there; the gravestones were jammed together like irregular teeth. Free of the 'miasmas' and shallow graves of older burial grounds, Tower Hamlets Cemetery was as pleasingly landscaped as Victoria Park, with gently curving footpaths and tall trees, the tranquillity only disturbed by the occasional scream of a locomotive on the new railway branch out to Essex.

Mrs Emsley was interred 'privately'. [1] At her graveside, there would have been tears from her niece, Elizabeth Gotz and from her nephew Samuel Williams. (If the commital had been in an Anglican churchyard women would not have been expected to attend.) However, amid their sorrow, there must also have been a stomach-lurching sense of insecurity. Neither of them were remotely well-off, and to an extent they had been reliant on the old lady's generosity. They both lived in houses owned by Mrs Emsley; Gotz was in Whitechapel and Williams in Limehouse, close to where Mrs Emsley had spent her childhood. Now the old woman was gone, that seemingly solid foundation was crumbling beneath them.

Walter Emm would have been there with his family. Samuel Emsley's daughters, Mary-Ann and Betty, would have been there with their husbands, John Faith and Henry Whittaker. William Rose, her faithful solicitor, and her apostolic minister friend Joseph Biggs, would have also attended. Biggs' church – if church is not too broad a term for the Irvingite sect – believed firmly in the book of John, in prophecies, in the power of the supernatural, and in the imminence of the Apocalypse. Biggs preached that there was a limit on the number of souls that would be saved, which was 144,000. Did he believe that Mrs Emsley was among them?

Even with James Mullins in custody and facing trial at the Central Criminal Court, all the mourners gathered around that wet grave would have known that this hideous affair was very far from being concluded.

One or two of them might have had reason to doubt the right man was facing trial. There was also one question that all those present would have been asking, though none of them would have had the bad taste to voice it within the cemetery: what was to become of Mrs Emsley's wealth?

At this stage, Mr Rose was administering the estate, or at least those properties stretching from the poorest corners of Whitechapel to the marshes of Barking that had been owned by

Mrs Emsley via trusts. The property that made up her share of the inheritance from the death of Samuel, that included all his books, furniture and plate, would have been administered directly by Whittaker and Faith, who were continuing to supervise all the works around the properties. Mary-Ann and Betty had been the main beneficiaries of their father's will, rather than the widow, but they too can't have helped speculating. The fact of Mrs Emsley's murder did not grant her hundreds of tenants a holiday from their rent obligations; as that money continued to accumulate, the Emsley relatives, some quite distant, were beginning to think about how best to lay their claims.

Many of Mrs Emsley's tenants were existing on a fringe of society that many well-off metropolitan Victorians were both horrified and fascinated by. Accounts of the ruinous state of property and health in the East End written by social observers were being published in ever greater numbers. Many commentators argued the vital importance of giving dignity to the very poorest, allowing them to prosper by lifting them from the moral degradation – adultery, incest, child abuse – that accompanied serious overcrowding.

For the first time, the government started to place an emphasis on intervention. Throughout the 1850s, increasing numbers of official sanitary inspectors were policing the parishes of London; the hideous cholera epidemics of 1853–54 had sharpened their powers. Every parish in London had a Board of Health, and these employed men who were empowered to enter premises.

The East End was not wholly composed of slums, though. In 1860, there were streets in Stepney that had sufficient elegance to lure the young middle-class professionals who were working in the expanding City of London nearby.

Around this time, there was also a stirring of commercial interest in widening property ownership. Advertisements in the *East London Observer* shouted about new building societies, about the possibilities of taking on partial ownership of houses with others (for rates not too far different from rents), and indeed about the idea of taking a loan (in other words, a mortgage) for an entire property in new suburbs such as Plaistow and Walthamstow.

For the insecure labouring classes, such prospects would have been beyond fantastical, which meant that the rental empire of Mrs Emsley would clearly remain extremely profitable. Mr Rose, looking down at her grave, would not have been able to keep his mind away from the nature of the struggle to come. Why had Mrs Emsley not made a will?

She had frequently told needy friends and relatives of her plans to leave the entire fortune to charities such as almshouses. There had always been a sense that she had been maliciously teasing those whom she considered to be in pursuit of her money; had she teased her killer similarly?

But there was one other possibility, one that would have been hanging heavy over the old lady's blood relatives: the possibility of secret family disgrace. The refusal to make a will might have been caused by Mrs Emsley's reluctance to confront her family's untidy history. She knew her father had not been a faithful husband, with rumours of children born outside of marriage. Her illiteracy might have sharpened this reluctance, for she would have had to dictate any will out loud to her solicitor. Mrs Emsley might also have been anxious that any will challenged in court would expose, rather than conceal, such things. As it was, the absence of any such legal documentation actually made the legal battles more certain.

As the soft wet clay closed over the casket and the mourners were led back through the dripping trees and twisting pathways, those relatives would have been oppressed with more than the weight of grief; they, and Mr Rose, would have sensed the storm to come.

The man accused of her murder, now sitting in the darkness of Newgate Prison, might have thought at one point that he would be favoured in some small way in the old lady's final wishes. Now, James Mullins was listening to the shouts and cries in the corridors and cells around him. He would not only have been fully aware of the hostility of his former police colleagues, but also that he was seen by the excitable public and the popular press as the epitome of wickedness.

18

'To Prove the Presence
of Blood'

∞

The smog-blackened walls of Newgate Prison were still evoking shudders – half-fearful, half-pleasurable – from passers-by. In an age when London was being bathed in new light, and its theatres filled with dazzling pyrotechnics, the old horrors of Newgate Prison and the Central Criminal Court which stood next to it on Old Bailey should have somehow seemed medieval. Yet there was something in the monolithic architecture of Newgate that forced a response of apprehension; the dark exterior walls were enormously tall; the lack of windows, or any discernible openings, reinforced that feeling of impenetrability, that what lay inside was another kind of world.

Few would have been more aware of this than the former policeman and convict James Mullins; a rare instance of a man who had seen the institution of gaol from both sides. Prior to his trial at the Old Bailey, set for late October 1860, he would surely have understood that he could shout at the top of his voice about his innocence, but to be held in Newgate was to cross some form of shadow-line, as if passing into purgatory.

As a literate man, Mullins would have been familiar, and possibly even enjoyed, the curious literary form termed 'the Newgate novel'. These 'penny dreadfuls' reached their height in the 1830s and 1840s, detailing the wild escapades of anti-hero criminals, and were knowingly unrespectable. By 1860, their thrills had been surpassed by increasingly ambitious stage melodramas, but Newgate's public executions continued to draw large, full-throated crowds. On ordinary days, the crossroads outside the prison, leading one way to Holborn and the other to the City, would be filled with the rich green and gold livery of omnibuses and the clamour of lawyers, stockbrokers and young clerks pushing through the crowds. On execution days, when hangings were carried out in the morning, usually at 8am, all modernity seemed suspended. Public executions were still carried out on a wooden scaffold directly in front of the prison. It was the sharp and unbeatable drama of mortality: a life for a life.

In 1840, twenty-eight-year-old Charles Dickens, already wildly famous for *The Pickwick Papers* and *Oliver Twist* (in which the criminal Fagin ended up in Newgate) went to see a public execution. The case was that of François Courvoisier, a valet who had slit the throat of his wealthy employer. Dickens attended with his friend Henry Burnett, and rather than mingle with the huge and uncontainable crowd outside the prison, went upstairs to a specially rented room overlooking the gallows. Dickens watched the condemned man, speculated that he had slept soundly ('for they always do') and observed how his lifeless body was cut down.

The author's real horror was aroused not by the hanging, but by the crowd. There was, he wrote years later, 'nothing but ribaldry, debauchery, levity, drunkenness and flaunting vice in fifty other shapes. I should have deemed it impossible that I could have felt any large assemblage of my fellow creatures to be so odious.' [1]

The Central Criminal Court had been remodelled many times over the decades. In the previous century, it had been a fairly open prospect, with the general public allowed free access to witness trials in progress. The popularity of the Old Bailey's trials, infinitely juicier than anything a writer could devise, caused wild sensation and overcrowding. Walls went up, gateways were narrowed, and admittance became strictly limited. It has been suggested that court records became scrupulously accurate at this point in order to compensate for the wider, clamouring public not having so much of a chance to see the English justice system in all of its transparent brilliance. Even though the exterior structure was built up, the interior of the Old Bailey had an airy dignity. Unlike the suggestion of darkness from Newgate, natural light was built into the main courtroom; large windows to the left and the right of the judge's bench were supplemented by hanging lamps. The light was arranged in such a way that those standing in the dock would have their faces strongly illuminated; it was felt to be vital that judges, lawyers and jurors could study the features of the accused as the case proceeded. Particular reactions would be noted, and later discussed, and might form part of the final judgement.

There was a wooden board – a 'sounding board' – situated above the dock. This helped with the acoustics, making the defendants' voices audible to all, especially in circumstances where distress or pure terror were choking them off.

Mullins sat in that dock on the morning of 25 October 1860. Unlike modern murder trials, which are conducted slowly and with glacial care, this was to be a relatively speedy business, lasting only two days. This was less to do with the quality of the evidence than the Old Bailey's schedules being packed tightly; the judges and juries had a great many cases to examine. There was no sense that this was unfair to the defendant. Indeed, in 1860, two days would have been considered a lengthy trial.

The proceedings had caught the imagination of many Londoners (not least in the East End where, as one clerk put it, Mrs Emsley's murder was still 'the talk of every taproom and bar'). There was some competition to be admitted inside the Old Bailey to watch proceedings.

In his first appearance in the dock, there was a poise and confidence about James Mullins. He immediately pleaded not guilty to the charge of murder, and the hearing began. Mullins 'appeared perfectly at ease, making frequent suggestions for the guidance of his counsel, and occasionally taking notes of the evidence'. [2]

The court reporter knew that readers would be fascinated by Mullins' physical demeanour, and noted that although he was described in the court papers as being fifty-eight, he 'looks hardly so old, though he wears spectacles'. The reporter added, 'in appearance, he is intelligent and rather prepossessing'. [3]

Mullins was being defended by a Mr J Best and a Mr Palmer; the prosecution was led by a Mr Parry. Also present was Mr Wontner, the lawyer who had been acting for Whittaker and Faith at the Thames Police Court hearing.

Prosecuting counsel Parry opened with the declaration that this was, 'one of the most cruel and barbarous murders ever committed'. The jury, he said, had all probably read or heard something 'of this most atrocious crime'. It was usual in so serious an investigation, he told the jurors, to tell them to put from their minds 'every preconceived notion . . . every fact that might have come to their knowledge beforehand' and simply focus on the evidence that was to be laid before them.

'A crime of this kind is generally committed in secret, and no other human eye witnessed it,' announced Parry. 'In order, therefore, to ensure a conviction for a crime thus secretly committed, the prosecution has to rely on a number of facts, each of greater or lesser importance, but all pointing in one direction and one alone. This is what is called circumstantial evidence.'

In the earlier years of the 1800s, there had been vigorous debate in Old Bailey cases about the use of circumstantial evidence (that is, evidence from which facts were inferred – missing knives, coincidence of timings – as opposed to direct evidence, which would be a straightforward eyewitness account of a stabbing, for instance). It seemed to most frequently occur in cases of alleged poisoning, of which there were quite a number at that time. Juries were repeatedly presented with this dilemma: the fact that someone had ingested deadly poison and the question of whether they did so accidentally or whether they were secretly given it by the accused could not be divined by any direct evidence. In an age before forensics or fingerprints, there could simply be no way of knowing what exactly had happened with those bottles of prussic acid and arsenic.

The debate continued for some decades afterwards. Both in his essay in *The Strand Magazine* and indeed in his Sherlock Holmes stories, the nature of circumstantial evidence exercised Arthur Conan Doyle enormously. In 'The Boscombe Valley Mystery', a Holmes short story, the detective summarises his creator's views:

"'Circumstantial evidence is a very tricky thing," answered Holmes thoughtfully. "It may seem to point very straight to one thing, but if you shift your own point of view a little, you may find it pointing in an equally uncompromising manner to something entirely different.'" [4]

The philosophical basis of circumstantial evidence was supported by a number of judges who felt that even if the greatest care had to be taken not to condemn the innocent, it still had a kind of moral force. The jurors would be able to divine guilt by an accretion of this evidence – the accused having been in the vicinity, or having had words with the victim beforehand, or having access to the murder weapon – and confidently deliver a verdict. This was what Parry was telling the Mrs Emsley jury, while acknowledging from the start that there was no direct evidence.

He admitted that while some considered this kind of evidence 'the strongest and best that could be adduced', others 'assailed it as unreliable'. However, in his own view, 'a series of facts varying in importance . . . each independent of the other, but all pointing in one direction only' were quite sufficient for a jury to rely on.

Parry turned to the character of the victim, who he described as 'a person of very penurious and peculiar habits who resided by herself'. Next to the fact of her widowhood was the fascination of her wealth. She was 'the owner of a considerable amount of house property, the rents of which she collected herself'.

He went on to describe how 'her peculiar habits were known in the neighbourhood; it was known she collected the rents every Monday; and it was also known that the sum that she collected on that day was considerable, amounting to 30*l*, 40*l*, even 50*l*. This was an important fact to bear in mind.'

Parry told the jury (composed largely of men of business and property) how Mrs Emsley's body was found; the 'marks of blows' and 'brutal violence'; he told how she was last seen alive on the Monday evening, 'sitting at the window of her bedroom'. He described how, from the next morning onwards, visitors and callers to the house received no answer. There was clearly no question that this was a murder; the only question for the jury to consider was 'the most awful and painful which any tribunal could put to them': who committed the crime?

The murder had naturally 'caused a great sensation' in the area, and Parry told the jury of the massive financial reward that was offered. At this point, having told them of Mullins' first approach to the police with his allegations against Walter Emm, Parry turned to the character of the accused.

He had, Parry explained, 'obtained a livelihood by working as a plasterer and a bricklayer. Formerly he was in the police force, both here and in Ireland. He was known to be a man of shrewdness and experience, and he was frequently employed by this old lady to do anything which might be required to her houses in the neighbourhood. He was, therefore, fully acquainted with her, and many years ago when in the police at Stepney, he was acquainted with her late husband.'

Throughout these opening remarks, Mullins 'exhibited perfect coolness and unconcern'. Parry then went on to describe the

Saturday evening some three weeks after the murder, when Mullins made his first approach to Sergeant Tanner about the mysterious package to be found in Emm's outhouse. According to the prosecution, Mullins 'substantially' said: 'You know, I have for some time been looking after [for] the murderer of Mrs Emsley. I have had my suspicions, and now I know the man.'

That man, of course, was Walter Emm. The court heard how Mullins had 'taken meals' at Emm's cottage several times; how Mullins had then stated he had been watching the cottage on the morning of Saturday 8 September, saw Emm emerge and go towards 'a ruin in the brickfield', emerge with a parcel which he took back to the cottage, then returned to the outhouse, but this time with a parcel that was markedly smaller. On making arrangements to go with the police to Emm's property the following morning, Mullins was anxious that he should not be left behind: 'Don't go without me,' he told Sergeant Tanner. Tanner replied, 'You may rely on that – I have taken down your statement in writing and whatever advantage is derived from it will be yours.' This was clearly a reference to the enormous reward fund, and Mullins replied, 'I will make it all right with you.'

The court was then told of that Sunday morning visit to Emm's cottage; the initial unsuccessful police search of his outhouse; and Mullins' furious exhortations to the officers to search more carefully behind the slab. The jury heard how the parcel was then found; the 'dirty apron string' with which it was tied up; and the motley contents of spoons, lenses, and an uncashed cheque.

It was here that the prosecutor made a vaulting leap: 'It would seem, therefore, as clear a proposition as could be proved in evidence that the person who really placed the parcel in the shed and who had in his possession this cheque was the murderer of Mrs Emsley.'

Parry explained his reasoning thus: 'Now, who did put the parcel there? The suggestion . . . one that affected the life of the prisoner, was that Mullins put it in the shed for the purpose of making a false accusation against Emm. This would be proved to the jury as clearly as though they had seen the act done and, if so, it showed the prisoner to be not only guilty of one murder, but guilty of an attempt to destroy the life of another person.'

There was seemingly no allowing for the possibility that the murder of the widow and an attempt to plant evidence were completely separate offences; that Mullins might well have done one without having had any hand in the other. Instead, there was something even more gravitational in the force of the reasoning that then followed. The jury was invited to ponder the preposterousness of Emm first murdering Mrs Emsley and then harbouring evidence which he carefully placed in his outhouse. They were further invited to consider that Mullins had been seen lurking around the brickfields in the days beforehand, and that a search of his Barnsley Street lodgings had yielded string and cobbler's wax that corresponded to those used for the parcel.

Emm had a good alibi for the night of the murder as well: he 'went to Stratford for the purpose of collecting rent belonging to the old lady there'. Four or five witnesses would depose that Emm was in their company up to nearly midnight, and Emm then went home and never left the cottage for the rest of the night.

'Moreover,' added Parry, 'by one of those providential circumstances by which sometimes innocence was established and guilt detected, Emm was not out of his cottage at all between eight and nine o'clock of the morning when Mullins declared he saw him depositing the parcel.'

On the question of Mullins' whereabouts, the jury was told how he was at work on a house in the neighbourhood until around six o'clock that evening.

'He had with him when he left a plasterer's hammer, which he had been using to knock away the ceiling.'

This hammer would be one of the most important pieces of circumstantial evidence. Doctor Gill had already said at the pre-trial, and would declare again before the jury, that it could well have been this instrument that was used to inflict such horrific wounds, as the edge of such a hammer 'corresponded' with the wounds above the old lady's left eyebrow. This hammer 'was afterwards found by the police at the prisoner's lodgings'. Even more damningly, Mullins had been seen by another witness at eight o'clock that night, 'at the corner of Grove Road' near Mrs Emsley's house. If he was innocent, he would have to tell the jury where exactly he was, if not there. This would be the only way to 'rebut the presumption which otherwise would be so strong'.

Parry also told the jury of one other crucial link in the story. On the morning after the murder, at ten past six in the morning, Mullins was met 'by a seafaring man named Mitchell passing through Stepney-green.

'If the prisoner had committed the murder, he was returning home in a circuitous manner,' he added, 'no doubt to escape observation. He appeared to be in a state of high excitement, his pockets were bulky and so struck was Mitchell with his appearance that he – before Mullins was apprehended – gave information to the police on the subject.'

Mullins' own manner, when confronted with this witness sighting, was, according to Parry, one of 'marked agitation'. This increased when articles were found in his possession that 'pointed clearly to his guilt': items that had been taken from the widow's house.

'Whoever the murderer was,' Parry told the jury, 'it seemed unlikely that he obtained any great amount of money, for after Mrs Emsley's death, 48*l* in notes, gold and silver was found secreted under some wood and coal in the coal cellar. A valuable ring which had belonged to the husband [Samuel] was found between the mattress and the bed. And it was pretty clear that the murderer had been baulked of his wished-for plunder.'

The jury at that point might have wondered if that had really been the killer's primary motive, for it would not have taken a thief long to reason that any valuables might be hidden in the coal cellar. Parry seemed keen to elide this further logical gap by pointing up what seemed to be a hugely incriminating act.

'A pencil case . . . was in the possession of the deceased and that pencil case was disposed of by the prisoner's wife only a day or so before he gave information to the police,' he revealed, before coming to the conclusion that, 'the cheque, the lenses, the metal spoons were taken by the murderer from the house that night.'

Again, a juror might have been justified in wondering why those items could not have been pilfered earlier. The prosecutor went on regardless with what he considered to be the clinching item of circumstantial evidence.

'Near the body, on the landing, was a considerable quantity of blood and in it was the partial imprint of a nailed shoe,' declared Parry. 'In matters of this kind, eyesight was the best guide and therefore it had been thought right that the board containing this impression should be cut out and laid before the jury.'

This was a striking moment of pure theatre: the blood-soaked floorboard, carrying with it all that horror of violent mortality. There is no record how the jurors reacted, but it is reasonable to assume that for every one who recoiled, there must have been another who was darkly fascinated.

Parry had not finished with the matter of the 'nailed shoe'. He told the jury about Mullins lodging in both Barnsley Street and the rooms in Chelsea, which were largely occupied by his wife. The landlady there saw 'a boot being flung out of the window'; this boot was afterwards found in the dust hole.

'The jury would see the impression in the board and compare it with the boot, and the witnesses would be asked whether the boot was likely to have produced that mark.'

At this point, the judge, Lord Pollock, sharply interceded. He doubted, as the report had it, 'whether such a question could be put'. Counsel, he declared, could only ask the opinions of witnesses where 'some peculiar skill was required in coming to a conclusion'. Otherwise, the impression of a shoe was not a matter for a witness to decide.

Parry relented, then added that some 'human hair was found sticking to the boot. The head of the poor woman was dreadfully beaten in and it is possible that some hair might have adhered to the boot of the murderer.' He also told the jury that since Mullins was a plasterer by trade, it was possible that 'in pursuit of his vocation', another explanation for the hair might be found.

Mrs Emsley was too careful and suspicious to open her door to strangers. Whoever gained access to the house that night must surely have been well known to her? There were 'no marks of violent entry' and there was good reason to suppose that Mullins would have had 'some business there' on the night of the murder, announced Parry.

Throughout the course of the hours beforehand, Mullins had visited Mrs Emsley to get the keys of various properties on which he was working. One of these keys, 'of a remarkable shape', had been given to him and was subsequently found in a basket along with other keys 'in the old lady's bedroom'. Mullins had also been helping Mrs Emsley by taking 'a quantity of paper-hangings' into the house; her body was found in the room where they had all been placed, and there 'could be no doubt that she was showing the patterns to some person at the time of the murder, and this would account for his getting access to the house'.

Curiously, this point would also seem to move the accusing hand away from Mullins towards any one of the men who had visited Grove Road in answer to her advertisements about wallpaper. Why would Mrs Emsley have been showing wallpaper she had no intention of bestowing upon her tenants to the properties' handyman?

In conclusion, Parry announced that in cases where the evidence was entirely circumstantial, such evidence had to be 'clear, plain, direct and incapable of any other reasonable solution than that which it was brought forward to sustain'. A crime of this kind, he averred, was rare; rarer still was it for 'a murderer [to] attempt falsely to accuse an innocent man'. If there was any doubt in the minds of the jury, he said, then Mullins too would be 'entitled to the benefit of the doubt'. On the other hand, if they felt this evidence pointed to 'one fatal conclusion', then no feeling of their own, however strong, 'as to the sanctity of human life would prevent them from discharging their duty firmly and unshrinkingly'.

It was time for the prosecution to call witnesses. The first to take the stand was Mrs Emsley's solicitor, William Rose. He recounted to the jury the extent of his client's property wealth, his acquaintance with her property maintenance man Emm, and the morning he was summoned to 9 Grove Road and found the old lady's corpse, together with Emm and Sergeant Dillon. Rose also told the jury that he had noticed the 'remarkably shaped' key in Mrs Emsley's bedroom in a basket with other keys.

Rose was then cross-examined by the defence counsel, Mr Best. He testified that he had no previous knowledge of Mullins and that he was better acquainted with Rowland. He also stated that Mrs Emsley's front door was latched, and not bolted. When asked to describe the crime scene, he talked of 'the pool of blood around the body of the deceased'.

Sergeant Dillon was next, telling the court of the scene of carnage he found. Once again, there was the dreadful bathos of the wallpaper; on the landing outside the murder scene were several large pieces, as well as a 'bloody footprint'. Inside the room, Dillon described how, 'there was a great quantity of blood about the body, a pool on the floor, and splashes on the wall'.

Dr Gill of Bow was now called, who started by recounting the state in which he had first seen Mrs Emsley's body: lying at full length on her left side, her clothes giving no indication of any preparation for bed. He told the court about 'the large opening of the back of the skull extending deeply into the brain'. The wound, he said, 'seemed to be the result of repeated blows and was quite sufficient to account for death'. These blows had been so violent that 'small portions of the skull were carried completely through the interior substance of the brain'. Added to these, Dr Gill told the court, were several other wounds, one of which, 'a contused wound inflicted over the left ear, which had driven in the whole of the temple bone on that side, would also have caused death'. In addition, there was a lacerated wound above the left eyebrow.

Dr Gill claimed that even before he had seen the hammer, he had formed a view on the sort of instrument used to inflict these horrific injuries. 'The blade end of the hammer corresponded in length with the lacerated wound,' he said, 'and in size and character, the wound was such as might have been inflicted' by it.

Under cross-examination, these certainties began to give way a little. It would be a matter of opinion, the doctor said, which of the wounds had been inflicted first. The body as he found it was 'very slightly' decomposed – under some circumstances, he said, the effect of decomposition would be to make the wounds expand. This would have made his measurements redundant. Dr Gill added that he did not think it was the case here, because the lacerated wound was comparatively dry.

It was a week, perhaps a fortnight, after his initial examination of the deceased's head that he first saw the hammer, recalled Dr Gill. He was forced to admit he never 'compared the hammer with the body'. He had been most assiduous, not only in measuring the wound above the eyebrow, but also probing its depth, and it was from these examinations that he had concluded that the lethal instrument was a hammer. Gill conceded under questioning that an 'instrument of a similar shape – a piece of iron sharp at the end, for example – might have caused it'.

Added to this, it was possible that the wound at the back of Mrs Emsley's head 'might have been occasioned by another instrument than a hammer'. The wound was certainly some inches in size, and whatever instrument was used, Dr Gill added, he imagined that blood must have adhered to it.

Could Dr Gill be quite sure of the time of Mrs Emsley's death? His opinion was firmly that she had been dead for three or four days when he saw the body, and that he saw her on the Friday in the middle of the day. If pressed, though, he conceded that he could not 'speak to a few hours, or even a day either way'. Mrs Emsley was last seen alive on the Monday evening; did this open up the possibility that she was murdered later than the Monday night?

The old lady's observant neighbour, Elizabeth Pashley, was called next. The entire occasion, the journey from Mile End into the city, being ushered into the Central Criminal Court, and to stand before such an assembly, must have been quite extraordinary for her. It is not difficult to imagine friends and neighbours gathering around her afterwards to talk about what had happened. Mrs Pashley told the court how she had last seen Mrs Emsley alive at around seven or eight o'clock on that Monday evening. At that point, the old lady was sitting at the first-floor window. Mrs Pashley was familiar with Mrs Emsley's routines; how she normally went to bed at around ten o'clock, and how she always closed her shutters at dusk. Mrs Pashley's first pang of disquiet was on that Monday night when she looked out of her window and saw that the old lady's shutters were still open around midnight. This was so remarkable, she told the court, that she noticed it 'particularly'.

The next morning, she said, the shutters were still not closed; and on the second floor, one of the windows was slightly open. Over the next couple of days, Mrs Pashley watched as callers came and went. Whereas in normal circumstances, Mrs Emsley would be sitting at her window ascertaining who the callers were, now no one was answering.

Questioned by Best for the defence, Mrs Pashley confirmed that Mrs Emsley never kept any servants and that 'very few men in working clothes went in and out'. Tradesmen, she said, were never admitted. Mrs Pashley was familiar with the figures of the property managers Mr Rowland and Mr Emm. She didn't know of any others, but had seen 'some persons enter occasionally'.

What of the gentlemen who had shown interest in buying some of that enormous quantity of wallpaper? One of them took the stand. John Cook, 'a builder, residing at Clapham' said he went to 9 Grove Road on the morning of Tuesday 14 August specifically for that purpose, but after knocking repeatedly, got no answer. Best asked him if he had had previous dealings with Mrs Emsley; Cook replied that he had known her for two years, 'but had never bought paper-hangings from her'.

Sergeant Tanner was called, and revealed to the court that Mullins had first been 'fetched' (called in for questioning) two weeks after the murder. That was the first time they had met. The second was that following weekend, when Mullins called on the police to tell them he had 'suspicions of a person', who was Walter Emm. Mullins had told Tanner he had been watching Emm at the brickfields – Mullins himself evaded notice, he said, by picking herbs. Tanner then told the court about the Sunday morning visit to the brickfields, the outhouse, and Mullins' increasingly frantic prompting for them to find the parcel, including those spoons on which were stamped the letters 'WP'.

Tanner recounted Mullins' reaction to being arrested along with Emm: 'Is this the way I am to be served after giving you the information?' Mullins was searched and they found his shoe tied with 'a piece of waxed string'. Tanner told the court how he went to Mullins' Barnsley Street lodgings and found 'tape' (or ribbon) on the chimneypiece that corresponded with the 'incriminating parcel'. Under cross-examination, Tanner said he didn't know if the bits of ribbon had been properly examined to check they had the same number of threads, but they seemed to him to be of the same kind and the ends of the ribbons corresponded exactly with each other. Tanner told the court that he had found a hammer at Mullins' lodgings.

Tanner recounted the scene at Emm's cottage and the discovery of the parcel. He told the court how he had made a search of the cottage and he wanted it to be known that he had not found a hammer inside. He conceded that since Emm was a shoemaker, it wouldn't in fact have been unusual for him to be in possession of one.

The next policeman to take the stand relayed an interesting conversation he had with Mullins at his wife's new lodgings in Chelsea (the family had moved) nearly a month after the murder.

'You know I am clever in these matters,' Mullins said, according to Sergeant Thomas. 'I have been working day and night to discover the murderer of Mrs Emsley, and I have found him out.'

'Whom do you suspect?' asked Thomas.

'The man Emm,' Mullins replied. 'No one had better opportunities than he had, as he was in the habit of taking to Mrs Emsley small sums of money, and would be admitted at any time.'

'Would she have admitted you?' asked Thomas, shrewdly.

'No,' answered Mullins, 'she would have called to me from the window.'

Thomas was the third policeman that morning at the brickfields, and he remembered finding some papers in Emm's house 'relating to business with the deceased'. After the events at the outhouse, Thomas not only took part in the search of Mullins' Bethnal Green lodgings, but also at Chelsea. In a back room, he said he found a spoon marked with the letters 'WP'. The spoon was then produced for the jury to look at.

Under questioning from Best, Thomas conceded that the spoon 'was of ordinary metal, such as was in common use'. The point was that the spoon was of the same kind as two others found in the parcel. The letters 'WP' were probably some kind of trademark, as opposed to specially engraved initials. With this, he was asked a little more about what he had found in Bethnal Green. Thomas said he saw no one else there; some people lived upstairs, but Mullins had the downstairs. The house, he said, was very small.

Either the judge or members of the jury were not satisfied with the evidence pertaining to the ribbon: was there or wasn't there proof that the ribbon that tied the parcel was from the same length as that found on Mullins' chimneypiece? Startlingly, it was Dr Gill who was recalled to give his expert judgement. He was happy to tell the court that the two pieces of ribbon corresponded perfectly, thirty-three strands within each. He had to admit to Best that he himself, 'was not engaged in the manufacture of tape but he was in the habit of examining fabrics he took an interest in under the microscope'.

After Inspector Thornton had given his account to the court of the brickfields and the search of Mullins' lodgings, corroborating what his colleagues had said, it was time for Mrs Emsley's friend Joseph Biggs to take the stand. He told the court that he 'knew the deceased and was in the habit of calling upon her on the Sunday evening'. Indeed, Biggs did so on Sunday 12 August. On the following Tuesday, Biggs said that he went to Grove Road to ask about some of the wallpaper, but there was no reply after he rapped on the door.

When asked about the exact nature of their friendship, Biggs confided in the court that Mrs Emsley used to, 'deposit her plate with him' – a means of keeping her money safe, but also, by implication, a gesture of great trust. He was asked about the metal pencil case and confirmed that some time before the murder, she had handed him a pencil case for safekeeping; then she 'took it away again'.

'Anything which the old lady thought was of no use to her, she was fond of withdrawing' from his safekeeping and then selling, said Biggs. At this point, the pencil case was produced. To the best of Biggs' belief, this was 'the one which she took away'.

However, he couldn't be certain of that. 'The pencil case,' he said on reflection, 'seemed changed in appearance from the time when he saw it.' Nonetheless, he believed it was the same.

An unusual weight of significance was being placed on the pencil case. Also asked about it was Mrs Emsley's niece, Elizabeth Gotz. She told the court how she had seen her aunt for lunch on Monday 13 August. While she was there, Mullins came to the house to ask for a particular key. She remembered having seen the pencil case on an earlier occasion and identified it as belonging to the old lady. On that day, she recalled, Mullins was busy on various of her aunt's properties, fitting keys and carrying out other maintenance work.

Even on a dull, dark autumn day, the large windows of the Central Criminal Court would have bathed the room with a light that brought out its sombre grandeur; the drama of the architecture, as well as the sensation of being called to speak at the Old Bailey before all these people, must have been awe-inspiring, especially for someone like Elizabeth George, Mrs Emsley's charwoman.

Mrs George related that even when she was in the house with Mrs Emsley, the old lady would still be extremely careful about callers, making sure she had thoroughly appraised and interrogated them from the window before any suggestion of opening the door. That last Saturday of the old woman's life, a huge quantity of wallpaper was delivered and it was Mullins who carried the rolls upstairs. Mrs George had seen him frequently on her Saturday cleaning shifts there, and it was the day that he came to be paid by Mrs Emsley. Mrs George remembered that Mrs Emsley paid Mullins six shillings, which she fetched out of her pocket.

There were other visitors that last Saturday: 'a short man' calling about the paper-hangings, whom Mrs George thought was called Mr Wright. He came and went while the cleaning lady went about her chores.

There was reportedly 'sensation' throughout the court as the next witness was called and took the stand: Walter Thomas Emm, who was, by now, a national celebrity. Officials had to calm down the assembled public spectators as he began his testimony.

'I am a shoemaker by trade,' he told the court. 'I collected Mrs Emsley's rents and did odd jobs for her.'

Emm related how he had been taken into custody and charged with having in his possession a parcel he had never seen before. He then told the court that the last time he saw his employer was 'at the end of Barnsley Street' on 13th August.

Next, he accounted for his movements on the presumed night of Mrs Emsley's murder, though there was no explanation as to why he had left it so long to do so. On top of this, given that the charges against him had been withdrawn, Emm's anxiety to demonstrate his innocence further had a curious sound of desperation.

'On the evening of the same day [as the murder],' he told the court, 'I went in a penny-cart to Bromley and Stratford. I got home at about half-past eleven. My wife and a woman called Buckle and a man named Rumbold accompanied me, and here is the toll-ticket we got that evening.'

The tolls were a remnant of the previous century; vehicles on the Mile End Road (as well as other London suburbs) were still required to pay a small sum for use of the road. The ticket Emm held up for the court also seemed solid proof; he had documentary evidence and witnesses to show he had been some distance away from Grove Road when the slaughter took place.

'On the solemn oath I have taken,' Emm declared, 'I had nothing whatever to do with the murder of Mrs Emsley.'

The day after his night at Stratford, he said that it was 'a quarter-past nine on the Tuesday morning that I got up, being unwell'. Indeed, it was only by about quarter past ten that he made it to the outhouse.

The cross-examination by Best began. When did Emm start to think there might be something wrong at Grove Road?

'I went twice to Mrs Emsley's on the Wednesday, in the afternoon and in the evening,' he recalled. 'On the Thursday I went again and received no answer. On the Thursday evening I began to think that something was wrong so I called the next door neighbour who said that he had been out all day. My wife was there in the morning. I determined that evening to tell Mrs Emsley's relatives. The next morning I found the house in the same condition.'

It was at this point that he had called for the solicitor, Mr Rose.

Next in the stand were the people who would confirm Emm's alibi: Mary-Ann Buckle, penny-cart driver Thomas Rumbold, and Emm's wife, Anne. They all testified to the truth of the journey to Stratford.

The effort to ensure Emm was completely exonerated did not end there. His daughter Susannah now took the oath. She told the jury about giving her father his breakfast at quarter-past nine on the morning after the murder. She then recounted her sightings of Mullins' presence in the brickfields near their outhouse.

Another sensation in the courtroom, this time veering towards the sentimental, broke out when Emm's ten-year-old son was called. The boy swore the oath and then told the court how he had seen Mullins in the brickfields, simply lying there 'with his handkerchief up to his eyes'. There were no further questions for the youngster. The impression of his brief testimony – that curious image of Mullins' stillness and even apparent despair – must have been strong.

Next came a witness who was near the old lady's house on the fateful Monday evening. Local tailor John Raymond testified that around ten minutes to eight that night, he saw Mullins emerge from a urinal at the end of Grove Road. Raymond said he had been waiting to enter the urinal himself. On leaving, he said, Mullins walked around by the Earl of Aberdeen public house in the direction of Mrs Emsley's house.

'Did you particularly notice the man Mullins?' asked Best.

'I did,' replied Raymond. 'He looked me up and down as if struck by my appearance.'

This retort drew a loud and unexpected laugh in the courtroom. One report stated that Mullins himself was seen to laugh. It is possible this was a form of nervous reaction to a sense of mounting tension.

When, Best wanted to know, did Raymond share this intelligence with the police? Raymond said that he went to Scotland Yard some days after the arrest of Mullins.

The judge wanted to know if Raymond had ever seen Mullins before. No, was the reply, not before 'observing him in the urinal'.

Raymond had 'read in the newspapers that [Mullins] was a plasterer, and he had noticed on the evening in question that the man in the urinal was a plasterer'. Best was interested in this point: how does one identify a plasterer?

'He had on what seemed to be a plasterer's coat,' responded Raymond. He had a good opportunity of seeing his face too, so much so that he had no difficulty in identifying Mullins among twenty other men at a police line-up.

Then came a startling intervention from Mullins himself: had not Mr Raymond had an opportunity of seeing him the day before the line-up when he was being examined by officers at the Arbour Square police station?

Raymond conceded that he might have done so.

James Mitchell, the dock worker who testified he had seen Mullins walking across Stepney Green near to dawn on the morning after the murder, reiterated his evidence, talking of Mullins' 'bulky pockets' and of how he 'looked very excited and trembled all over'.

Under questioning, Mitchell stated that 'he was not afraid' of Mullins when he saw him, 'but was a little alarmed to see a man in so excited a state'. When he heard about the murder, he 'came to the conclusion that the man he had met was connected with it and he gave information to the police'.

It wasn't wholly the spirit of justice that motivated Mitchell; after having heard Mullins being discussed everywhere after his arrest, Mitchell went to the Clerkenwell House of Detention, where, he told the court, he saw Mullins and 'knew him to be the man' he had passed on Stepney Green that morning. He told the court he had not heard of the reward that had been offered for information, but confessed that he did expect to get a portion of that money.

Next on the stand was William Rowland, one of the other rent collectors who worked for Mrs Emsley. Like Mullins, Rowland was a former policeman. He told the court he had seen Mullins on the 13th doing some work at one of Mrs Emsley's houses. He then saw him again on the Wednesday. On the Friday, the day the body was discovered and the news spread through the east, Rowland saw Mullins again working on a house occupied by a Mr Gaffney. The man had asked if the two labourers 'had heard of the death of an old lady in Grove Road'. At this, Rowland said, Mullins 'fell into a tremor, and his countenance changed'. Rowland said that he later found that 'the work Mullins was doing was very slovenly done'.

Rowland said he had met Mullins again a couple of weeks later, and his appearance was very much changed. The two men went for a drink and there seemed to have been a rather charged conversation: Mullins declaring confidentially that he had a suspect for the murder in mind, and Rowland replying that he thought the police's suspect was a very different person altogether. Rowland told the court he knew about Emm's trip to Stratford on the evening of the 13th.

Again, it seemed a little striking that it was only now that Rowland should have corroborated Emm's alibi, because no one was suggesting at any point that Emm needed one.

Under cross-examination, Rowland seemed a little less certain of himself. He recalled how, the day after the murder, Mullins abandoned the plastering job he was working on, claiming he could not finish until the carpenters working at the same house had finished their work. Rowland said that was not the case about the carpenters' part in the job.

Did Rowland ever see Mullins wearing the 'billy-cocked hat' that several other witnesses had mentioned? He replied that he had not. Rowland was asked by Best about another matter: the allegedly fierce row that had taken place between Mrs Emsley and one of her tenants called Smith.

The lawyer might not have been aware that the same Smith had written an aggrieved letter to *The Times* a few weeks beforehand, denying he had taken anything from Mrs Emsley or that he had threatened her. In court, Rowland retold the story of the row and suggested that it was only his intervention that had prevented things from becoming even uglier.

Another of Mrs Emsley's tenants, Isaac Tyrell, swore the oath and told the court that he 'knew' Mullins and had seen him at work at his house on the day of the murder. Tyrell confirmed he 'had then a hammer, the ordinary hammer used by plasterers'. Mullins did not finish the job in hand that day and did not return until the Wednesday.

In terms of the jury, the next witness seemed particularly dangerous for Mullins. Thomas Pryor, a Chelsea pub landlord, took the stand to relate how, on 8 September, Mullins' wife Catherine had entered his establishment with the aim of selling a silver pencil case. Pryor agreed to buy it.

'It was not straight,' he said, meaning the pencil case itself. He straightened it himself, then cleaned it, 'as it was very dirty'.

The spots of blood observed on it subsequently must therefore have materialised after Pryor bought it, not before.

He told the court that when he read of the apprehension of Mullins, he thought it best to hand the pencil case to the police. Pryor's testimony implanted in the jury an impression of James and Catherine Mullins in a partnership of crime.

Catherine Mullins' landlady, Anne Cooper, was called. She shed a little light on the family's domestic arrangements, telling the court that 'Mullins did not sleep regularly at her house'. Mrs Cooper recalled that when Mullins was there in Chelsea, 'a boot was thrown out of the window'. Court ushers produced the boot in question, showing it to the jurors and judge.

The bloodied floorboards from 9 Grove Road were brought back to the courtroom. On the stained board had been drawn the impression of a boot. The actual boot was then placed in the outline, and 'it was found that there was a correspondence between them,' according to the court report. 'Two nails in the boot particularly corresponded with marks on the board and there was a hole in the centre of the sole of the boot in which there seemed to be a soaking up of blood.'

The judge was moved to interject. Who had made the pencilled boot outline on the board? That person was Dr Gill. The judge then stated that 'it appeared to him that the pencilled outline of the boot was not taken from the boot itself, but was wholly imaginary.'

Dr Gill, returning to the stand, told the court once again that he had examined the boot with a microscope and found three hairs in different parts of it. The hair, he said, corresponded with that of Mrs Emsley, 'some of which he had in his possession'. Under questioning, Gill was forced to be a little more precise. Yes, he conceded, it was the case that 'human hair was used by plasterers' as part of the mixture. However, he had also examined the silver pencil case with his microscope and had found blood on it.

'The microscope,' said Gill, 'was an infallible test to prove the presence of blood.'

Best jumped in. Could Dr Gill be certain about the provenance of this blood? At this, Gill was forced to admit that he 'could not say it was human blood on the pencil case. There was no test for discriminating human blood from other blood.' (Indeed, in the first Sherlock Holmes story published twenty-seven years later in 1887, Watson meets Holmes while he is at work with test tubes in St Bart's Hospital, formulating his own fanciful method of testing blood stains. In real life, it was not until the turn of the twentieth century that techniques for distinguishing human from animal blood were found.)

The final witness for the prosecution was another of Mrs Emsley's tenants. Elizabeth Fuke, who lived at Jane Street, recalled how Mullins visited at the beginning of August to carry out work. Just as Mrs Fiske told the Thames Police Court, Mullins had complained to her that the old lady would not allow him money to buy sufficient materials; that she would 'not even allow herself a farthing's worth of milk to her tea; that it was a pity such an old wretch should be allowed to live'. Best probed her a little – did Mullins perhaps expand on these thoughts? No, replied Mrs Fiske, he simply 'spoke of her penurious habits generally'.

Parry announced that these were all the witnesses for the prosecution. Best asked for an adjournment until the following day as there were defence witnesses he was going to have to call. Lord Pollock agreed; he and the jury would be examining the bloody floorboard and boot more closely, and it would be better to do so in daylight. It had been a long day and the court adjourned at half-past five.

Reports did not convey the state of Mullins' spirits as he was led back to the holding cell. Even in the darkness of the prison, he may still have presented an optimistic face to his gaolers. However, at some point during the night the terror must have overwhelmed him; for the man who faced the court the next morning looked entirely different.

19

Sufficient for the Day
is the Evil Thereof

❧

At ten o'clock on the morning of Friday 27 October 1860, James Mullins was led back into the dock of the Old Bailey. According to one account, he 'looked a great deal care-worn'.

The experience of standing trial for his life must, in some perverse way, have been exhilarating as well as frightening; but while the adrenaline would have raced constantly in court, the silence of a dark cell in the small hours would have been a different matter. Come the morning, that long night was showing on his face. Mullins was sick with anxiety for his family. The full extent of this fear would emerge later.

The jury had stayed overnight at the London Coffee House, overseen by officers of the court. This was to prevent both the public getting access to them, and to stop talkative jurists accidentally getting into unwise conversations. From the start, Mullins was observed to be paying 'close attention to the proceedings' and making notes. [1] Mr Best, for the defence, rose to speak to the jury.

Before calling the first witness, Best gave an introductory

address outlining his themes. He talked, *The Times* reported, of the 'heavy and distressing responsibility' devolved upon himself, plus the 'fearful and important duty which the jury had to discharge'. He reminded them that 'in this land, every man was presumed to be innocent till he was legally proved guilty, and to weigh impartiality in the stern scales of justice the evidence brought before them'.

Strikingly, in view of the torrents of excitement from newspapers, Mr Best asked the jury, according to *The Times*, to 'dismiss from their minds the fearful state of the outer world – where they read, day after day, that murder is stalking through the land'.

Best continued, reminding the jury that Parry, for the prosecution, had told them, 'murder was most frequently committed when there was no eye to witness it, save the all-seeing eye of God – that it was a deed of darkness, usually perpetrated when the rest of the world was at rest'. Best explained that this meant Parry had presented them with an array of circumstantial evidence – 'greater and lesser facts'.

Immediately addressing one of these facts, Best discussed the idea that Mrs Emsley was always extremely cautious about whom she allowed into her house. Yet, the defence counsel added, it 'appeared that this woman had bought a quantity of paper-hangings' and was 'desirous of selling' them.

'It might be inferred, therefore,' declared Best, 'that ... seeing she had paper-hangings to sell, and considering her penurious habits, that she would not be so careful of the admission of persons as at other times, and that other men besides the prisoner Mullins would get easy access to her house.'

Continuing, Best said that 'on the very first blush of the case', there was good reason to believe that 'other persons' might have obtained entrance to the house on the night of the murder.

He then said he thought the jury would agree that the murder was committed 'between seven in the evening and eight on the following morning', since the old lady had been seen 'by two respectable females' sitting at her window at seven o'clock in the evening and in the morning, callers who knocked could not gain admittance.

The question, said Best, was: 'Who committed the murder? And how did his learned friend endeavour to bring it home to the prisoner?'

Best turned to the matter of Mullins 'lodging information' against another individual, and explained to the jury the simple motive for this act: the enormous cash reward.

'As early as the 28th of August, the prisoner was in communication with the police on the subject of the murder and continued to be so from time to time so that Mullins, actuated by the motive of the reward, had from the first been in communication with one or other of the police.'

At this point, Best rather neatly swivelled attention away from the obvious inference that Mullins, using stolen goods, had attempted to frame another man, with an aside on the use of financial rewards in such cases. There was, he said, 'extreme danger' in offering such vast sums. 'In former times,' said Best, 'it was the custom to give people what was called "blood money" and they all knew the fearful consequences that resulted from that practice. Happily those days have gone by, but still, who could doubt that evil results from the system of offering rewards?'

Slyly, Best sought to shift some of the emphasis on to the policemen Mullins was talking to. He reminded the jury of that attested conversation where Mullins had told Sergeant Tanner that 'I will see you all right.'

'There seemed,' said Best, 'to be a perfect understanding of what was to be the result of the work they were engaged in.'

Why, asked Best, did the police make such a listless effort in that Sunday morning search of Emm's brickhouse and his cottage? They had told Mullins to stay back, but then 'very carelessly' carried out the examination of the premises. Mullins, he said, was anxious to see what was going on and at last came forward to exhort the police to look behind 'that bloody slab'. The parcel was found, and, Best said (again, rather smoothly), that 'his learned friend' declared Mullins was the man who put the items in the parcel and so, 'having committed one murder', he 'then attempted to commit another'.

Best said he 'would afterwards deal with this part of the case in a broad and distinct manner'. He wanted the jury to separate the theft and the parcel from the murder of the old lady.

'A search was made of the prisoner's room at Barnsley Street,' explained Best, and there was found some ribbon that corresponded with the ribbon tied around the parcel and some cobbler's wax. Meanwhile, at the Mullins' Chelsea lodgings, there was a hammer and a boot in the dust hole which was presented as having nails that corresponded with a footmark in Mrs Emsley's blood. Besides this, Best said, there was 'a pencil case said to be marked with a spot of blood', though he did not think 'the jury were likely to rely much on that supposed spot of blood on a pencil case'.

Best moved on to addressing the prosecution's case that Mullins had been seen 'in the neighbourhood' of Mrs Emsley's home on the night of the murder, 'and this evidence [the prosecutor] tried to strengthen by the extraordinary testimony of a dock-labourer who spoke of an apparition he had seen early in the morning'. This labourer, said Best, laid emphasis on the bulkiness of the man's pockets; he hoped the jury would bear in mind that only a very few small articles had been taken from the old lady's house – so small that they could scarcely have filled a man's pockets.

In addition to this, continued Best, was the observation of the solicitor William Rose, who found a key in a basket in Mrs Emsley's bedroom and said it was a key that 'had been given to Mullins'. However, 'there was nothing to show that this key had not been given back by Mullins to the old lady [at an earlier time]'.

There was also a vital forensic point for the jury to bear in mind: in the upper rooms of the house where the murder had been committed, witnesses spoke of the great splashes and pools of blood.

'The person who committed the murder,' said Best, 'could not fail to have splashes of blood on his clothes. Blood is not easily got rid of.'

Yet 'not a particle of blood' had been found on any of Mullins' clothes.

Best then turned on Dr Gill and the flaws in both his evidence and reasoning, making a clear suggestion of professional neglect. Gill had described in great detail the hideous nature of the wounds but 'they all knew how dangerous it was to conclude that a wound was inflicted with a particular instrument' when testimony otherwise was vague. If Dr Gill had not taken a note of the length of the wound at the time, could his memory of it be counted upon to be accurate? Especially since he claimed to have seen the hammer in question a fortnight after the murder, when in fact it was considerably longer than that.

That was not all. In Dr Gill's testimony about the footprint, did the boot produced really correspond to the marks on the floorboard? Best told the jury that 'evidence arising from footmarks was of a very painful character' in the sense that it was almost preposterously unreliable: 'very many working men, and ladies and gentlemen, wear boots and shoes of a similar kind'. When it came to the configuration of nail marks, who was to say how many pairs of boots in London had been manufactured in the same way? In addition to this, Best said, the jury were perhaps more competent than him when it came to observation, but when he himself examined the boot, he found it had three nails. The impression on the bloodied floorboard was of two.

That same examination of the boot had found no trace of blood, yet surely the leather would have soaked up a certain amount of Mrs Emsley's blood? Indeed, it should have been suffused. Yet the leather seemed clean, and that boot had not left any kind of a stain in either of Mullins' dwellings.

The boot had apparently been thrown from the window of his Chelsea lodgings on the day the family moved from Orford Street to rooms in nearby Oakham Street.

'Where was the other boot?' asked Best. 'Was only one found? It is, to say the least, singular that only one boot should be forthcoming.'

Then there were the hairs found on it. The boot had been found in a dust hole, smothered in ash; a hole in which a great deal of other matter had been dumped. Human hair frequently made its way into such places. More than this, human hair was used in mortar, 'as they all knew'. So as far as this part of the evidence went, there was nothing to be laid at the feet of Mullins at all.

What about the spoons, of which the prosecution had made so much? Was there really anything 'so peculiar and exceptional' about them as to make the jury think they were the exact same spoons that had been taken from Mrs Emsley's house? What about the lenses in the parcel? No one had actually mentioned that these items had ever been in Mrs Emsley's house near the time of the murder. When lenses were mentioned, they had been there 'some considerable time beforehand'. The defence was striving to persuade the jury to interrogate these everyday items, to see them not with the sinister slant given by the prosecution, but as rather ordinary, and in themselves unremarkable.

What about the cheque given to Mrs Emsley by Pickering the 'chymist'? It was 'still in his possession' at twelve o'clock on the day of the murder. Might it not be possible, asked Best, 'that she might have given it away to someone else in the way of business? It was not a crossed cheque and might have been passed anywhere'.

Further still, what about the silver pencil case? Like the spoons, 'there was no evidence to prove it had been in the possession of the old lady for three weeks before her murder'. Mrs Emsley might have lent it to Mullins, perhaps to measure something, and he simply retained it.

Now Best was coming to the thorniest part of his defence: how to account for the extraordinary saga of the parcel in Emm's outhouse? If he was not accusing Emm, then how exactly could he explain it?

To tackle this, Best employed a devious gambit. It was, he said, 'no part of his duty to throw this crime on anyone'. Best added that it was simply sufficient for him to show the jury that there was reasonable doubt to assume the man in the dock had committed the murder. Moreover, the jury was not to think 'that he charged any human being with the commission of the murder'.

Suddenly, and after some misdirection, the defence counsel rather startlingly turned on Walter Emm – just as the man in question had clearly feared. This was why he had taken such trouble to demonstrate his firm alibi for the night of the murder. The court, said Best, had Emm's testimony that on the night of the murder, he had been in a pony trap with several associates going to Stratford. What, the defence asked, were Emm's 'antecedents'?

'He collected rents for the old lady and was in constant communication with her. It was very singular that Emm should have gone to her house twice and found no admission, and have sent his son once with the same result, and yet should never have thought of giving information that he suspected something was wrong, though, in a conversation with his wife, he expressed a fear that something was wrong.'

Best added that he merely thought that this fact deserved the attention of the jury.

He added he should also like to know how 'the friends of Emm remembered so distinctly the evening on which they had gone to Stratford'. A lot of time had elapsed 'before their minds were called to the subject'; more than this, 'one striking incident in the examination was Emm pulling out of his pocket a turnpike ticket to bear out his evidence'.

The defence lawyer did not expand on his own thoughts about the pony trap and turnpike, or the exact provenance of the toll ticket, save that the jury had to consider whether Emm 'had cleared himself in their minds' from the charge originally brought against him when he was arrested with Mullins. The prosecution's case rested on Emm being cleared and the burden of guilt then falling wholly on Mullins, who the prosecution had said went about making up the parcel of Mrs Emsley's bric-a-brac to ensure Emm was found guilty of murder.

The prosecution, said Best, was also placing emphasis on the evidence of Mr Raymond, who had seen Mullins at the public urinal on the night of the murder. He wanted to put it to the jury, 'as men of intelligence and judgement', whether Raymond's recognition of Mullins was to be relied on.

'Our criminal annals are full of mistakes of identity, committed even by experienced persons,' said Best. 'To depend on evidence of identity was at all times dangerous, but more especially so when the life of a human being was in danger.'

Raymond, said Best, had only given Mullins 'the mere casual glance of a man coming out of a urinal'. In a moment, the man he had seen had gone, and yet Raymond had taken to the witness box to swear that he had seen Mullins. Furthermore, Raymond had claimed Mullins had been wearing a 'billy-cock hat' that night; Rowland, Mullins' colleague, had told the court he had never seen him in any such hat.

Best said that he had no wish to speak of the motives that might have influenced Raymond to come forward, which implied that Raymond was motivated by the prospect of a financial reward. It was possible, with all the pub discussions about the murder taking place across London, that Raymond had heard a description of Mullins.

Then there was the witness James Mitchell, the dock labourer who said he had seen Mullins on Stepney Green at around five o'clock in the morning on 14 August. Like Raymond, said Best, Mitchell had heard all the news and speculation around Mullins before he came forward; he had even admitted that he had been drawn to the prospect of the reward.

What of Mullins' colleague William Rowland, who had testified that on the days following the murder, Mullins seemed 'very much agitated' and left jobs unfinished? This could be answered with the fact that Mullins was clearly very busy and had multiple jobs on hand; it was not at all an unusual circumstance for such a worker to leave one job and then come back to it a short time later. Nor was Mullins avoiding Rowland. 'Did the jury think' that a man haunted by murder would have gone back repeatedly to the colleague who was talking to him about it?

At this, Best delicately broached a question of class (and perhaps, subliminally, of London views of the Irish) when he put it to the jury that 'Mullins belongs to that class of society in which they might expect a man guilty of murder, and agitated and excited about it, to have taken refuge in liquor to drive away his care. But nothing of this kind was traceable in his conduct.'

Moving on to the hammer, Best explained that nothing could be drawn from it against Mullins, since it showed no trace of blood. Moreover, there was no proof that a hammer was the instrument with which the murder had been committed.

The rules of the court at that time meant that if Best called witnesses for the defence, they would first be cross-examined by the prosecution. The prosecution would then be entitled to conclude the entire case before the judge and jury, thus giving the prosecuting counsel the final influential word before the jury retired to consider their verdict. As a result, calling defence witnesses was, as Best knew, a risk. That said, the instructions he had received from Mullins was that the witnesses should be called.

Best then announced to the court that these witnesses would 'disprove the evidence given as to the place where Mullins was said to have been on the night of the murder – and to show where he actually was'.

Best was going to call Mullins' family to testify, just as Emm had been allowed to call his. In addition, he was going to call witnesses who had not only seen Mullins at key moments, but also witnesses who had seen curious activity around Mrs Emsley's house after the murder. Best reminded the court of 'one of the greatest privileges of an English tribunal': the fact that guilt had to be 'brought home' by legal proof. The jury would have to ask themselves on what elements of the circumstantial evidence they were prepared to rely.

The defence counsel then addressed one of the key points against Mullins, that he 'put the things into the parcel from the wretched motive of getting the reward'. Best appealed to the jury not to be led by this.

'Do not set up in this court an altar to an unknown god,' he continued strikingly, 'the god of prejudice.'

Do not, he added, make the man in the dock 'the first sacrifice, the first victim whose blood would be sprinkled on that altar'.

Possibly unwisely, Best invoked Judas in pleading for Mullins' life to be spared if there was even 'a feather' of doubt. 'Let him go forth free and let him end his days in misery,' said Best. Rather that, he concluded, than if in the future 'the real murderers of that poor old woman' were to come to light when Mullins was hanged.

Apparently underwhelmed by this stirring address, the jury simply asked for a pair of compasses to measure the bloody boot print on the board. The judge, with seeming impatience, told them that he doubted if any great importance could be attached to the comparison.

It was time for Mullins' family to have their voices heard in the great chamber. Best was possibly gambling that the children would evoke sympathy from the jury. But this was an undeniably risky manoeuvre.

Mullins' teenaged daughter Mary was the first to be sworn in. On the day of the murder, she said she was living with her mother in Chelsea.

'My father then lived at Barnsley Street,' added Mary. 'I have three brothers: James and Thomas lived with my mother, John with my father.'

She was directed immediately to the mystery of the silver pencil case.

'I have seen the pencil-case in the possession of my brother James,' she said. 'I don't know where he is now – he is a sailor. I saw the pencil case last June and since then I have seen it in my mother's possession. She had it a fortnight before my father was taken [arrested].'

Mr Parry for the prosecution began his cross-examination. Where was Mary Mullins when she heard of the murder of Mrs Emsley?

'I was in service . . . living at 9 Sloane Terrace with Mr Gibson,' she replied. 'I first read of it in the newspapers.'

Mary saw her father on the Saturday after the murder, then, a little later, when her father was arrested, the calamity rippled outwards.

'Mr Gibson dismissed me from my situation on the Monday after my father was taken into custody,' explained Mary. 'My master read the case in the newspapers and told me I had better go. That was the only reason for my dismissal.'

Mary had been badly hurt, and damaged in terms of her own prospects, by the reports and gossip around her sacking, so this was a rare chance to receive a hearing.

'I was not sent away because I was seen removing a stone in the kitchen and was thought to be concealing something there,' she continued. So why did she remove this flagstone? She had, she said, 'dropped a shilling down a hole and wished to find it. I did find it, but not in anyone's presence.'

No one at all?

'The little girl, my fellow servant, found me taking up the stone,' said Mary. 'I called her afterwards to hold the candle. I never offered her sixpence to say nothing about it.'

There were some supplementary questions. How often did Mullins stay in the Chelsea lodgings? Only on a Saturday night, was the answer. Mary spoke a little more of her situation at Sloane Terrace. It had paid her twelve pounds a year, and when she was fired she was given eighteen shillings as notice.

When questioned about the location of the flagstone she had moved, Mary explained that it was 'by the side of the fireplace, and there was a hole near the fender'.

It is not quite clear how such testimony, even if it spoke of an obvious injustice and snobbery on the part of her employer, could have helped her father in any material way.

Next to the stand was Mullins' sixteen-year-old son, Thomas. The boy's story had an element of pathos that might have elicited sympathy. But prosecutor Parry was ready for him.

'I am a labourer, and occasionally assist my father in his trade,' Thomas told the court. He also stated that he remembered that Monday 13 August, 'on which day I was staying with my father in Barnsley Street. My brother was also staying with us. I was doing nothing and remained home all day. My father was out at work. He came home from his work that evening at a quarter to seven.'

What, then, of that crucial night?

'He did not go out any more that night,' Thomas explained. 'He slept in a little bed by himself, and my brother and I slept together in the same room.'

What about Tuesday morning, after this uneventful evening and night?

'We got up about half-past seven,' recalled Thomas. 'When my father got up, he water-washed the passage and stopped the nail-holes. He was at work upon this till noon. Then, about half-past twelve on the Tuesday, he had his dinner and went out. I did not go with him.'

Did Thomas recognise the boot at all?

'I have cleaned my father's boots and he never had such a one,' said the boy.

Then there was the matter of the 'billy-cocked' or 'wide-awake' hat seen by witnesses; Thomas denied his father owned such an article.

Parry persisted with his questioning, asking of Thomas' brother James.

'I last saw my brother James about three months ago,' said Thomas. 'He was at home at the time of the murder.'

When, asked the prosecution, did James leave home?

Thomas was by now flustered. 'No, he wasn't at home at the time.'

'Why,' asked Parry, 'did you tell me he was at home?'

'I made a mistake,' responded Thomas, now floundering badly. 'He left three or four weeks before the murder.'

'How is it,' Parry calmly enquired, 'that you can now tell me so glibly when he left? You told me just now something quite different.'

'Yes – because I had it in my mind,' replied Thomas. 'I do not know where he is now. He went away in the *Mechanic* [a ship], bound to New York.'

What of Thomas's own employment? How had he been earning his keep around that fateful August?

'I was working at a greengrocer's named Pinnock in Marlborough Road in August,' Thomas said. 'I left there on the Saturday, I went down to my father's on the Monday morning.'

In an echo of his sister's testimony, Thomas told the court: 'I have only done one day's work since the murder.'

Parry seized on this; had Thomas been sacked by the greengrocer?

'I was not dismissed by Mr Pinnock,' the boy said. 'I left of my own accord. That I will swear.'

Was he quite certain about his movements on those days?

'I am quite sure I left on the 12th of August,' said the boy. 'I slept on the Sunday night in Orford Street. My father was there and left about six o'clock on the Monday morning. I went up to

Barnsley Street about noon. My brother John was there. I went out for a short time, but with that exception we were in the room all day together. My father came home to his dinner and we all dined together.'

The prosecutor wanted to know more about these domestic arrangements. His questioning threw a sharp light on to what some members of the jury might have seen as the disordered nature of life in the poorer parts of the East End. Meat and bread were eaten that day, but where in the house did they dine?

'There is no table in the room and only one chair,' explained Thomas. 'We had supper on the Monday and went to bed at nine o'clock, my father sleeping on a trestle and sacking, my brother and I on some canes or rushes. It was twelve o'clock before we went to sleep. I don't know why we did not go to sleep at once – because we could not I suppose.'

Thomas told the court he stayed in Barnsley Street 'the whole of Tuesday' and 'slept again in the room with my father'. He 'continued there' until Thursday and then took himself back to Chelsea. Thomas had been looking for work in Bethnal Green and Mile End, but was at pains to point out that 'on the Tuesday' he did not go out 'for more than quarter of an hour'.

The prosecuting counsel asked when Thomas first learned of the murder.

'I first heard of the murder on the Saturday evening [the 19th] when my father came home,' he answered. 'It was then I remembered where I had slept on the Monday night.'

Who else shared the house? There was another lodger called Mrs Musick. She had three children who 'lived in the room which my father occupied', said Thomas. Were they there that Monday night as well? Thomas replied that he 'did not recollect whether or not they had slept there on the Monday or the Tuesday night'.

He then told the court that his last night in Barnsley Street was on the Wednesday after 13 August. At this, Thomas recalled that on the Monday, there had been some argument, and 'Mrs Emsley would not allow Mrs Musick to remain in the house.'

What had happened? Was she forced to leave?

Thomas said that he didn't know 'where she slept on August 13th'. He believed 'she used to sleep in the back-kitchen when my father was in Barnsley Street', and the 'children used generally to sleep in my father's room'. He recalled sleeping in that room with the children himself.

Thomas was dismissed from the stand; now his older brother John was called. This young man was also about to become hopelessly entangled in his account of those nights in the Bethnal Green lodgings.

'I live at number 1 Rose Court, East Smithfield, and am a dock labourer out of employ,' John told the court. Thus the jury now knew that three of Mullins' children were unemployed.

'I remember my father living at 33 Barnsley Street,' said John. 'I lived there with him. I was there on Monday August 13th. My father and brother – the last witness – were there on that day. My father went out at his regular time in the morning, about eight. He came home about twelve to his dinner, and then went out to his work again. I saw him next a little before seven o'clock. He sat til eight o'clock, and went to bed at nine. I went to bed also in the same room. I did not go to sleep for some time afterwards.

'I got up the next morning [Tuesday] at half-past seven o'clock and my father rose at the same time,' he continued. 'After breakfast, he water-washed the passage and stopped the nail holes. At half-past twelve o'clock, he had his dinner and went out, saying he was going to Cambridge Road to work.'

John also agreed with his family about the boot and hat.

'I never saw the boot produced in all my life,' he stated, before going on to say, 'my father never wore a billy-cocked hat.'

Parry was struck by a thought: perhaps Mullins did not wear such a hat, but did John ever wear one?

'At times in Ireland,' replied John. 'I might have had one for about a month.'

Why was he now out of work?

'I have not done any work for four months because my health would not allow me,' said John. 'During that time, I have lived in Barnsley Street. On the Saturday before the murder, my father slept at Little Orford Street. On Sunday night I slept at Barnsley Street with my father. On Monday morning he had his breakfast.'

At this, John stumbled over himself and seemed muddled.

'I made a mistake in saying he slept at Barnsley Street on Sunday,' he said.

Parry was silky in his intervention: 'You said so distinctly just now.'

Parry then asked if the Mullins family' had had breakfast at Barnsley Street on the Monday morning?

'I can't say,' said Mullins' son, miserably. 'You speak a little too fast for me. If you speak a little easier, I shall understand you.'

There was laughter in the court at this point. The boy tried to recover himself.

'I did not sleep there on Tuesday night,' he said. 'I went up to Orford Street on that day. I can't say how long I stayed there.'

He was certain that when in Barnsley Street, he 'did not go out on the Monday'. So what were the sleeping arrangements on that fateful Monday evening?

'My brother slept with me that evening,' said John. 'I believe that the Musick children slept in the kitchen but I will not swear that. They would either sleep there or in the room. They certainly slept in the house.'

How long did young John Mullins tarry in Barnsley Street that week? He recalled that he left to go to Chelsea on the Tuesday evening, and he believed that Mrs Musick would have seen his father 'water-washing the ceiling'. Where was Mrs Musick now?

'I don't know where she is,' said John. 'She is out of the way.'

Parry pressed him on this. Clearly Mrs Musick would surely

have been a most valuable witness to Mullins' comings and goings that Monday? John testified that he had 'tried to find this Mrs Musick', but had failed.

None of this had gone well for Mullins. Instead of offering a solid alibi, his sons' stumblings and inaccurate memories, plus the miserable fact of their workless states, had instead created a cumulative picture of a shiftless family with an uneasy relationship with the truth. Their accounts seemed to underscore a sense of chaos, among themselves and their fellow tenants; the firm borders of domesticity appeared to dissolve.

At the time, the social observers and journalists who descended on areas such as Bethnal Green mesmerised their readers with accounts of transgressive and curiously primitive-seeming behaviour; the decencies of family life replaced by the queasy squalor of poverty, forcing strangers to share each other's space promiscuously.

The next two defence witnesses had a story that produced a ripple of shock around the court, for they were in effect naming another man as a chief suspect in the murder. This was the moment that would haunt Arthur Conan Doyle as he chewed over the case forty years later.

Caroline Barnes was the neighbour who lived across the road from Mrs Emsley. She told the court how she recalled seeing Mrs Emsley on Monday 13 August, but then, crucially, added that as she was looking at the house on the Tuesday morning, she 'observed someone moving the paper-hangings in the next room. This was about twenty minutes to ten o'clock. I saw the right hand window opening a little way.' She said she 'could not tell who the person in the room was'.

Sensationally, the defence counsel now had a witness who seemed to have an answer to this: a builder called James Stephenson.

'I had occasion to go to Grove Road on Tuesday morning, August 14th,' he told the court. 'I called in at number 3 on business at half-past ten. In walking down the road afterwards, I saw a tall man come out of a garden, with some paper-hangings under his arm, apparently from number 9. In turning the corner, I met the man face to face. It was Mr Rowland.

'His manner and conversation were very flurried,' continued Stephenson. 'I said, "Hallo! Are you in the paper line?" He said, "Yes. Didn't you know that?" "No," I said, "or else I might have given you a job or two."'

Stephenson then told the court he had subsequently given this information to Scotland Yard.

The idea this testimony presented was disorientating. As Mrs Emsley's body lay in a glistening pool of blood, one of her employees, who possibly dealt the fatal blows, had either stayed with the body all night and then chosen to leave with the stolen articles and wallpaper in the bright glare of morning, or even more bafflingly, had blankly returned to the bloody house for the wallpaper.

Parry was swift with his cross-examination. Was Stephenson quite sure he had the right house?

'I am not aware that a house was being papered at the time next door to number 9,' replied Stephenson, adding that he did not recognise 'Mr Rowland until he was close upon me.'

There was a brief interlude as one more witness, Michael Gaffney, testified that Mullins had been working at his house on the morning of Tuesday 14 August.

The case for the defence over, the flurry of supposition produced by the accounts of Caroline Barnes and James Stephenson had caused clamour among the jury. They wanted to see William Rowland recalled to the stand.

Lord Pollock remarked to the jury that 'no question was put to Rowland yesterday about this matter' and that he did not think the case was 'one which called for fresh evidence'.

He added that Stephenson had said that this man had 'apparently' come out of 9 Grove Road; whoever the man he saw was, 'he might have gone to the door [of that house] and come back again, or he might have come from another house'. However, Pollock said, the jury were free to ask Rowland a question. The foreman stood and addressed the question to the judge: was it really Rowland who had come out of the house, or indeed any adjoining house?

Rowland was now called back to the stand.

The judge asked him: 'Do you know James Stephenson?'

'I do,' said Rowland.

'Did you see him in Grove Road on the 14th of August?'

'I did not,' said Rowland. 'I was not near the place.'

'So you did not come out of any house in Grove Road that day?' asked the judge.

'No,' said Rowland, 'but I met Stephenson some days before near the Grove Road with a bundle of papers under my arm. Perhaps I may be allowed to explain that I have known Stephenson for some time and I have always laboured under the impression that he was not quite right in his mind.'

At this, there was a great echoing of laughter through the court. There did not seem to be anything more to ask Rowland, and it was not recorded how Mullins reacted to his colleague's testimony.

One further witness was called: a laundress called Caroline Brinson, who wished to contradict what Mullins' sons had told the court. Her aunt, she told the jury, also lived at 33 Barnsley Street – an invalid who was being cared for by fellow resident Mrs Musick.

Mrs Musick 'went away' she explained, and Miss Brinson went to take her place in the caring duties on the Tuesday 'after the murder'. She told the court that that morning, Thomas Mullins was there, 'but not the other brother', and that the house's passage was water-washed 'on the Thursday', and not the Tuesday. According to reports, the defence counsel simply 'made a few observations' upon this new evidence.

It was time now for the prosecution, in the form of Mr Parry, to summarise the entire case for the jury. It seems curious now, with perhaps a more acute sense of the balance of justice, that this privilege should have been accorded. His attack on Mullins and the defence witnesses was unsparing. Parry started by saying that the witnesses had hardly done 'the prisoner at the bar a service' and that his learned friend, if left to his own judgement, would have been wiser not to call them. Parry dismissed Mullins' daughter's testimony, claiming that a daughter 'was not the most trustworthy witness in the world'; to save her father, she might have been apt to 'strain her conscience'.

When it came to Mullins' sons, Parry accused them of straight-forward lying. Could the jury be under any doubt, he said, that 'these youths came for the purpose of deceiving them? They had been evidently tutored to give their evidence, which from the beginning to the end of it was entirely false.'

'Would any one of the jury believe that they were speaking the truth?' asked Parry. Even Thomas Mullins' stumble was held to be deliberate. He 'thought to excite a laugh by telling counsel he was going too fast for him' as an effort to 'throw counsel off his guard' while he thought of what to say 'to save his father from his perilous condition'.

Then there was the matter of the water-washing, and on what day it was carried out. This, according to Parry, proved that the evidence of 'the young men' and all other defence witnesses was 'totally untrustworthy, totally false or inaccurate', while the boys had come there deliberately to 'tell a lie'.

Addressing the testimony of the neighbour who saw movement in the house following the murder, Parry declared that it had been comprehensively contradicted by witnesses for the prosecution. What of the builder who saw Rowland with the wallpaper? That witness' manner was 'flighty and dramatic and not like that of a sober steady man'.

Parry told the jury that it was now a matter for them to decide if the guilt of Mullins had been 'brought home', 'clearly and unmistakeably.' He believed he had demonstrated that the murderer certainly was not Walter Emm; members of his family as well as independent witnesses could prove where he was on 13 August. Parry added that it could not have been Emm who placed the parcel in the outhouse. 'If Mullins put the parcel in the shed, could there be a doubt that he committed the murder?'

Again, two crimes conflated; now Parry amplified the blood-curdling rhetoric, telling the jury that this was 'one of the most heinous crimes ever brought before a court of justice'; that he could not remember such a case as this, even in court archives 'teeming' with 'records of human depravity'.

This, Parry told the jury, was not a case in which they had to creep their way through darkness – 'the broadest daylight had been thrown on the circumstances connected with the murder'. The prisoner, he argued, 'murdered the old lady for the sake of money'. Mullins 'no doubt imagined that he would find a quantity of money in her purse'. Yet, he was 'baffled in that object'.

This was a man who had told a tenant that the old lady 'should not be permitted to live'. Since the murder, he had been thwarted in his quest to find money ('he had stained his soul by this enormity'). What was Mullins to do? In order to 'secure something', Mullins made an accusation against Walter Emm.

For those who would say that the man who planted the parcel and the man who murdered need not be one and the same, 'this was utterly erroneous'. Whoever obtained the items found in the parcel must have 'got possession of them before any human being but one knew of the murder'. Doubt had been thrown on the ribbon that tied the parcel up corresponding with ribbon in Mullins' lodgings, but 'sometimes very trifling articles . . . led to the detection of great criminals'. What was Mullins doing with cobblers' wax, save to 'fix the charge' more securely on Emm? Then there was the pencil case and the hammer, even if there was no blood on it. Mullins was a 'crafty cunning man' who would have got rid of any 'marks of blood'.

Also, what about the house key found in the basket of the old lady? The prosecutor's logic at this point seemed labyrinthine; Mullins, said Parry, obtained it from her niece, so was it not 'probable' that he 'took advantage of the paper-hangings' as a reason to get into the house and then committed the murder? He did not explain why the key might be linked with the wallpaper and instead swiftly moved on.

What then, Parry asked the jury, of the boot thrown from the window? The witnesses who saw Mullins in the vicinity of Stepney Green? The 'pure fabrication' woven by his sons about his having been in that night? Yes, one of the eyewitnesses, Mr Raymond, had been motivated by the reward, but he had been 'nine years in the employment of his present master and had all the appearance of a respectable person'. How about the witness who had seen Mullins just before dawn? Could he not have spent the night in the murder house searching for money, then emerged; might the 'billy-cocked hat' have been some kind of disguise? That, said Parry, could 'not be known', but the jury were told to 'take into consideration the cunning of the man'.

Such a summary, with so many new allegations and suppositions thrown in suggestively, would be outrageous today. There is no record of Mullins' reaction, save that occasionally he leaned over to have words with Best. Does there come a psychological point of stillness when an individual on trial for his life, whether guilty or innocent, suddenly finds the intense struggle futile?

20

'The Life of a Man
is too Sacred'

❧

As the pale lamps in the Central Criminal Court flickered, Lord Pollock turned to the jury and gave his own summary of what he understood the case to be. There could be no doubt that the murder had been prompted by 'desire or gain', and that the 'probability' was that the old lady's killer was someone she knew – for a stranger, a questing thief, 'would have taken care to tie her up in some way or other then left her'.

Yet the judge also wanted the jury to think about the circumstantial evidence: the ribbon, with its thirty-three strands, which he himself had examined, and of which there might well be thousands of examples all over the city (and, he added, the ribbon he had looked at was thicker than that alluded to by the prosecution). He himself did not see why undue weight should be attached to Mullins allegedly being seen near the victim's house. The hammer? A perfectly common plasterer's hammer; very little had been added in terms of evidential weight by bringing it into court.

The mystery of the parcel in the shed? Well, it was for the jury to decide if Mullins could simply have had a better idea than the police of how best to search for it, as opposed to being the man who planted it. This was a case in which a great deal of the evidence and facts 'seemed to point neither way'. More important to his mind was Mullins' statement that Mrs Emsley 'would not have admitted him' if he called at her house; if the jury doubted that, then there would be a reasonable ground for wondering why he had lied.

The judge agreed that whoever placed the parcel in the shed was the murderer. Since the items in the parcel were by themselves valueless, why, for instance, would Emm be concealing them, as opposed to destroying them as evidence of a crime? Emm had a ticket to show he had been on that pony trap to Stratford on the night of the murder, so he was 'exculpated'. The question remained as to who made up that parcel. With regards to the cheque, which the prosecution said had 'passed out of Mrs Emsley's possession' and thence into the hands of the accused, the jury had a right to ask Mullins for an explanation of exactly how; the same went for the spoons and the lenses.

Lord Pollock told the jury that 'the prisoner was not to be convicted on suspicion only'. They were also told to think about the term 'circumstantial evidence'.

'If a man were seen coming out of a room,' he said, by example, 'that was circumstantial evidence to prove that he had been in the room.' It would be a terrible mistake, he added, to apply the term to the 'idle dreaming of the men who alleged they met Mullins on the evening of the murder'.

He quoted Lord Tenterden: did the evidence bring to their minds that firm persuasion, that degree of conviction, that the prisoner was guilty? 'It was to the interest of the public that no innocent man should suffer, and it was also to their interest that the guilty should not escape.'

Lord Pollock continued on this theme for some time, perorating on checks, balances, the dangers of surmise, but also the degrees of certainty. With an appeal that they 'do justice to the prisoner', the jury retired to consider their verdict.

This was just before five o'clock on the second day of the trial. Mullins was returned to his holding cell; the judge and lawyers may have availed themselves of some refreshment. As it happened, the jury took a little under an hour before they returned to the court, and Mullins was once more brought to the bar to hear their verdict.

There was, according to reports, a 'breathless silence' in the court. When the clerk asked the foreman of the jury to pronounce, that silence continued a little.

Then the verdict came.

'Guilty.'

Lord Pollock turned to Mullins and asked him (as was the form in all such cases) 'what he had to say' and 'why sentence should not be passed upon him'.

It was here that the court reports noted Mullins' 'slight Irish accent'. He was not slumped in defeat, though; rather, he was observed to speak with 'much energy and firmness'. Indeed, this was the first time that judge, jury and onlookers would have caught the full measure of his intelligence. Anyone taken aback by the guilty verdict – anyone who doubted that he was the murderer – might have found his words poignant. Yet those convinced that he was the killer would have been alert to some curious omissions in his plea.

'My lord, will you allow me a few words?' said Mullins. 'I am not guilty. I know that I have not many days to live, and I am now speaking the truth. I am most happy to have had such a trial – an attentive jury and also such able counsel, who have done so cleverly for me in my defence. On Monday the 13th, I was at work in Temple Place, repairing some houses. I remained there till between six and seven o'clock. After then I returned home to my own place and, as the Lord is my judge, and I shall see him before long, I remained in my own place until I had my supper.

'After supper I went to bed and remained there until eight o'clock or so the following morning. One witness has told your lordship that he saw me in the urinal at the corner of a public house, the name of which I now forget. I solemnly declare before my God that I am telling your lordship and the court at large the simple truth. I was at home at the time and I was in bed at the time when the other witness said he saw me early next morning at Stepney Green. I say he could not have seen me there for I was in my bed.

'Now, as for the boot and my hammer. My hammer was not used by me in any way to hurt any man, woman or child. And as to the boot, I protest before my God I never saw it till I saw it at the Thames Police Court. Never did I see it before, never did I wear it. I solemnly declare that before all here present.

'What I have stated now are the real facts as the Lord is my judge, and He shall judge me before long. I was in my own bed. Never did I go out of my own place from the time I left my work in Temple Place until eight o'clock the following morning. And my heart' – with this, Mullins dramatically struck his chest – 'is light at being able to tell all my friends about me [in the court, he meant] that what I say to you now is the real truth.

'I am extremely obliged to the jury and I am happy to have had such a patient jury. I am obliged to your lordship, also, and to the gentlemen, both against me and for me – Mr Parry and my own able counsel. I am happy to say that Mr Best has done very well for me, not forgetting my attorney Mr Wood, who has taken more trouble than I would expect a man in his class to take. He has done all he could to find witnesses for me and as yet I am sorry to say that I have not paid him. What I have said are the real facts.'

There was no mention of the parcel, of Emm, or of the items stolen from the old lady's house. There was also no mention of Mrs Emsley herself, at least not directly. Those ranged against Mullins might have found a slightly ingratiating note in his praise for the jury that had just condemned him to death, and something jarringly sugary about his warm words for the judge and the prosecution. On the other side of this, who knows what anyone might say when the certainty of violent death is near? How might a naturally articulate man, seeing the horrible inevitability of what was coming, seek to swerve and alter the course of events? Mullins was, to an extent, babbling; he was clearly as fixated on conveying a certain intelligent and deferential tone as much as putting new facts across. As a former policeman, would he have been setting his sights on the possibility of an appeal?

Lord Pollock reached for the black cap and placed it on his wig. Addressing Mullins directly, he began his sentencing.

'James Mullins, you have been convicted of the crime of wilful murder upon the person of Mrs Emsley on the 13th of August last. You have yourself, I think, very properly commended the patience of the jury and the propriety of conduct shown by the counsel concerned in the case, even by those retained against you.

'The jury, after a trial of two days and after patient deliberation, have found you guilty. You have addressed the court upon the evidence against you. It would have been more satisfactory to me if you had addressed your observations to some parts of the case which was considered by me as really bearing against you. Instead of that, you have confined your remarks entirely to those parts of the case which I pointedly in some measure warned the jury to pay very little regard to. Not that these matters so proved by some of the witnesses were untrue, but because it appeared to me that they were not of a nature justly to prove the crime contained in the indictment. They might form reasonable grounds of suspicion but it appeared to me that they did not furnish any pregnant proofs against you.

'Had you been desirous, in your address to the court to meet what I considered to be the really grave part of the evidence against you, you would have told us whether you were in possession of the cheque or not, and whether your accusation against Emm was true or false.

'If you were in possession of the cheque, you would have told us how you came by it. I mention these points to show that the remarks you have made appear to me to be entirely beside the case which has been proved against you.

'The jury have found you guilty and without some explanation of your conduct – an explanation which you have not furnished – without some evidence, of which there does not appear to be any in existence, I own that I do not see how any reasonable person can come to any other conclusion than that your charge against Emm was altogether false, and that you were responsible for the possession of those marks of guilt contained in the parcel.

'The murder of this helpless old woman was a wicked, cruel and aggravated crime. The unhappy sufferer may have felt little as she was probably deprived of sensation by the first blow. But it is manifest that whoever committed the murder took good care that there should be no possibility of recovery, and that life should be utterly extinct. I endeavoured to leave the case entirely for the consideration of the jury. I am still of the opinion that some of the circumstances urged against you, instead of increasing the weight of evidence for the prosecution. But with that conclusion I am bound to state I am perfectly satisfied, and with the evidence before them uncontradicted as it was and unexplained, as part of it might have been, I do not see how they could come to any other.'

Lord Pollock could not quite disguise a sense of puzzlement, if not doubt, as Mullins sat silently, listening to the sentencing.

'It only remains for me now,' declared the judge, 'to entreat you to make the best use of the time which may be spared to you before the execution of the sentence. It is my duty to pass the judgement which the law provides for the punishment of so awful a crime. If you can even now make it manifest that you are innocent of the charge, I do not doubt that every attention will be paid to any cogent proof laid before those with whom it rests to carry the sentence of the law into execution.

'That duty, however, does not belong to me and I have only now to order that you be taken to the place whence you came and thence to the place of execution, there to be hung until you shall be dead, and that your body be buried within the precincts of the prison where you shall last have been confined prior to your execution.'

Mullins, who had listened to all of this 'unmoved', as one report suggested, but also 'with great attention', according to another, now turned and start moving 'at some haste' from the dock, flanked by court officers. [1] The jury was discharged.

Despite the judge's wording, execution was not expedited as it would have been in an earlier age; that is, with the prisoner led through the passage back to Newgate Prison and thence immediately to the scaffold outside it. Instead, Mullins was escorted to one of Newgate's condemned cells. An illustration from 1873 depicts a larger than usual space, furnished with table, chair, bed and additional stools for the officers who were assigned to keep close watch on the prisoner until the sentence was carried out; this would have been less to do with fear of escape and more a precaution against another form of escape, via suicide. The watch was incessant and carried out in shifts. From the moment he got there, Mullins had broken out of what had seemed an unusual calm and was now in 'an excited state for some time', all the while protesting his absolute innocence. Those watching over him had a duty to make sure that he did not harm himself.

In the cell, small privileges were granted. When the judge had told Mullins to make best use of his time, this was in the knowledge that he would be given access to writing materials. Outside the cell, as soon as judgement was pronounced, those representing Mullins were already beginning fresh work. The date for the execution had been set for November 12th, some two weeks later, and there was an appeal to be made.

Any appeal was going to have to be made against powerful headwinds of public opinion, helped along by a hugely excited press.

In *The Spectator*, the leader-column the day after the conclusion of the trial proclaimed that Mullins' conviction did much to 'reassure the public mind' at a time when so many other crimes seemed to go unsolved (including the child murder at Road). Indeed, the paper continued, justice itself had a lucky escape, for Mullins' diabolical plot had been to try to trick the judiciary into 'murdering' Walter Emm for the crime that he had committed; if Emm had hanged on Mullins' planted evidence, there would have been a 'lasting stain' on England's legal system. [2]

For *The Times*, this was 'one of the most extraordinary' stories that had 'ever been told in a court of justice'.

'Although the case was one of circumstantial evidence, the guilt of this man was proved beyond all reasonable doubt,' declared the unsigned leader. 'The murder for which [Mullins] is to die was in the highest degree cold-blooded and cruel; but even the guilt of this is, perhaps, surpassed by that which he meditated when he laid his plot for the ruin of Emm. To commit a crime and then to pocket the reward offered for the discovery by falsely denouncing another man is a refinement of villainy which almost borders on romance.'

The paper praised the 'lengthened trial' of two days and pronounced on what it considered Mullins' psychological motives to have been.

'In many cases, the murderer cannot rest, but is impelled by an irresistible force to talk of his crime, and to do something to avert the suspicion which he fancies is about to light on him . . . he was urged on by an uncontrollable desire to give public suspicion an object' and the result was his attempt to 'sacrifice Emm'. Mullins, the paper declared, was a 'wicked old man', and that he would 'go to his doom without pity from anyone'. [3]

This was not the case. Mullins' wife and children would have felt horror and fear. They were facing the prospect not only of seeing him hanged, but also their lives being tainted with the dark disgrace. In the days that followed, Mullins seemed to suffer intolerable agitation about what was to become of his family. To those around him, he never stopped asserting the essential fact of his innocence.

Mullins did not give up hope; he and his legal adviser, Hubert Wood, started to put together appeals directed towards the Home Office. Various written representations were made, protesting his innocence. They also insisted on the possible guilt of Emm. Mullins had grown so agitated that he had started to refer to himself in the third person.

One letter, addressed to the Home Secretary, read: 'James Mullins wishes to explain some difficulties against him at the trial. These are chiefly the alibi proved in favour of Emm on the Monday evening, and the hour at which he states he saw him deposit the parcel.

'There may be two suppositions with regard to the time of the murder, one placing it on Monday night, the other on Tuesday morning – in either case, no proof against me; first, if committed on Monday, my children, who alone could prove or swear that I was at home all that night from seven o'clock.

'He also wishes that Mrs Musick should be found . . . as she could probably swear that she knew him to be at home that night or evening. The alibi in favour of Emm would only show that he did not commit the murder on Monday night; but yet he might have received the parcel from the man who did.

'In the second supposition, that it was committed on Tuesday morning, no evidence was given to show that Emm or any other person may not have committed it, as the alibi was proved only for Monday. Yet it was distinctly sworn by Mrs Barnes, living opposite, that she saw some person moving papers in the top room on Tuesday morning.'

As Mullins argued: 'Why should this woman's evidence not be believed, when she had the daylight?' [4]

Indeed, beyond the walls of Newgate, there was the very faintest glimmer for Mullins when that neighbour, Caroline Barnes, came forward to the police once more. She in turn produced another witness, a local tradesman called Davidson who had been with her at the time. He too remembered seeing the open window and movement within Mrs Emsley's house.

In Mullins' representations to the Home Office, this was clear evidence that the murder had not taken place when thought and that these accounts placed him in the clear. In Newgate, Sheriff (Sir Andrew) Lusk – a City banker and recently appointed dignitary who acted as an intermediary with the Home Office – discussed this angle further with Mullins; he was still insisting that Emm, and not he, should have been the chief suspect.

Sheriff Lusk listened to this with some apparent impatience, and told Mullins that he was willing to make further representations in the 'proper quarter' if the prisoner would at least address the matter of the stolen cheque and the other items found wrapped in the parcel in Emm's outhouse. Mullins, according to one account, 'became almost angry' at this and said: 'Oh, Emm hid them. He put them in the parcel. I know nothing about them.' [5]

Was this the statement of a man so irredeemably bad that he was determined to see an innocent man's life taken in order that his might be saved? That was clearly the official position (and also the view of a great many Londoners, who would a few days later be out in the streets making this opinion loudly heard). Was it undiluted wickedness, or was Mullins so desperate that he convinced himself? Something in his alternating fervour and anger suggests a man who could not quite understand why no one else would share his belief.

There was also that lasting sense of grievance to do with a sense of persecution.

'Prisoner submits that he was not convicted from legal evidence,' wrote Mullins to the Home Secretary, 'but through prejudice; and he trusts that the Hon Home Secretary will consider the whole case without prejudice and prove to the world that the life of a man is too sacred to be taken on mere suspicion.' [6]

Hubert Wood added in a note about Mullins 'not giving any account of the possession of the cheque', remarking that 'in accordance with the principles of the laws of England, no man is bound to criminate himself, and even if Mullins had been a receiver, he would not be liable for murder'. [7]

The clear hope held by Mullins, his family, and to some extent, his counsel, was perhaps that the sentence of death might be commuted to that of transportation. There were still, even in 1860, convict ships bound for the other side of the world, although it was extremely unusual for them to carry convicted killers. The ultimate hope was that the trial evidence was so very circumstantial that there was simply too much doubt to execute Mullins; that the Home Secretary might 'sift' and 'purge' all 'extraneous matter' from the accounts that the court heard. By doing so, the authorities might guard against a dreadful miscarriage of justice by sending him in penal servitude to Australia for life (where, presumably, his wife and family would be able to join him).

Mullins' moods swung wildly as he wrote numerous letters with his generous supply of pens and ink. At one stage, he genuinely believed that he would receive a free pardon and walk from Newgate without any further stain on his character. He was telling everyone he saw that not only was he guiltless of murder, but also of any kind of participation in such an act.

In this curious suspended period, Mullins apparently also became very inclined towards religion. Even as a Catholic, he attended Protestant services within Newgate. This was noted, and Mullins at last requested that he should be able to see a Catholic priest. The governor saw no objection, and over the course of the next few days, local priest Father O'Callaghan visited Mullins often. It is possible that the authorities were hoping that Mullins would offer a full confession to the priest, but this was not the case.

Mullins was also visited a few times by Catherine, his sons and his daughter. On one of these occasions, it was clear that he was feeling more fatalistic. Mullins gave each of them a lock of his hair for remembrance. He had also sent out a request to the sheriffs at Newgate to get in touch with Sergeant Tanner, as he wanted 'the articles that had been taken from him' by the police to be disbursed among his children. This suggested that hope was fast flickering. In all normal cases, any personal articles belonging to a condemned prisoner would be passed to the Crown after his or her execution. In this instance, the sheriffs of the court decided that the items were of such a trifling value that there would be no harm acceding to the prisoner's request.

Indeed, the paucity of the items gave a powerful sense of bathos: here was 'a pocket-book', a 'small purse or port monnaie', 'a comb', 'a pencil case' (not the silver one discussed at the trial) and 'a small foreign silver coin, about the size of a threepenny piece'. [8]

The Mullins family was in serious financial difficulty. With all three of the children out of work and the eldest son at sea (and therefore presumably limited in his chances to make sure remittances were sent to his mother), each meal must have been hard-earned, as would have been the roof over their heads. Mullins' efforts to get his trifling goods passed to them had a very serious practicality. Apart from the locks of his hair, there would be nothing else in the world left to remember him by, as everything would be sold. Perhaps even the locks of hair would be on sale as well: even as late as 1860, there was a thriving subterranean market for macabre mementoes of executions and murder.

Mullins himself had a strange request. He wanted the return of his plasterer's hammer, with which the prosecution had alleged he had brained Mrs Emsley. This might have been part of his campaign to protest his innocence: to reinforce the idea that he had never used the implement as any kind of weapon, that it was a spotless tool that should be passed on to his son. Curiously, this was the one request with which the authorities would not comply. In the eyes of the court, the implement was a murder weapon and, if anything, ought to be retained by the police. Perhaps they feared it would be offered for sale.

The Mullins case meanwhile had caught the attention of the Society for the Abolition of the Punishment of Death. This group was quite different to those who were just opposed to public executions, such as Charles Dickens. The society demanded wholesale penal reform. The abolitionists had strong roots in the Quaker movement. Many wealthy businessmen and society hostesses were supporters, and there were strong links with similar movements in America and continental Europe. In the case of Mullins, members of the society made representations to the Home Office to have his sentence commuted.

On 18 November, the Home Secretary sent word to the governor of Newgate. The prisoner, stated the Home Secretary, had 'transmitted' a number of 'different memorials' and facts to his office. They had, said the minister's equerry, been 'anxiously' considered, but 'after communication with the learned judge by whom the prisoner was tried' and after 'further inquiry into the facts of the case, he can discover no ground to justify him . . . in advising any interference with the due course of the law'. [9]

This message did not come through until quite late on the Friday evening, a little after Mullins had gone to bed. The governor, possibly out of a sense that sleep was precious to the condemned man, decided not to disturb him there and then with the news, for it was after all the final irrevocable confirmation that the noose would be tightened around his neck.

The next morning, the governor, together with several of his court sheriffs, told Mullins that 'he no longer had any hope in this world and must prepare for the fearful sentence that awaited him'.

Mullins, according to one report, 'appeared to be prepared for the pronouncement and did not betray the least emotion'. He did, however, have this to say to the governor and his men: 'Well, I will not go before God with a lie in my mouth, but still I am innocent of this murder.' [10]

He was to be hanged outside the walls of the prison at eight o'clock on Monday morning. As the hours counted down, Mullins' wild shifts of temperament became increasingly pronounced. He talked more with Father O'Callaghan, then sat down at the wooden table in his cell, still watched over by a court sheriff, to write his final note. It was, in its own curious (and well-written) way, sensational.

'I, James Mullins, do make the following true statement against the charge of murder which has been committed on the night of August 13th upon Mrs Emsley, at Grove Road Stepney, the foul crime and charge of which I have been found guilty through the most false and gross perjury that has ever been given in a court of justice. I do most solemnly declare before my God and the public that I came home from my day's work on Monday evening August 13th, between the hours of six and seven o'clock, as was sworn to by a man named Tyrell, where I had been that day at work at no 1 Temple Terrace, Collingwood Street, Bethnal Green.

'When I returned to my own home, as I have stated, I remained with my two sons in my room talking to them until supper, and I afterwards retired to bed, I do declare that I did not leave my bed until eight o'clock next morning, August 14th.

'I also solemnly declare that the witness from Hoxton, named Raymond, a tailor by trade; and Mitchell, a dock labourer – I confess to my God that every word they have sworn against me was totally false and untrue. They swore their falsehoods in the hope of obtaining the produce of my blood; and as was stated in the cross-examination of Mitchell, by the highly-trained counsellor Mr Best, the above named men have made my wife a widow and my poor children fatherless.

'There was the boot produced which they found in a dust-hole at 12 Orford Street Chelsea, which house I left three weeks before that boot was found. This boot belonged to a man named Mahoney who had lived in the front parlour of the said house and who had left some time before. He now lives in Prince's Street, Drury Lane. This man came forward on Friday evening; but it was too late for him to give evidence that the shoe was his. He had cast it away when living at the above-named house. This shoe may have created an effect upon the jury; but I solemnly declare I never saw the boot until it was produced at the Thames Police Court.

'As regards Sergeant Tanner's evidence, he did not do me justice as to what was done in the shed. I drew first his attention to some bricks and wood that were near the flag at the door. This he never mentioned in the court. The flagstone was the only thing he mentioned, in order to make it appear that I must have had some knowledge of it, although I believe Emm to be innocent of the murder of Mrs Emsley.' [11]

The significant words are those that remain unsaid. If Mullins was declaring his own innocence – and now, startlingly, the innocence of the man of whom he had been convicted of trying to frame – then who did he believe responsible? The letter itself appeared to have been amended and rewritten by Mullins throughout the course of the night; those crucial lines concerning the innocence of Emm had been a second draft. The original lines had been thoroughly crossed out and it was impossible to read them.

Mullins concluded his letter with what sounded like a cry of frustration: a sense of disbelief that his account had not been listened to.

'I declare I never came out of my room from between six and seven on the Monday evening, the 13th, until I got up from my bed on Tuesday, the 14th. My two sons slept in the same room with me and they both swore at the trial that they did so. I ask any man with a family, if any charge was brought against them, however unjust that charge might be, who they could apply to under such circumstances, except their own family, to clear them of it.

'My children proved the truth, but the truth would not do, the truth was not believed, but those who proved nothing but lies and swore my life away by the blackest and foulest perjury ever given; I make this statement in order that the public may know that my life has been taken away by the most gross and false evidence ever given in a court of justice, all through the hopes of getting money.

'I say that they have no right to any part of the reward and I hope they will get none of it.'

What then followed was a final appeal that his wife and children should not be made to suffer. Mullins must surely have been aware of the braying note of most of the newspaper coverage and felt shudders of concern about the repercussions.

'I beg most sincerely that all the religious and charitable people of England will extend their hand to my poor widow and fatherless children in order that they may gain a livelihood for themselves. The Rev Mr O'Callaghan of 22 Finsbury Circus has kindly consented to receive any donations for my poor family, who are in great destitution through this charge.'

He finished by giving his 'best thanks' to 'Mr Hubert Wood of 4, Coleman Street Buildings, my solicitor, and my counseller [sic] Best for the kind attention paid to my case, and I also thank the two sheriffs, the governor, and Dr Gibson.' (12)

If the public had been expecting some last-minute confession – and the subliminal expectation was that, as an Irish Catholic, surely Mullins would do anything now to save himself from the everlasting fires of hell – then the letter would have been a profound disappointment. Yet, the gaps were haunting. If Emm wasn't the murderer, then who was? What of Mrs Emsley's possessions? What reason could Mullins have had until the very last to stay completely silent on the pilfered objects and cheque?

There was, purportedly, one other letter, apparently written to one of his sons, and relayed the next day to the author of a 'broadside'. Broadsides were, in essence, souvenirs of executions: printed sheets consisting of descriptions of the murder case, the apprehension of the killer, vividly illustrated with a large woodcut of the hanging, and accompanied also by some terrible doggerel about the murderer and his fearful crime. One particular broadside made the claim that this was the only one of Mullins' letters that would be disclosed to the public. As such, there is good cause to be very wary. In theory, there was nothing to stop the broadsides making things up. However, amid the uncharacteristically flowery style, there are a couple of details that do have a ring of authenticity, and point to a possible psychological complexity that made Mullins so curiously reticent in court.

'Dear son,' Mullins is alleged to have written (though to which one of his sons the broadside did not make clear), 'the head that wields the pen that writes this note will be motionless and stiff. This brain, thy father's brain, will cease to think, and the heart will cease to beat, 'ere you read these my last lines . . .

'Government has treated me badly. I had thought, even if I failed to prove my innocence, that the services I rendered them would have been taken into account. Not so.'

The alleged letter ended on a note of high Victorian melodrama.

'The gallows is out, people are gathering around, the clock is going on and I must die . . . The last hour that I can live on earth has come. Farewell, farewell! Pray for your unhappy father, James Mullins.' [13]

With all due scepticism applied, the line in the letter about the way the government had treated him has the possibility of authenticity. It is likely that since his attempt to infiltrate the Ribbonmen, the humiliating demotion to railway police work, the dull job in the goods yard, the conviction for pilfering, and the six years spent in Dartmoor, Mullins had been boiling with resentment; not simply because the government had failed to look after him, but that Whitehall had failed to appreciate his intelligence and potential and had utterly failed to promote him to a rank and status that reflected his true abilities. The government had not only betrayed him, but also the future prospects of his family. Mullins had turned on his own countrymen out of loyalty to the Home Office and had placed a terrible strain upon his own marriage by doing so. Even if he had murdered Mrs Emsley, and still in this letter there was no suggestion of any confession, then surely, he might have thought, all of his past services should have coloured the sentencing?

On his last evening alive, Mullins did not see his family, but he spent a little more time in the company of Father O'Callaghan. He 'paid the closest attention to the reverend gentleman's exhortations'. Early on Sunday evening, Mullins retired to the bed, watched closely by the officer on guard. As with his sworn evidence about that sleepless and restless night in Barnsley Street on 13 August, so Mullins' sleep was observed to be 'broken'. [14]

21

They Brought
Opera Glasses

❦

The clouds enveloped the dome of St Paul's that night; the rain coursed down it in dancing rivulets. The pavement and roads at the base of the high walls of Newgate Prison were sloppy with dung and mud. In the restlessness of his final night, James Mullins would have heard the hourly chimes of nearby churches. In the darkness before daybreak, this iron clamour was accompanied by the noise of activity; the sound in the street of three horses dragging vast apparatus through the wet gritty mud of the roads; the sharp report and echo of stakes being driven into the ground.

If Mullins had been listening very closely, he might also have detected the faintest hum; the low noise of conversation among an ever-growing crowd of people near the prison who had begun saving their places as early as one o'clock in the morning, despite the wind and insistent torrents. For the putative spectators, a night in the cold, enlivened with laughter, drink and even outbreaks of dancing, was worth it to secure a good vantage point.

Mullins already knew his death was going to draw a very large crowd; he had been debating with himself, and with Father O'Callaghan, about whether he should give a speech on the scaffold. Over the last few centuries of public executions, this had become something of an expectation for Londoners.

The stakes driven into the grounds around Newgate and Smithfield Streets were there to support crowd-control barriers. The noise made by the three horses struggling up the hill from three o'clock onwards was due to the gallows they were dragging behind them. The structure underneath the cross beams, over which the condemned man would be dropped, 'had the appearance of a gigantic cistern or box' and in the eyes of one reporter, rather recalled 'the cart in which the dead bodies' were conveyed to the pits during the times of plague. [1] Before the sun rose, a number of workmen would help in reassembling the structure before that ever-swelling mass of excited spectators.

Some of those Londoners were viewed by reporters as 'roughs'; those same journalists were busy prompting these people into giving their own verdicts on Mullins. 'The epithets and adjectives used in speaking of his crime of crimes were of too emphatic a character to render them presentable in print,' wrote the clearly delighted journalist for *Reynold's News*. [2]

One fellow needed little encouragement to say he regretted not having the job of executioner himself; if it was down to him, he would have the greatest pleasure in putting the rope around the prisoner's neck, putting 'the cap over his face' and then kicking the bolt that would send Mullins into eternity.

When the bell of St Paul's struck the hour of six, Mullins rose from his bed. It would have been necessary to bring light into the condemned cell; the morning was dark and cloudy. Father O'Callaghan was there by Mullins' side immediately. In that cell, they waited and talked quietly; by half-past seven, presiding aldermen from the City of London arrived, including Sheriff Lusk.

Outside, executioner William Calcraft – a famous veteran of the job who had presided over many such occasions – was making his way through the slippery streets. On nearing Newgate, he saw the quite extraordinary and boisterous crowd. Indeed, the closer he got, the more he had to start pushing his way through tightly packed bodies. Near the main entrance, Calcraft was stopped by a policeman; he told the constable exactly who he was, yet it seemed he was not believed. How many others that morning had tried to get past the policeman also claiming to be the famed hangman? With time now starting to press, Calcraft reportedly lost his temper and a scene began to develop just outside the prison; he was spotted by one of the prison officials, who came forward to rescue the executioner from the incredulous constabulary. Calcraft, by this stage almost levitating with rage, threatened to bring charges; gradually, as he was led inside the prison, away from the cheerfully jeering mob, his temper cooled and he addressed himself to the sombre duty in hand.

Just a few minutes before eight o'clock, the governor of the prison, Mr Jones, went to Mullins' cell, accompanied by the prison chaplain Rev Davis, chief warder Mr Humphreys and the hangman. Mullins was introduced to each in turn. He handed a note to one of the presiding sheriffs, telling him: 'This is the only statement I have to make, and I wish that it should be made public.'

It appeared that in his long discussions with Father O'Callaghan, Mullins had decided not to make a speech from the scaffold, though he was still within his rights to do so. The gathered crowd would have been expecting, if not hoping for, this gripping element of theatre. As a former policeman, Mullins might well have had experience of witnessing public executions; as an intelligent, reflective man, he might have understood that last-minute bellowed protestations of innocence would surely have had the effect of goading the spectators into an almost ungovernable roar of rage. The crime of attempting to frame another man was viewed as especially heinous.

Mullins now faced his executioner. The condemned man was led out, through passages of pale brick and stone, to a yard just within the prison walls; through the door beyond lay the gallows. It was here that Mullins, now observed to be 'trembling', had his arms pinioned with straps by Calcraft. One of the sheriffs asked Mullins if he had any more to say.

'No, I have nothing more to say, except that my family are put out of work and are quite destitute in consequence of this,' said Mullins, 'and I hope that the charitable and religious public will do something for them, in order that they obtain a livelihood.' [3]

Mullins reminded the sheriff that he himself had promised to do what he could for the family; the sheriff replied that he would not forget his promise, and that he would also make sure that his other requests concerning the distribution of that small number of worldly goods would be carried out.

The priest leaned in and whispered something in Mullins' ear. Whatever it was O'Callaghan had said, Mullins nodded earnestly, 'apparently in assent'. Then the door of the yard was opened and before the condemned man, outside the wall of Newgate, was the prospect of the wooden scaffold. Beyond this, a crowd that was now not just noisy, but manically restless.

The priest was the first up the steps to the gallows; Mullins, his arms pinioned, followed him 'without any assistance'. From this elevation, under that slate-grey November morning sky, he would have been able to see the full terrifying size of the assembly gathered to see him die. Some estimates put the numbers at 20,000; others suggested it was more like 30,000. The streets and passages that ran off the main junction were full. Some observers were convinced this was the largest crowd ever drawn for a Newgate hanging. Due to the wooden barriers, there were also bad-tempered bottlenecks; witnesses saw fights breaking out among men and women alike. Another observer, comfortable in a room looking down at this mass of Londoners, saw people jumping up and down on the spot, clearly in an effort to get a better view of the scaffold. This had the effect of sparking violent reaction as jostled spectators punched the offending jumpers.

Mullins, his eyes level, would have seen the more rarefied class of observers in turn; in all the windows of the houses facing and around the prison, there were middle-class men and women, all in fine clothes. 'The owners of the houses opposite must have reaped a profitable harvest,' wrote one reporter. [4]

A hush fell as Mullins climbed the scaffold. It seemed clear that everyone was waiting for the condemned man to offer his last words. As Calcraft readied the noose, Father O'Callaghan leaned in towards Mullins and again said something very quietly into his ear. From Mullins, there was no further word, but the two men shook hands. The silence from the massed spectators was broken by the odd cry of 'Bravo, Mullins!' Again, the theatrical nature of the term suggested not support, rather blackly comic gratitude for the dramatic spectacle.

The noose was placed around Mullins' neck. Mullins had dropped his hands in front of him and his head was bowed, apparently in prayer. He was 'placed under the beam, and he evinced some trepidation as he took his place on the drop', reported the *Evening Standard*. [5] Calcraft adjusted the rope, then he too shook hands with Mullins.

It was time.

'The bolt was then drawn,' ran a report, 'the drop fell and the culprit appeared to die almost without a struggle.' [6]

The opera glasses and telescopes in the windows of the houses opposite were fixed on the man dangling 'like a pendant' from the gallows; the spectacle, cruel as it was, must also have been curiously empty.

Even as Mullins was asphyxiated, there were those, a few journalists among them, who were convinced that this was not the end of the matter; that the real killer was still at liberty.

Indeed, almost as soon as Mullins' body was interred within the walls of Newgate, questions were being asked.

There was also the intense public interest in what would now happen to Mrs Emsley's vast property empire. Who, if anyone other than Queen Victoria, would gain from it?

Also: what if the murder and the toxic question of inheritance were more closely linked than the police – in the desperate hurry to secure a conviction – had been able to see?

22

Numbered with
the Dead

❧

The golden prospect of immense wealth cast a deep, cold shadow. The Victorian imagination was haunted by piles of capital and property as high as the city's dust heaps. People ached with desire for the money that would make them gentlefolk, releasing them from the unending strain of insecure income. Conversely, it seemed universally understood that for those who were not royal or aristocratic, unearned wealth would always carry some form of stain. It could never be perfectly clean.

After the hanging of Mullins, the focus turned eagerly to the riddle of what was to become of Mrs Emsley's riches.

Already, cases and claims were being prepared for the Court of Chancery. Mrs Emsley had not left even a suggestion of a will and there was absolutely no indication given, even verbally, about how she intended her estate to be distributed. Of course, she had relatives and friends, many who had worked for her; almost as soon as Mullins was in his prison burial plot, various parties were seeking legal advice.

And as this happened, some people were now openly questioning if it really had been right to execute Mullins and whether his conviction was safe. The oblique question asked was if the obscenity of Mrs Emsley's riches could have provoked quite a different killer, with quite a different motive?

The *Illustrated Times* published a storming editorial a few days after the execution: 'They have hanged Mullins, to the great delight of everybody except perhaps the enlightened jury who are said to have discussed his guilt on the night preceding his sentence over a capital supper with a liberal allowance of grog. We except these highly intelligent persons from the general attribution of joy because after all, it cannot be pleasant to them to find, after convicting a prisoner upon the shabbiest, shallowest evidences of supposed guilt ever brought forward to mislead a jury, that strong evidence exists that Mullins did not commit the crime for which he suffered.

'We have already pointed out the rottenness of the so-called circumstantial evidence against this defunct ruffian . . . taking the presumptive testimony against him at its utmost value, it went no farther than to prove his possession of the property of the murdered woman and hence, constructively, his complicity in the crime.' [1]

However, the theory of this was that Mullins was nonetheless complicit; indeed, the journalists believed that he had 'planned the murder', but someone else carried it out. The paper pointed to the eyewitnesses whose testimony was dismissed by the judge as 'idle dreaming'; the hammer which had never been measured with the fatal wound and which bore no trace of blood; the ribbon, which may or may not have matched; the boot with the three hairs, 'not even proved to be human'. [2] Yet against this was the enigma of Mullins' silence on his possession of Mrs Emsley's property. At the very end, the paper noted, Mullins had declared Emm to be innocent. What was stopping him naming the true murderer?

At this, the *Illustrated Times* lapsed into a decorous silence, musing only that the 'ties' between Mullins and the actual murderer might have been so strong that he was anxious that only one soul should go to the gallows, not two. The newspaper left its readers to draw their own conclusions, as the laws of libel meant it could go no further. It could not print what perhaps a number of its readers had already been saying over those heated pub discussions: that Mullins' accomplice in the murder was one of his own sons.

The newspaper raised the question of how Mullins might have come into the old lady's possessions if he had not stolen them. The answer, left to the readers to surmise, was that he had commissioned the crime and the articles were brought back afterwards.

If the journalists were reflecting what a number of people had already been speculating about, how might the sequence of events on the night of 13 August – however improbable – have progressed?

We would first have to imagine Mullins in a state of perpetual rage about the old woman and her miserly ways; her refusal to even adequately cover the expenses of his building materials, as well as her sharp and sardonic nature. We would also have to imagine Mullins at home in Barnsley Street with his elder son John, the unemployed dock worker. Perhaps the pair of them were working each other into ever greater heights of anger about the sheer extraordinary injustice of Mullins having been brought so low as to depend on the goodwill of a capricious widow.

Was this then a robbery that went terribly wrong? Can we imagine John Mullins making his way past the gas-lit shops on the Mile End Road towards Grove Road? Did the young man arrive before the sun went down, before Mrs Emsley locked up for the night?

Under what circumstances would she have let him in? Like everyone else, she would have interrogated the lad from her window. Could he have claimed to have been on an errand from his father?

If it is possible that he could have made it past that initial barrier of suspicion, what would have led Mrs Emsley to go upstairs with him and stand in that lumber room with the wallpaper? Could the boy have been claiming that his father wanted to buy some?

If all of this is the case, we would have to imagine the situation darkening quickly; John Mullins perhaps demanding that Mrs Emsley tell him where any valuables were kept, the old lady threatening to raise the alarm, then, in a moment of panic, John reaching for his own plasterer's hammer, striking the blow that caved in her skull, then, in a terror, stealing the only items he could immediately find in the house.

To imagine this – a blood-drenched young man trying to wipe his hands clean on Mrs Emsley's dress, which he has hoisted up – we would also have to leave John Mullins sitting there in the gathering darkness of the widow's house as the sun finally set. No one had been seen entering or leaving that evening, so we would have to leave him there with the dead body until such time in the darkness of the small hours when he could steal out and slip through the quieter streets without his bloody clothes attracting attention. We also have to imagine that John Mullins was able to find a route home so quiet as to not pass any night wanderers.

After all this, we also have to imagine the boy making it back unseen to the room in Barnsley Street, his pockets full of the lenses, silver pencil case and cheque that he had managed to gather up. We have to imagine him looking at clothes drenched with an old woman's blood, and we have to imagine his father was there, greeted by this horrific sight.

At the trial and the inquest beforehand, various witnesses testified that James Mullins seemed in a state of high tension in the days following the murder. Could this have been the reason? John commanded to stay in Barnsley Street while James tried to give the impression that he was as baffled and shocked by the murder as everyone else?

In terms of robbery, John would have failed. We would then have to envisage James, with his policeman's eye, looking at what had been stolen and knowing that if they were ever found in Barnsley Street, the truth would be instantly divined. How best to dispose of them?

We would then have to imagine that James Mullins was even more evil than the Old Bailey jury could have guessed. In the early days of the police investigation, there was never any suggestion that he or any member of his family were credible suspects; rather, the inquiries were pursuing 'foreign-looking' gentlemen, rackety relatives or angered tenants. In other words, all Mullins would have had to do would be to get rid of those items permanently: a small hessian sack and a short walk down to the Thames would have been sufficient. The true wickedness, if we were to pursue this line, would have been revealed the moment the reward was offered. Not merely to protect his son from a murder charge, but to plot to claim the fortune of £300 by pinning the murder on an innocent man would indeed have been the act of a man steeped in melodramatic villainy.

Then we would have to imagine the subsequent reversal of fortune; Mullins' failure to see that Emm would have a strong alibi; the parcel of Mrs Emsley's items now not passed on to the guiltless party, but instead left in the hands of the killer's father. To pursue this line a little further, we then have to imagine Mullins, aghast with his own stupidity, helpless to frame any new kind of defence as K Division started accruing its circumstantial evidence. All he could do at the end, right up to the scaffold, was to swear that he himself was not the murderer, and to stay silent on the provenance of the stolen items for fear of incriminating his eldest son.

That is the logical extension of the reasoning of the *Illustrated Times*, but it does not convince. Fundamentally, it fails to address the central question of motive. Mullins would have known very well that miserly Mrs Emsley was most careful about not having valuables or cash in any great quantities in her home. Any burglary would have been speculative at best. Another distant possibility is that rather than being sent out by his father to commit the crime, what if the young lad had conceived of it separately?

Again, there are difficulties. Mrs Emsley might have known John by sight after seeing him with his father, but it is highly unlikely she would have let him in her home, not at least without there being more of a commotion – which her acutely observant neighbours would have doubtless registered.

We might imagine instead that the youth had found some means of breaking in through the back of the house, and that the old lady was with her wallpaper in the lumber room as he crept up the dark stairs. But then his sudden appearance would surely have caused her to cry out with anger?

Could John perhaps have terrorised Mrs Emsley into silence? She was a tough old woman, though. Threats from the roughest of her slum tenants had little effect on her; she appeared to find them amusing.

Her neighbour would surely have heard raised voices, and most certainly a cry. However, there was nothing. Even the attitude in which the old lady's body was discovered, still holding the rolls of wallpaper, suggested the attack was a complete surprise.

Additionally, the pressure that would have been felt by a murdering son seeing his father go to the gallows for his crime is extremely difficult to imagine; how could such a young man testify without being overcome? In the final visits to the condemned cell, which were all supervised, surely there would have to have been some sign or indication or unconscious slip in the conversations that father and son would have had in the shadow of the noose?

None of this seems plausible.

The *Illustrated Times* did not foresee the next stage in the tragedy: the eruption of a bitter fight over the disposal of Mrs Emsley's extremely profitable empire. If the paper had realised that this conflict was coming, and if it had then examined the proceedings of these legal battles and the Emsley relatives who fought them, the journalists might have started to form more psychologically convincing theories about the nature of her assassin and about what had led to that bloody night. The answer to the slaying was more likely to be found in the bitter courtroom confrontations that followed Mullins' hanging.

At the end of 1860, it was still looking a distinct possibility that one of Mrs Emsley's satirically-voiced fears, that Queen Victoria would be the main beneficiary of her wealth, might well have come true. While her estate was in probate, her affairs were looked after by her solicitor, William Rose. Across all of her properties, the everyday business of rent-collecting and maintenance continued. Emm was still a form of property manager, and while the more financially desperate tenants no longer had to face the prospect of a visit from the acidic old lady, they were still very much expected to pay up or face eviction.

Mrs Emsley's step-relatives were already provided for well. The people who had the most urgent interest in the old lady's affairs being settled were, initially, her niece Elizabeth Gotz, and the nephew who had not been called at the trial.

Samuel Williams, the son of Mrs Emsley's brother, was the presumptive heir. From the start, as the inheritance case made its way towards the courts, there seemed on the part of the family an anxiety that there should be perfect precision and accuracy on how these matters were reported. Elizabeth Gotz had a letter published in the *Morning Advertiser* in the summer of 1861, just as the lawsuits were being prepared, to make it quite clear that 'the claim set up in Mrs Emsley's property' was through the lineage of the widow's brother, not the sister. [3] There was, said Mrs Gotz, only one sibling, and no sister. The reason for her worry on such a seemingly small point would later become apparent.

This was just the start. Samuel Williams – who in his own right was not very far away from poverty – now found himself facing a powerful enemy in those courts of chancery: the man who had looked after so many of Mrs Emsley's affairs. William Rose claimed that he was a mortgagee of the murdered lady, and as such was owed a large sum of money from her estate by means of repayment. Williams retaliated by filing a bill in chancery for the 'purposes of upsetting that mortgage'.

The word 'chancery' reflected perfectly the violent and some-times arbitrary switches of fortune that those who pursued cases found themselves suffering. In turn, Rose informed the Attorney General that as Mrs Emsley had died without stating any of her intentions – 'without heir or next of kin' – Williams forfeited the right to be regarded as heir. The court agreed; the old lady's affairs – after consultation with the Master of the Rolls – were to be handled as a temporary measure by a specially appointed receiver. This was an auctioneer at Pall Mall called Henry James Peachy. He was to receive 'the rents and profits of the freehold and leasehold estates' and also to 'collect in her outstanding personal estate'. [4] This was a reference to the evidence that the police still held from her house: the money and silver that had been found in the cellar, plus the ring and the cheque.

It is perhaps worth reflecting for a short while on a possibility that was briefly examined by the K Division at the start of their murder inquiry, but then abandoned: that the killing of Mrs Emsley might well have been at the hand of some relative, in straitened circumstances, and gasping for some of her money.

If we consider for a moment that Williams was her murderer, the scene is somehow a little easier to evoke than that of a prowling Mullins lad. A shoemaker seriously struggling day by day to find enough work even to pay for a decent meal; an aunt who lives little more than half a mile up the road; an evening visit, a plea for a loan of some cash; harsh homilies from the old miserly lady about her own (imagined) financial difficulties. Perhaps the middle-aged shoemaker has brought one of his cobbling implements with him; perhaps the old lady has beckoned him upstairs to start talking about her current obsession, the surplus of wallpaper; and perhaps in that moment, the struggling man has mistaken her eccentric singularity for deliberate cruelty.

Such a crime then – if any such thing had happened – would have been borne of anguish, a sense of deprivation combined with a lethal misinterpretation of taunting. We might perhaps imagine in the aftershock of the blood-splattered violence the nephew sitting with the body in the steadily darkening house, paralysed with horror. We might envisage him waiting hours – hideously aware that there was no chance she was alive – before leaving the house, crossing over Grove Road and trying as far as possible to keep to the shadows of the Regents Canal towpath as it wound past the vast Stepney gasworks, which rumbled and glowed throughout the night, and then down back to the small terraced house in Salmon Lane.

Of course, there was no such suggestion that Williams was even a suspect, but the legacy of Mrs Emsley was set to cause this man a great deal more stress. Not only was he facing rival claimants, his case was also being disputed by the Crown, which itself continued to show a serious interest in seizing this vast amount of East End property. In the summer of 1862, almost two years after the murder, a new case came before the Court of Probate. It was titled 'The Queen's Proctor v Williams – The Stepney Murder'. The Crown was now raising a startling new objection to Williams being the heir: Mrs Emsley had been illegitimate.

The carefully handwritten deposition, with the official seal of the 'probate court', made an inventory of all the properties that the Crown had a particular interest in, from the Irish labourers' dwellings in Angel Lane, Stratford, to the slightly more upmarket houses in Bow and Limehouse. There was also, poignantly, a list of the contents of 9 Grove Road, from table cloths and sheets to books. These remnants remained in a state of suspension, subject to the decisions of the court. Even these scraps were now in jeopardy, due to the accusation that Mrs Emsley had been a bastard.

Williams was called to prove that the Crown was mistaken about his aunt's parentage. For a poor shoemaker with no previous experience of having stood in such a courtroom, or having dealt with professional lawyers, or having been faced with the prospect of reading enormously long and densely written court documents, the process must have been exhaustingly stressful. As he took the stand in that humid, dark hall in 1862, he surely had to concentrate very hard on the prize that so many threatened to snatch out of his reach.

'My parents were named Samuel and Mary Williams,' he told the court. 'They are both dead. My father died in 1830, and my mother some time after that date. They resided at Stone Stairs, Broad Street, Ratcliff. I remember my father's funeral. It took place in Stepney churchyard [St Dunstan's], where Mrs Emsley née Williams had been christened in 1790. My mother married a second time, her second husband's name being Edward Wilson . . . My father was a shoemaker. Mrs Emsley, the deceased, generally called him "Sam" and he used to call her "Mary".

'My parents always spoke of her to me as my aunt. I lived in one of her houses to take care of her property for her. My sister Mrs Gotz lived in another of her houses.'

Williams was now placed under searching cross-examination. Could he be absolutely certain about the provenance of his great-uncle and aunt's marriage?

'I first searched for the certificate at Lambeth,' he said, adding that he never knew of any half-brothers or sisters. Nor had he ever heard in the local neighbourhood that Mrs Emsley had had any relations but her brother.

The lawyer for the Queen's Proctor had a shocking disclosure to make: that a family called Spencer was also claiming kinship with Mrs Emsley, and that Mrs Emsley's upbringing was attended with some obscurity. Samuel Williams protested that he had never before heard of these Spencers.

When Elizabeth Gotz took the stand, she repeated much of what her brother had said; no one had any grounds for suspecting that Mrs Emsley's father had lied about who her own mother was. The Crown then produced a surprise seventy-four-year old witness called John Sherman, who knew Mrs Emsley over sixty years previously.

'She was then living in Gin Alley, Ratcliff, with her father and mother and brother,' he announced.

This, in terms of the law as it stood, was straightforward. A wedding certificate from 1780, between Samuel Williams and Mary Poupard, was produced. The Queen's Proctor, having heard from other interested parties, had a serious allegation to make: that Mary Poupard was not, in fact, the mother of Mary Emsley. He alleged that Samuel Williams had also cohabited with a woman called Mary Spencer, and not only was *she* the true mother of the murdered landlady, but that she had another sibling, and a range of other nieces and nephews, who had not received their proper legal acknowledgement.

Williams the nephew must have listened on with mounting horror as the QC dragged another allegation before the public gaze: that Williams himself was a bastard, and that his own father had cohabited with various women, one with the surname Graham, and another called Polly Armstrong. The result of this would be that the undeclared relatives would in fact have a far greater claim on Mrs Emsley's money than he did.

During that hearing, more witnesses were brought forward to see if there could be any further clues gleaned from the words of Mrs Emsley herself about her family, and if she wanted any side of it to be favoured with her money. One of the trustees she had employed to supervise her funds was called. Mr RA Simmonds told the court that Mrs Emsley had gone so far as to ask him to be an executor; but, he added, 'she intended to leave her property to charities, as she had no-one particular to bequeath her money to.' According to Simmonds, she 'said nothing about her relations'.

The brother of Mrs Emsley's late husband was called. Edward Emsley, who had 'a good position' at the Charing Cross Post Office, said she had told him that if she made no will, 'her property would go to the Crown'. Emsley also declared that he had never heard her mention the Williams family (a declaration that must have upset her nephew). Led on by the QC, Emsley also said he had heard Mrs Emsley 'speak of a person who she said was her half-sister', but he could not recall that woman's name. Under cross-examination, he revealed that Mrs Emsley had told him about her property going to the Crown not a month before she was murdered.

Another of Samuel Emsley's brothers was called. Thomas, a clerk with the Inland Revenue, told the court a simple, self-interested story: that the old lady had told him she was going to make a will in favour of him and his brothers, and that she had said: 'If I don't, the Queen will get my property, and I am sure I don't want that, Thomas.'

It turned out that Thomas Emsley was yet another of Mrs Emsley's rent-collectors, but he didn't get paid for the work. He had, he said, been promised payment, but he was as sceptical about getting it as he was about her promising to make her will. Meanwhile, Mr Rose the solicitor told the court he had not even realised Mrs Emsley had living relatives until after she was murdered; the money had always been intended for almshouses.

The Queen's Proctor produced a witness, Elizabeth-Ann Bachelor, daughter of Ann Spencer. Ann was in turn the daughter of Mary Spencer, whom the court contended was the real mother of Mrs Emsley. In other words, the contention was that Ann Spencer had actually been Mrs Emsley's sister. The court heard that Ann had been sufficiently close to her sister that she apprenticed her daughter Elizabeth-Ann to Mary and her first husband, John. They all lived together for four years amid the dusty poverty of Brook Street. One more knot for the court to untie was that Elizabeth-Ann testified that her own father's name was Druce, and that she had two brothers. All claimed half-kinship with the murdered widow.

In an era when so much of the city's population had been destroyed by disease, when the graveyards groaned with dead husbands and wives, there was nothing unusual about labyrinthine family trees, of second and third marriages, of children with competing claims. Nor indeed was the court interested in any questions of morality, abandoned wives or partners, or children who could not be quite secure in their legal status. There was simply one question: was it right that Mrs Emsley's nephew, Samuel Williams, was in pole position to receive her incomes? In the course of the acrimonious proceedings, there were two non-family witnesses who might have felt strongly that they also had a claim to some of the estate. Walter Emm was called, as indeed was Joseph Biggs. Emm, whose fame still elicited comment in the local press, reiterated that Mrs Emsley had scarcely referred to relatives, still less an extended family. He had the delicacy not to mention his own financial disputes with the old woman before she died; her apparent promises to sell a couple of her more rundown properties to him, and then her apparent reversal. There were indications that since then, the Emsley family, in the form of John Faith and John Whittaker, were continuing to employ his services, so perhaps the comfort of security (when employment was becoming ever more precarious) was more valuable than the prospect of an extended and potentially ruinous battle in these courts.

Biggs also received a warm, though faintly mocking reception from the lawyers and jury alike. He explained to the QC that he had sometimes collected rent for Mrs Emsley. The QC was slyly interested in Biggs' own financial interest in the case. Biggs conceded that he had on many occasions proposed marriage to Mrs Emsley, and that while she had never said yes, she also 'never directly refused him'.

Biggs told the judge he had never been paid by Mrs Emsley for any of his services, which included writing letters, receipts and accounts. Equally, he was quite certain that Mrs Emsley would never have wished to see him destitute. There came a point when both the judge and QC were clearly teasing Biggs. Did he have any intimation that she might have left him something in a will? She had, according to Biggs, actually asked what he would like her to leave him. He apparently told Mrs Emsley that such a thing was not for him to say.

Added to this, Biggs insisted, his motives were not mercenary – he merely wanted 'to do her all the good he could'. The lawyers seemed thrilled to hear this and asked to hear more. Biggs told the court that he 'rendered her all the assistance I could in spiritual and temporal things'. She occasionally came to his chapel in Bishopsgate, but not as often as he would have liked. Someone in the court had remembered an old teasing accusation from the murder trial, so Biggs was once more forced to angrily deny that he had frequently enjoyed drams of pineapple rum with Mrs Emsley. They had beer together, he clarified.

Even in a case as fearsomely complicated as this, with so much depending on scraps of certificate manuscript from the previous century and on the testimony of elderly neighbours recalling scenes and events from decades previously, the judge was relying on a jury. It decided that, despite what the court had heard, Mrs Emsley was in fact legitimate, and that her mother had in fact been the 'Dutchwoman' Mary Poupard. Equally, they felt that the Spencer side of the family, although half-siblings, also had rights. Their mother, whose married name was Colchin, was recognised as a half-sister of Mary Emsley. While the nephew Samuel Williams was permitted to continue administering the estate, the jury decided that Elizabeth-Ann Bachelor and the Druce brothers (descendants of the Spencers) should get a say. On this occasion, the Crown lost out.

That was by no means the end of the affair. It took a further ugly turn in 1864 after Samuel Williams had sold off some of Mrs Emsley's houses. A man called George Frederick Spencer came forward, claiming to be 'heir-at-law' to Mrs Emsley and staking his own claim upon her property. He struck an aggressive financial blow at Williams, and indeed at his tenants. Spencer visited the terraces of Stratford and Bow and told the inhabitants of the houses to stop paying rent to Williams because the properties were his by right.

Williams hit back, through the luckless tenants, telling them in turn that if anyone dared to withhold rent, he would arrange for the immediate seizure of all their goods.

The situation for the tenants was hideous, and some were convinced they would have to start paying double-rent to Williams and Spencer. As a result, a certain number abandoned their homes, clearing out by moonlight. It is possible by this stage that both Williams and his sister Elizabeth had come to see the inheritance as poisoned, that the endless legal battles were corrosive to the soul. At this point, their names fade from view in the court records. The sale of even a modest proportion of the houses, of ever-increasing value in an expanding city, would likely have made them both perfectly comfortable. So, who would get the rest?

By means of a climax, the Court of Chancery had found yet one more twist. There were now branches of the Spencer-Druce clan who were making bitter claims among themselves. By 1869, nine years after Mrs Emsley's death, a new case was brought before the Master of the Rolls. This time, William Spencer, who claimed to be a half-nephew of Mrs Emsley, took up the case against the children of Elizabeth-Ann Druce, who had been acknowledged as a half-niece. In court, the legal representatives of the Spencers argued that their branch of the family now had sole rights over the remaining properties and freeholds. They also suggested that the Druce branch of the family was illegitimate, alleging something close to bigamy by one James Druce, who had lived in Witney, Oxfordshire, and who had not, as supposed, had children with Elizabeth Spencer. Even the court authorities seemed forced to acknowledge that this was an unusually complicated case of 'voluminous' character.

The Master of the Rolls, having absorbed all the documentation and new marriage certificates that the case demanded, found in favour of further subdivision of the wealth of Mrs Emsley: the Druces, as well as the Spencers and Williams, would all be granted their share.

Yet it is the unflagging determination of all the parties in these various chancery cases that points the way to another, possibly more plausible, solution to the mystery of Mrs Emsley's murder.

There was one person in particular who had an unusual degree of access to the old lady, and a large measure of her trust. All parties believed they deserved a share of her wealth, even if they had never had any kind of contact with Mrs Emsley. However, one person who did have that contact may have for some time, we might imagine, felt rather ill-used by her. Could it have been the case that by murdering Mrs Emsley, this person was then inadvertently saved by the foolish actions of an employee called James Mullins?

23

The Fever of Fear

❧

There were two fundamental mysteries that lay at the heart of Arthur Conan Doyle's fascination with the murder of Mrs Emsley. Firstly, what manner of person could enter, and then, having committed the savage and senseless deed, leave the home of a paranoid and voluble old lady without being seen or heard?

The second question was what sort of a murderer, no matter how deranged, would stay in the house of his victim all night long? The court testimony of Caroline Barnes revealed that there was someone in the house the morning after the slaughter.

Conan Doyle wrote that, the following morning, Mrs Barnes 'saw someone moving paper-hangings in the top room, and that she also saw the right-hand window open a little way. Now, in either of these points she might be the victim of a delusion, but it is difficult to think that she was mistaken in them both. If there was really someone in the room at that hour, whether it was Mrs. Emsley or her assassin, in either case it proved the theory of the prosecution to be entirely mistaken.'

'Besides,' added the author, 'is it not on the face of it most improbable that a man should commit a murder at eight o'clock or so in the evening, should remain all night in the house with the body of his victim, that he should do this in the dark – for a light moving about the house would have been certainly remarked by the neighbours – that he should not escape during the darkness, but that he should wait for the full sunlight of an August morning before he emerged?' [1]

Improbable, yes. However, to paraphrase Sherlock Holmes, when one has eliminated the impossible, whatever remains, however improbable, might very well be the truth. Indeed, there was one man, widely overlooked, who would have willingly lingered throughout the night in that bloody darkness.

To get to the core of the mystery, we must recreate that grey evening of 13 August 1860. We must imagine Mrs Emsley's killer walking along Grove Road, with the noise of the horse-drawn traffic around him, opening her front garden gate. The lady, sitting at her window, as is her custom, sees the figure instantly. The distinction is this: even if neighbours such as Mrs Barnes see the figure as well, they don't especially notice him; certainly not sufficiently enough to recall weeks afterwards. He is simply too familiar. Broadly, the witnesses remember only the remarkable visitors to that house. And nor would Mrs Emsley question him out of her window, leaving him on the doorstep. Instead, she goes downstairs immediately to let him in.

The old lady is conceivably displeased by the visit. This figure has been wheedling at her for some months now. Perhaps on this occasion, he is doing so with extra urgency. The courts were told that the candles in Mrs Emsley's house were unlit that night. We can infer from this that she has no wish for her visitor to stay very long; they would be sitting and talking in lengthening shadow.

We can imagine Mrs Emsley beckoning her familiar visitor upstairs to that lumber room, by means of further discouragement, as the shades of that cloudy August evening deepen. She was, as the courts heard, monomaniacal about that surplus wallpaper; her detailed discourse concerning all the different rolls and patterns might be another sly means of making a prolonged visit disagreeable.

She clearly does not detect danger. Perhaps the man who is with her is also not fully aware of what he is about to do. Now we can imagine her standing with this figure in that fast-darkening lumber room. The man is possibly staring at the back of her head as she, holding wallpaper, talks with her usual sharp tone.

What triggers the lethal frenzy? What does she say that causes the murderer to strike? Given her caustic wit and harsh taste for teasing, it is very likely something to do with her plans to disburse her wealth.

Mrs Emsley's cruel goading, the promise of money made and then withheld, possibly sparks a deeply repressed rage. As the man stares at the back of her head and listens to that harsh voice, he is no longer aware of her humanity.

The first blow is a lightning strike seemingly from nowhere, yet the storm has been building for months. Now, as the killer and wallpaper alike are hit with hot sprays of the old lady's blood (she has been slain so swiftly that there isn't even time for her to make a noise) it is time to overturn two assumptions made by the police.

The first, that the motivation for the crime was theft; the second, that the murder weapon was a plasterer's hammer.

In the inquest and the trial, Dr Gill seemed a little suggestible when it came to the question of the lethal instrument. The tardy examination of the corpse, and the decomposition and resulting enlargement of the wound in those warm days, made it impossible to be precise. Indeed, the hammer in question, when presented as evidence, had, as the defence pointed out, no discernible trace of blood. So perhaps it was another heavy object, more frequently found perhaps than plasterers' hammers.

Something such as the heavy brass handle, carved and patterned, of a gentleman's walking stick; the kind commonly used by a great many men. The edge of such an implement, deployed in fury, would produce the same savage, yet horribly precise, wound on a skull.

The motivation was clearly not theft. One extraordinary detail from the inquest was, for some reason, never even mentioned at the main trial. Detection was a developing art; at that time, no one could see any significance in the fact that Mrs Emsley's dress and petticoat were not only bloodied, but had been pulled up over her head, leaving the lower half of her body exposed. For an assailant to do that suggests a level of compulsion and frenzy rather beyond a simple robbery.

The kind of man who could then stay there in the dark with the corpse – and whose hands were seen through the windows the next morning – was a man who knew that after the killing, obscenely stained as he was, that he should keep vigil and pray as Mrs Emsley's soul embarked upon the longest journey.

Such a man would be the apostolic minister, Joseph Biggs.

As heard in court, Biggs had proposed marriage to Mrs Emsley on many occasions, always with the words 'the will of the Lord be done'. She had repeatedly refused him, presumably with that humiliatingly caustic manner she used with everyone. She made repeated vague promises to him about her will, but also appeared to taunt him with it, asking him what he thought he should be left.

She never paid him. Biggs wrote her letters and kept the accounts of her rented properties. He knew exactly how much money she was accruing and he also knew that precisely none of it was going to charity. All her spare funds went into yet more property.

Biggs' church was constantly looking for donations. He had managed to get Mrs Emsley along to a couple of his services, but there was not a penny forthcoming.

The minister was not at all well-off. He told the court he lived in Pollard's Row in Bethnal Green, which was adjacent to the fevered slum of Old Nichol. He was surrounded with piggeries,

278

cat-meat factories and streets glistening with blood and dung. He was also surrounded by properties belonging to the Emsleys. Biggs would have been acutely aware of many stories of desperate tenants.

It is worth looking a little closer at the nature of the church, or sect, to which Biggs belonged. The Catholic Apostolic Church, a body that was Presbyterian in origin and had nothing to do with Rome, stood out among the many jostling religious sects of the day, and always attracted satirical comment for its perceived eccentricities. It was founded by a Scottish preacher called Edward Irving (hence the term 'Irvingite') some thirty years previously, and in its heyday attracted some of the most fashionable (and wealthy) worshippers, such as the banker and MP Henry Drummond and the poet Samuel Taylor Coleridge.

The essayist Thomas de Quincey described the charismatic Irving as a 'son of thunder', [2] but fellow writer Thomas Carlyle recoiled from the shouting, foaming apostolic congregations who claimed to have effected resurrections.

Each branch of the Church was presided over by a priest referred to as an 'angel'; in turn, the angel appointed deacons and deaconesses. The Church believed in the reality of the Apocalypse of St John and taught it almost to the exclusion of all else. The world was to be destroyed in plague and fire, Christ would return, and they, and a very few of their followers would, at the site of each church, be drawn up into the air towards Heaven. The Church believed in the power of prophecy, in the reality of the supernatural, and in the healing miracles of the laying on of hands; it also believed in the divine wisdom to be learned from speaking in tongues.

For all that, the Church could see very well the brutal hardships and grimly circumscribed lives of the people around them, the squalor and disease that bore off too many young souls, and it worked in each parish to help alleviate the sorrows of the poor. The church was reliant upon rich donors; Mrs Emsley would have been a fine benefactor. It seems likely that this was one reason for Biggs' repeated proposals of marriage. Each rebuff would have been more stingingly humiliating and cruel than the last.

So it is time to imagine Biggs in that now silent lumber room, Mrs Emsley's corpse at his feet. The dropped walking stick – its brass handle clotted with gore and hair – is in the way of the spreading pool of blood.

He might be looking down at his smeared hands, wiping them with a manic fury on the white hems of her petticoats. Then, with a wrench, pulling up the dress and petticoat high enough to partly cover the head and exposing her stockinged legs, trying to get the blood off.

After this humiliation on her body, we might imagine Biggs' rage subsiding and the fever of fear setting in. Would it not be his duty as a pastor to watch over Mrs Emsley and pray as her soul began its voyage? She died unredeemed; and there were subterranean beliefs in that era of souls becoming trapped in mirrors, or possessing the living. Therefore, it would be seemly to hold vigil.

This is how a man might stay in such a room, rather than fleeing; how he and the old woman would be gradually ingested by the darkness of the night. Biggs would be aware of the noise of the world elsewhere: the low roars of the railway, the drunken voices from the pubs.

Across that landing, he can probably see through her bedroom door the distant yellow brightness in the window of the house opposite; the neighbour with her newly installed gaslight who can be seen flitting back and forth, sometimes coming to have a look at the street below, her shutters open.

It is for this reason that Biggs would know he cannot light any candles, as he could be glimpsed in the flickering illumination. By now, he may not even need that meagre light. His eyes have probably adjusted to the shadows. It is even possible to imagine him, prompted by urgent nature, moving down through the dark house and out into the back garden to relieve himself, then moving back upstairs, perhaps with a little water from the scullery, to return to the old lady in that lumber room and to continue praying that her miser's soul will be allowed a taste of the joys of eternity.

He will not have seen any significance in the print of his boot being left on the landing. As the judge in the Old Bailey observed, there must have been countless men in London at that time who wore very similar footwear.

Faint and almost hallucinatory with horror at what he has done, we can imagine the black hours flowing like liquid for Biggs. We can hear the regular striking of church bells obscured by the deeper humming resonance of the nearby gasworks.

In the grey light of the morning, he might be lying on his side, awaking on bare boards, facing away from her body. He will be jagged with stiffness, but the nausea is more pressing; he is desperate to get away from that suffocating sweetness. Without thinking, he stumbles from that back room. We might see that a strip of wallpaper that lay on the floor has become stuck to his hand. The smell from the body is unbearable; he walks to the room at the front of the house, takes a hold of the bottom edge of the sash window and raises it.

The movement is seen by the neighbour, Mrs Barnes. She notices the wallpaper, and the hand, but not his face.

That strip of wallpaper is still stuck to his hand. It is smeared red and black with blood. Very quickly, he draws back from the window towards the door, back towards the room in which the body lies. He realises, even in his semi-lucid state, that he might have been seen.

Now Biggs understands he must stay in the house during the day. This is the point at which reason and sanity begin to reassert themselves. He understands that if he leaves the house now, any number of people could see him.

Downstairs, there is a knock. Biggs' heart skitters with fright.

Another knock at the front door, brisk, hard and impatient. He closes his eyes.

Despite the increasing horror of the smell and the awareness of flies coming through the open window, he is as still as a rock. When there are more knocks later on, he stiffens his nerve. They don't know. No one knows.

After a taste of the water, we can envisage Biggs returning almost to a trance, impervious to the bustle of the traffic outside, the voices and occasional sharp raps at the old lady's door.

By evening and then deep night, he knows it is time to leave. The gaslight in the house opposite has been extinguished; the hiss and sigh of the locomotives on the railway has ended; the drinkers from the corner pub have returned to their homes. It is now past midnight, in the early hours of Wednesday 15 August. Biggs hovers behind the front door for some minutes, then opens it. He surveys the dark street, steps out, and as quietly as he can, shuts the door behind him.

With his bag and the stick that struck the blow, Biggs knows he must walk calmly up the sparsely lit Grove Road, then through the even darker streets that run along the side of Victoria Park.

His clothes are black, so the dried blood does not show. He is an old man, a trusted pastor, walking late at night. Of the many drunk, desperate, lust-filled, lost souls roaming the East End, there are none that will consciously see Biggs as a suspicious figure. He makes it back to Pollard's Row, with its stench of animals and urine. Back home, it is simplicity itself to burn the garments and wash the stick.

We might imagine Biggs has recovered his nerves and wits by the afternoon. When he knocks on that door in Grove Road after lunch on Wednesday, he does so firmly, so the lady opposite can be in no doubt that he has visited. In a further gesture; he writes on a card with the message that he called, and pushes it under the door.

Now we might see Biggs standing tall, making himself perfectly conspicuous as he turns and walks away. He will tell the courts he pushed the note through her door on Tuesday. Small untruths can be pardoned when set against the greater good of redemptive works.

What, then, of the man who would instead be condemned? How might James Mullins' part in this nightmarish affair be explained?

His is perhaps a story of a man lost in a labyrinth of deceit. It is actually more than likely that Mullins really was witnessed walking the streets of Stepney that fatal night, and that his sons were indeed lying with a carefully and identically worded story. There would have been a very good psychological reason for Mullins' nocturnal restlessness. After six years in a stone cell inside Dartmoor, he would need to see the stars and moon wheel above him, the sense of the planet turning beneath his feet. There would be a compulsion that made him hate confined spaces.

But how best for a convict to explain this to a hostile and suspicious court? Better and safer to construct a story about staying indoors for a simple supper.

In logical stages, Mullins' desperate tangle becomes clearer. On 17 August, the decomposing body of Mrs Emsley is found. In the wake of this, aside from the sheer shock of the killing and the accompanying anxiety about the loss of income, Mullins – who has been called in for routine questioning by the police along with a few others, and who has not been treated as a suspect – now feels a cold dread.

We might surmise that for some time, this convicted thief has been pilfering from the old lady. Small items that he calculated she would not immediately miss; even a cheque on the day she was later supposed to have been murdered.

It is likely that Mullins is quick to see, as he would have done as a police inspector, that such items, if found, would immediately make him the main focus of suspicion. A man without stain might be able to convince the police of the truth, but a man like him who has served time and had a quarrelsome relationship with his old colleagues? That is quite a different matter.

Indeed, William Rowland, another former policeman, with whom Mullins has shared a few rums, has told him to his face that he suspects him.

We can imagine the vertiginous moment for Mullins as he realises that the mourning ring for Mrs Emsley's first husband, which he took some time ago from her bedroom, could conceivably be traced through a line of illegal sellers back to his family, who have helped to sell on articles like the silver pencil case.

After a few days, even this seems to go quiet. Mullins reads in the newspaper that the officers of K Division are looking at the prospect of foreigners, possibly even a group of Frenchmen who have been suspected of violent burglary.

This is the point at which the second tragedy begins its inexorable cycle. There is also the matter of Mullins' long-nursed resentment at the course of his life. Did he not render valuable and life-threatening service to the Home Office in Ireland? Did he not deserve higher rank and recognition, rather than demotion to railway duties in Poplar? Should there not have been a degree of leniency, even understanding, over the minor matter of the goods yard pilfering? That house on Grove Road perhaps gives Mullins a chance to show all those who wronged him that he is a superior detective, that his intelligence can track the killer down while the idiots of K Division blunder about chasing immigrants.

The police investigation is porous; the officers are talking promiscuously to journalists in local pubs. It is easy to glean that, aside from a few missing items, money has been found in the cellar. The killer did not look there. If the killer was a robber, Mullins probably reasons, then he was an abject example of one.

He thinks about all those hundreds of tenants, those who live in the better properties, and those who live in the reeking courts. Is the killer a man aggrieved at the eviction of himself and his family? That would have required some sign of break-in at Mrs Emsley's house, and no matter how horrible a state her body was apparently in, she did not die fighting off a stranger. His thoughts drift to the inheritance. That too is no secret; the old woman laughing harshly and all that talk of almshouses. Now he thinks of the most faithful of her retainers. William Rowland is an idiot. He has been eyeing the wrong colleague.

Mullins has of late become acquainted with Walter Thomas Emm, who has invited him to take tea at the brickfields. Mullins is aware that Emm, although devoted to the Emsley family, has been feeling let down by the old lady in the matter of those shabby houses near the one in which he lodges. This had been Emm's chance to become a man of property; to take on the mortgages of these houses from the old lady would finally give him a firm foundation in the economic quicksands of London. However, lately she has disputed the transfer of the mortgages, and her reluctance and chicanery has hurt him.

Mullins can now see it with a horrid, yet exciting, clarity. Emm is one of the very few people to whom Mrs Emsley would grant access day and night. He's a man she would trust so much that as she turned around away from him to blether about wallpaper, she would not remotely anticipate the swing of a plasterer's hammer.

Mullins reads of the reward: a sum of £300 and all the blessed security for his family it could represent. Money fairly earned as well, for Mullins has been observing Emm. He knows he has been seen by Emm's children, but it matters little. Mullins thinks he has been looking at the calm façade of a vengeful killer. So certain is he of his insight, that he is further inspired to take those pilfered articles and, by planting them on Emm's property, guide the police swiftly to him. Once he is confronted, the man will surely dissolve and confess.

The tragedy now reaches its third and final act. Mullins, in his increasingly fiery certainty, behaves almost like a child as he summons K Division. He is overexcitable on that Sunday morning. He is like a small boy dragging the adults by the hand.

His charade with the paper package would be laughable if it were not contemptible. When Mullins is arrested with Emm, his indignation and fury are perfectly unfeigned. Can this sergeant and inspector not see? Now comes the chill of horror: if the police (who before long will have appraised themselves of his former career and conviction) believe that Mullins stole those items, they will also believe that the blood is on his hands. It is as if a maze is being constructed around him, the walls rising higher. He will have to navigate his way through with careful silence.

They surely cannot believe he killed the old woman. But the theft, and what will be seen as the attempt to pervert the course of justice, poses another terrible hazard: if he receives another long sentence in prison, perhaps ten years or even longer, there is a chance he might die behind bars. After all, he is no longer young. More than that: his family, complicit in handling some of the stolen goods, might also face prison.

Mullins is dazed, but the immediate anxiety is about gaol for theft and subterfuge, and about making the police see that Emm is the guilty man. Mullins knows he himself is innocent of murder, and it seems almost too abstract to imagine the police can make any such accusation seem credible under examination.

Then comes that short period in the Clerkenwell House of Detention; the knowledge, from what his counsel tells him, of the line that the newspapers are taking. There has been reporting of the scene at the inquest when he confronted Emm. This was portrayed as the snarl of a violent man against a wronged innocent. It is now that Mullins properly feels the danger. Yet if he calmly confirms that he did steal those items, then he will be tying the noose around his own neck. He must reason it through.

In the meantime, how does Biggs respond to all the public talk of the murder suspect being Mullins? Surely, even if his heart is calcified against the old woman, there must be a pang for this man? Biggs will have known about the thefts and he would also see how Mullins has wickedly attempted to have another man condemned to death for the sake of enriching himself. We can envisage that the preacher shares a certain belief with Mullins that it is impossible for the law to find an innocent man guilty of such horror.

This is how Biggs is able to take to the stand as a witness; how he is able to present a mild face, even as that coarse laughter about his marriage proposals to Mrs Emsley grows louder. Even in the great court room of the Old Bailey, the preacher is quite sure that there will be sense and reason.

Even to the last, Mullins was certain he would not be hanged. Then, the final, exhausted, bitter surrender to the hostile establishment. Forced to stay silent about the sordid truth in order to spare his own family from jail and disgrace, in the hope that they at least might salvage new lives.

We can imagine Biggs in his poor parlour, the coals ticking and glowing in the hearth, reading of the sentence of death. Like Mullins, he is quite sure the sentence will be commuted and that the man and his family will be allowed to forge a new life in Australia. The confirmation of the hanging, to happen on the Monday morning, might taste a little like iron in his mouth. Yet he may believe that mortal men cannot judge the tide of life.

Perhaps at the Bishopsgate chapel, Biggs redoubles his efforts among the local poor of Old Nichol to give them some kind of relief from their hunger and illness. Some of them are tenants of the late Mrs Emsley, and her agents are still walking the streets to collect the rents of a dead woman.

It is grotesque that even in death, Mrs Emsley has the power to torment. Perhaps that makes it easy for Biggs to attend and testify at the various court cases among relatives scrambling for her money in the subsequent months and years. She did, after all, say that she had no wish for him to be destitute.

24

'Sin's Long Pilgrimage'

❦

As he was preparing his Sherlock Holmes novel *The Hound of the Baskervilles* for serialisation in *The Strand Magazine* in 1901, Arthur Conan Doyle addressed what was, for him, the crux of the Emsley case: the scent of injustice.

'In the fierce popular indignation which is excited by a sanguinary crime,' he wrote in 'The Debatable Case of Mrs. Emsley', 'there is a tendency, in which judges and juries share, to brush aside or to treat as irrelevant those doubts the benefit of which is supposed to be one of the privileges of the accused . . .

'But when one looks back and remembers how often one has been very sure and yet has erred in the issues of life, how often what has seemed certain has failed us, and that which appeared impossible has come to pass, we feel that if the criminal law has been conducted upon such principles it is probably itself the giant murderer of England.' [1]

Conan Doyle's unease at the sentence of death visited on Mullins was based on a belief that there had long been a serious flaw in the English judicial system; one that had been properly answered elsewhere.

'Far wiser is the contention that it is better that ninety-nine guilty should escape than that one innocent man should suffer, and that, therefore, if it can be claimed that there is one chance in a hundred in favour of the prisoner he is entitled to his acquittal,' he wrote. 'It cannot be doubted that if the Scotch verdict of "Not proven", which neither condemns nor acquits, had been permissible in England it would have been the outcome of many a case which, under our sterner law, has ended upon the scaffold. Such a verdict would, I fancy, have been hailed as a welcome compromise by the judge and the jury who investigated the singular circumstances which attended the case of Mrs. Mary Emsley.' [2]

The principle of the 'not proven' verdict dates back to the eighteenth century, and is still part of Scottish law today. (Although at the time of writing, there is debate about whether it should continue.) In practical terms, it means that if the jury were not quite certain of the guilt of the accused, even if the evidence pointed strongly towards it, the verdict of not proven would result in the accused being released. There could be no custodial sentence after such a judgement. But it also means that the verdict could not be appealed against. In other words, even though the accused has been discharged, the ambiguity of the not proven verdict would always hang over him. In 1860, this meant that one might be saved from the gallows, but could never escape suspicion.

For Conan Doyle, 'not proven' seemed an acutely apt phrase for the case. Unlike the less attentive jury in the case, he was haunted by that uncanny sliver of evidence provided by the neighbour, Mrs Barnes.

Admittedly, Mullins did not make for an attractive defendant. However, that awful, itching doubt could not be dispelled.

'After reading the evidence one is left with an irresistible impression that, though Mullins was very likely guilty, the police were never able to establish the details of the crime,' wrote Conan Doyle, 'and that there was a risk of a miscarriage of justice when the death sentence was carried out.'

Nor could he quite fathom what the judge had been thinking.

'To allude to the possibility of a man's innocence and at the same time to condemn him to be hanged strikes the lay mind as being a rather barbarous and illogical proceeding.' (3)

Summarising the trial, Conan Doyle was leaving it to his readers to assume the role of Sherlock Holmes. He was inviting them to pore over the mysteries and ambiguities. For Conan Doyle, the crime appeared to remain impenetrable; he could not even qualify his instinct about Mullins by imputing a motive to what would otherwise appear to be quite a motiveless crime.

But the article was, in itself, another form of clue for the millions of devotees of his Holmes tales, for it seemed to make clear where at least some of the inspiration for his detective had come from. In the story of Mrs Emsley – which had continued to echo down the late Victorian years – was the murky atmosphere of a city charged with the possibility of violent death; also the idea that rigorous, inductive reasoning might be able to analyse elements such as the glimpses of moving wallpaper and windows being opened, and whom a widow might allow to enter her otherwise secure house after sunset. From those disparate and baffling particulars, a reader might be able to summon a perfect recreation of the night of a murder.

For all the wilder adventures of Holmes and Watson, Conan Doyle was fascinated by that curious and macabre blend of the fantastical and domestic: victims of uncanny crimes found in the most resolutely ordinary London houses, in the most drably undemonstrative streets. In *The Sign of Four*, the bland villas of Upper Norwood in south London are imbued with sinister gothic potential; the victim found in a locked upper room having heard a prophecy of death.

And of course, the first Holmes novel, *A Study in Scarlet*, featured a body found in a frowsy south London house, in a bare room, flat out on the wooden boards, arm outstretched. Like the jurors who were taken into 9 Grove Road to view the body of Mrs Emsley, arm outstretched to the door, so the corpse in Conan Doyle's fiction became the spectacle for the detective, his companion, and an eager public.

James Mullins himself passed from life into another sort of story. In November 1860, even as his still-warm corpse was being cut down from the gallows, his body was about to serve its undignified duty as a form of public spectacle. There was a craze for explaining criminal and psychopathic tendencies by referring to the shape of the offender's skull: a practice called phrenology.

It had been formulated at the turn of the century by German anatomist Franz Gall, whose theory was that different parts of the brain controlled different inclinations and impulses. An artist might have an enlarged artistic portion, or 'organ' of the brain; a killer might have an abnormally distended section of the brain that would be linked with violent impulses. These irregularities would be detected in the various bumps and curves of the cranium, which was assumed to have moulded itself precisely to the brain.

Among some sections of fashionable society, as well as a few scientists, the idea had enjoyed a vogue. By 1860, phrenology was being dismissed by more rigorous scientific thinkers, but there was still a substantial public appetite to read about it. The readers of the *Manchester Guardian* were given this intriguing exploration of the mind of James Mullins after an 'expert', C Donovan, had felt the contours of his lifeless head.

'All heads, well or ill-developed, from the philosopher's to the fool's, conform to a certain type,' wrote the phrenologist. 'In the numerous casts of murderers . . . the fact is plainly seen. There is a ferocious type of head . . . which may be termed the low military . . . the greedy animalised, or sensual type . . . the low sneaking woman-and-child-killing type . . . the head of Mullins is precisely of the sneaking type – having the least possible development of the coronal region – the seat of the organs of the specially human faculties. [4]

'The head of Mullins is of the lowest sneaking type,' continued Donovan. 'It would have been very difficult indeed to have fitted him by ever so good an education, for a position of trust. All the higher elements of humanity were down to zero in his mental atmosphere.

'He had a quick, acute intellect; was intellectually clever; morally, a dunce. In him was no obtuseness of the mental faculties. If not "wise to know", he was "quick to learn". He was observant, smooth, specious, crafty in the highest degree. He had been through "sin's long pilgrimage" and arrived, after many weary journeys, at the terminus where such sinners receive their due.' [5]

Just a few weeks later, James Mullins' likeness found further macabre fame when it was exhibited in the halls of Madame Tussaud's waxworks. The exhibition had featured a 'Chamber of Horrors' almost since its inception in the late 1830s. Crowds poured in to gaze at recreations of real-life murder scenes, lit with gas and coloured lights. While the Chamber was still very much present in 1861, the management had an idea for moving the spectacle a little upmarket. Like phrenological analysis, there was now a spuriously educational element to the gallery, and it was suitably extended with a new scientific-sounding name.

'New additions', announced the advertising. 'A full-length portrait model of the murderer James Mullins, with a plan of Emm's house and shed where the parcel was found . . . are now added to the Chamber of Comparative Physiognomy'. [6]

The suggestion was that there was indeed art, if not science, to reading a man's soul in his waxen face. The truth was that this was the same old ghoulish attraction repurposed and aimed at the middle classes. In death, Mullins was a household name, an object of such wickedness that refined people were invited to study his wax cadaver for clues to morality.

While his simulacrum glowered under red lights, Mullins' bereaved family withdrew into obscurity. Catherine and her daughter

Mary vanished from public view. The sons, John, James and Thomas, were also swallowed into anonymity. This would partly have been through choice; their own opportunities would have been circumscribed by being widely known as the family of a notorious executed killer.

Others also continued to feel the repercussions of Mrs Emsley's murder. Walter Emm, though completely cleared of suspicion, suffered financially, having had to pay for his legal defence. His friend Henry Gordon wrote to the *Morning Advertiser* just before Christmas in 1860 to appeal for readers' charitable donations.

'Maliciously charged with so awful a crime, poor Emm had to obtain loans of money from his friends – he being but a poor shoemaker, with a young family to support,' went the letter. This was faintly disingenuous, given Emm's secondary career as property manager, but Gordon did also mention 'the still greater loss to him . . . by the death of Mrs Emsley'. [7]

As to Mrs Emsley's stepdaughters and sons-in-law, there were soon to be fresh tragedies. Betty Faith, the eldest daughter of Samuel Emsley and wife of John, died in 1864 aged just thirty-five. Five years later, her own daughter Letitia died aged eleven. Mother and child were both buried with Samuel Emsley in Tower Hamlets Cemetery. John Faith continued to reside in the home he had shared with Betty, and was a prominent local vestryman, attending to such concerns as funding for the local workhouses. In 1867, he remarried, taking the hand of Mary-Ann Docwra, who hailed from Stoke Newington.

Mrs Emsley's other stepson-in-law, Henry Whittaker, continued to manage the properties acquired by Samuel Emsley together with Faith. From time to time, he would get into legal disputes with tradesmen that would end up in court. He died at the age of forty-seven in 1870.

Slipping deeper into the shadows than most was the preacher Joseph Biggs. Occasionally, he was called as a witness in the increasingly fraught court battles over the properties of Mrs Emsley. On each of these occasions, he found himself required to repeat that none was on more intimate terms with the widow than he, that she had never positively dismissed the idea of their marriage, and that it was certainly her intention that he should be acknowledged in the disbursement of her wealth.

Then, silence. Biggs, rather like the Catholic Apostolic Church for which he preached, seemed to fade from view. As the church attracted fewer and fewer congregants, so Biggs seemed to disappear into the anonymity of the streets.

In 1861, while the crowds were flocking to see the exhibit of Mullins' waxwork, the poor of the East End were increasingly becoming live exhibits to an activist middle class that was ever more determinedly examining the housing of the area. As well as social-housing pioneers such as Angela Burdett-Coutts, Octavia Hill and Helen Bosanquet, the districts of Shoreditch and Shadwell were being sought out by figures such as Samuel Barnett, who became vicar of St Jude's in Whitechapel in the 1870s. Together with his wife Henrietta, he established Toynbee Hall, the purpose of which was to bring both educated and uneducated classes together to work on alleviating the poverty and distress in the streets all around. In 1869, just a few streets to the north of Old Nichol, an astonishing gothic structure of model dwellings, funded by Angela Burdett-Coutts, was built. Colombia Market brought a range of dignitaries to east Shoreditch for its ceremonial opening. These solid, airy, well-designed dwellings stood as a rebuke to the dark, overcrowded houses all around.

Even before charities such as the Peabody Trust made their campaigns for decent property even noisier, the government had already become more interventionist. There were even visits to the East End from home secretaries. Eventually, Parliament passed 'The Artisans' and Labourers' Dwellings Improvement Act' of 1875. The idea was that local authorities would be authorised to demolish the very worst of the slums and sell the land to private companies and bodies such as the Peabody Trust and the East End Dwellings Company for the express purpose of building secure, hygienic homes.

The governmental impulse was both humanitarian and also watchful. Long after the Chartists had faded away, different forms of political unrest were fomenting. Mullins' work as a spy among the Ribbonmen had been an example of early British efforts to undermine a growing Fenian movement. By 1860, that movement had multiplied many times, partly aided and funded by the increasing Irish diaspora in America. Following the Great Famine, perceived as the moment at which official oppression turned to murderousness, Irish ill-feeling towards the British government was searing, and young recruits to a new, violent form of resistance were easily found in the east of London. In 1867, there was a bombing in Clerkenwell; in 1883, the first coordinated attack on London's underground railway, in which many were injured, but miraculously, no one lost their life.

Even though the term 'East End' was a synonym for slums, its streets were always more varied. Charles Booth's famous poverty maps towards the end of the century show that amid the pockets of black-edged streets (the black denoting poverty so dire that these areas were 'criminal'), there were also very many pink and red-edged squares and terraces, ranging from working-class families in steady, good labour, to the even better-off middle classes. The fascination today, in a London that is just as sharply segregated, is the Victorian proximity of wealth to near-starvation and death; warmth, comfort and security next to lives so chillingly precarious that the next meal was never assured.

If the shadow of Mrs Emsley were to walk the streets of Ratcliff, Limehouse and Mile End today, she might marvel at what remains from her lifetime. Streets that were built and mapped out in the 1840s still exist. She could walk down Salmon Lane and pass some of the houses she owned when they were quite new. The brick and paintwork, she would see, are as bright (if not brighter, thanks to cleaner air) as they were in her day.

She could walk on to York Square, where rooms in the houses were once marketed towards the smart new breed of young clerk; the houses themselves touted as sound investments for landlords. Those houses today are prohibitively expensive to many, but these are still streets where young professionals pay rent to live. Mrs Emsley would find it all curiously familiar.

At the Regent's Canal through the short tunnel under the Commercial Road, Mrs Emsley would find herself at Limehouse Basin. Above her head, the handsome stretch of brick viaduct where James Mullins suffered his hideous accident, and still carrying passengers today in the form of the Docklands Light Railway. Before her, the dock has been transformed into a marina for dazzling white yachts, and the squat, industrial warehouses have been replaced with smart apartment blocks. She would taste the relatively clean air with amazement, and might even be able for the first time to see fish in the water.

Newell Street would still be familiar, with its eighteenth-century houses that once belonged to captains and wealthy merchants. Behind it, the white Portland stone of Hawksmoor's church of St Anne is still there. Its strong, plangent bell would have been a constant throughout Mrs Emsley's life, but the church itself is brighter than it ever could have been when she was young.

Beyond, where once the masts of the great cargo ships were forested in the West India Docks, Mrs Emsley would now gaze on the glittering silver towers of Canary Wharf. Perhaps they would not need much explanation; much like the old docks and elegant eighteenth-century warehouses that survive – the warehouses now millionaire's apartments – these towers instantly suggest a close concentration of immense wealth. Yet she might also look at all the streets that lie around this citadel of riches and immediately understand the gulf. Just a matter of yards away, deprivation still exists in Poplar and the East India Dock Road. Streets that were poor in 1860 still ache with poverty today.

Closing the loop on Mrs Emsley's life is the large, green churchyard of St Dunstan's, where she was baptised in 1790. On top of the church's square tower, tall enough to be seen by sailors floating up the Thames from the Isle of Dogs, is a flag, the sort that has flown there ever since the docks were brought to the mighty river.

Through property speculation, Mrs Emsley played her part in building today's city. Much of her portfolio, in areas such as Bromley-by-Bow, has long vanished. Some houses were hit by bombs in the Second World War, others by the wrecking balls of local councils. However, some things have remained unchanged since 1860. From all around the world, people want to live in London; the forces of economic gravity still pull many of them to the east of the city. Landlords still thrive on renting-out properties; some subdivide rooms and let outhouse dwellings in back gardens which, for the purposes of official inspection, are termed garden sheds. Into this mire of squalid accommodation, of small rooms filled with bunk-beds, windows and ventilation sometimes severely limited, ever more tenants move.

Landlords often claim their own livelihoods are precarious; that mortgages and loans mean they have to pull in all the rent that they can. The story never changes.

In Fyodor Dostoyevsky's novel *Crime and Punishment*, published in 1866, a rich old lady, a miserly moneylender, is murdered with a hatchet by a student called Raskolnikov. His guilt goes undetected, which in turn feeds his increasingly feverish state of mind. Hanging over it all is the question of his motive. He tries to rationalise the hideous crime by pointing to the misery the old lady was causing to others, and by citing his own poverty. Yet in the aftermath of her murder, Raskolnikov neglects to take the vast amount of money she had in her apartment. His own explanations for his bloody actions grow ever more ambiguous.

Is it a species of nihilism? An early form of terrorism against the smothering oppression of capitalism? Is it possible even for Raskolnikov to feel remorse for what he has done?

In the end, after he confesses, he escapes death and is exiled to Siberia for eight years.

By contrast, the hanging of James Mullins left nothing but a deeper silence over the murder of Mrs Emsley; the silence of that dark house as she lay dead, her blood trickling under the door, and her killer sitting with her in that darkness, trying to understand what he had done.

Notes

Chapter Two

1 – Police report, National Archives, ref: MEPO 3/62
2 – As above

Chapter Three

1 – As reported from the inquest in *The Times*, Aug 21st, 1860
2 – As reported in *Morning Chronicle*, Aug 19th, 1860
3 – This was part of Dr Gill's later deposition to the inquest in the
   Railway Arms hotel, reported in many newspapers on Aug 22nd, 1860
4 – Police report, National Archives, ref: MEPO 3/62
5 – As part of Dr Gill's deposition to the inquest, Aug 22nd, 1860
6 – As above
7 – Police report, National Archives, ref: MEPO 3/62
8 – As above
9 – As reported in *Morning Post*, Aug 21st, 1860
10 – Police report, National Archives, ref: MEPO 3/62
11 – As above
12 – As above
13 – As above
14 – As above
15 – As reported in *The Times*, Aug 22nd, 1860

Chapter Four

1 – As reported in the *Evening Standard*, Aug 21st, 1860
2 – As above
3 – As above

4 – As above

5 – Arthur Conan Doyle, 'The Debatable Case of Mrs Emsley',
   The Strand magazine, May 1901

Chapter Five

1 – Arthur Conan Doyle, 'The Debatable Case of Mrs Emsley', *The Strand*
   magazine, May 1901

2 – Henry Mayhew, *London Labour and London Poor* (1861 three-volume edition,
   Cass)

3 – Cartwright's poem to be found in 'East London' by GF Bosworth (Cambridge
   University Press, 1911), held in Tower Hamlets Archives, Bancroft Road, E2

4 – As above

Chapter Six

1 – As reported in *The Times*, Aug 24th, 1860

2 – As above

3 – As above

4 – As above

5 – As above

6 – As above

7 – As above

8 – Police report, held in the National Archives, MEPO 3/62

9 – As above

10 – As above

11 – As above

12 – As reported in *The Times*, Aug 27th, 1860

13 – As above

14 – As above

15 – As above

16 – As above

17 – Police report, held in the National Archives, ref: MEPO 3/62

18 – As reported in *The Times*, Aug 25th, 1860

Chapter Seven

1 – A copy of this certificate is held in the Tower Hamlets archive, ref:
   P/SLC/1/21/7/1

2 – As reported in July 1794 by the periodical *European Magazine*

3 – A copy of this certificate is held in the Tower Hamlets archive ref: as above

4 – *The Maul and the Pear Tree – The Ratcliffe Highway Murders* by
   TA Critchley and PD James (Constable, 1971)

5 – As above

6 – As quoted in *Limehouse Through Five Centuries* by JG Birch
   (The Sheldon Press, 1930)

7 – Nov 25th, 1839; the case can now be found on oldbaileyonline.org

Chapter Eight

1 – As reported in *Marylebone Mercury*, Sept 1st, 1860
2 – *Morning Advertiser*, Sept 19th, 1836
3 – As above
4 – *History of the County of Middlesex*, ed. J Cockburn (London, 1969)
5 – As above
6 – A copy of the marriage certificate is held by Tower Hamlets Archives ref: P/SLC/1/21/7/1
7 – Advertisement in the *Morning Advertiser*, May 24th, 1852

Chapter Nine

1 – From the play 'The Miser of Shoreditch', attributed to Thomas Peckett Prest, circa 1855
2 – Police notice of reward for information, in circulation Aug 27th, 1860
3 – As reported in *The Times*, Aug 27th, 1860
4 – As reported in *Morning Post*, Aug 27th, 1860
5 – As above
6 – As reported in *The Times*, Aug 27th, 1860
7 – The fight in the Edinburgh Waverley tea-rooms, Rhodeswell Road, reported in *Morning Post*, Aug 29th, 1860
8 – As reported in the *Evening Standard*, Aug 29th, 1860
9 – George Smith's letter to *The Times*, Sept 4th, 1860

Chapter Ten

1 – As related by police witnesses in later court transcripts, in the Thames Police Court, in late September 1860
2 – As above
3 - As above
4 – As above
5 – As above
6 – As above
7 – As later reported in newspapers such as *Morning Chronicle*
8 – As related by witnesses under oath in later court transcripts
9 – As above
10 – As related in the *Evening Standard* Sept 10th, 1860
11 – As reported in *The Times*, Sept 10th, 1860
12 – As reported in court transcripts

Chapter Eleven

1 – Minutes concerning the Mile End workhouse in Tower Hamlets archives: 'The Minutes Book of Meetings of the Vestry of the hamlet of Mile End Old Town 1860-61' ref: L/MEO/2/5
2 – Contracts for provisions, Tower Hamlets Archives, ref: L 7048 3531
3 – As above

4 – Parish records/scrapbook, as held in Tower Hamlets archive ref: LC FOO 714

5 – As per note 2, above

6 – The development of which as discussed in 'Modern Methods of Artificial Illumination' in *The Journal of the Royal Society of Arts*, Aug, 1909

7 – From *Twice Around the Clock* by George Augustus Sala (Houlston and Wright, 1859)

8 – As later related in court transcripts

9 – From *What I Saw In London* by David Bartlett (Derby and Miller, 1853)

Chapter Twelve

1 – As reported in the *Morning Chronicle*, Sept 15th, 1860

2 – As above

3 – As reported in *Observer*, Sept 16th, 1860

4 – As above

5 – As reported in *The Times*, Sept 16th, 1860

6 – As above

7 – As above

8 – As reported in *Observer*, Sept 16th, 1860

9 – As above

10 – As reported in *The Times*, Sept 16th, 1860

Chapter Thirteen

1 – As reported in *Morning Chronicle*, Sept 17th, 1860

2 – 'The Debatable Case of Mrs Emsley', by Arthur Conan Doyle, *The Strand* magazine, May 1901

3 – As reported in *The Times*, Sept 27th, 1860

4 – As reported in *Manchester Guardian*, Sept 27th, 1860

Chapter Fourteen

1 – *Policing Victorian London* by Phillip Thurmond Smith (Greenwood Press, 1985)

2 – As above

Chapter Fifteen

1 – Letter to *Manchester Guardian*, Nov 9th, 1844

2 – As reported in *Manchester Guardian*, Nov 22nd, 1860

3 – As reported in *The Times*, Nov 22nd, 1860

4 – As above

5 – As above

Chapter Sixteen

1 – As reported in *Reynold's News*, Nov 24th, 1860

2 – As above

3 – As above

4 – As above

5 – As reported in *Morning Post*, Dec 21st, 1853

6 – As above

7 – Letter to *The Times*, Oct 25th, 1860

8 – Henry Mayhew, writing in *Morning Chronicle*, November 1859

Chapter Seventeen

1 – As reported in *East London Observer*, Oct 12th, 1860

Chapter Eighteen

1 – Charles Dickens, the *Daily News*, Mar 9th, 1846

2 – As reported in *The Times*, Oct 26th, 1860

3 – As above

4 – From 'The Boscombe Valley Mystery' by Arthur Conan-Doyle, featuring in *The Adventures of Sherlock Holmes*, published 1891

Chapter Nineteen

1 – As reported in *The Times*, Oct 27th, 1860

Chapter Twenty

1 – As reported in *The Times*, Oct 27th, 1860

2 – From *The Spectator,* Oct 27th, 1860

3 – As reported in *The Standard*, Oct 27th, 1860

4 – Mullins's letter reproduced in *Morning Chronicle*, Nov 3rd, 1860

5 – As reported in *Morning Chronicle*, Nov 10th, 1860

6 – As quoted by *The Times* Nov 10th, 1860

7 – As above

8 – As reported in *Morning Chronicle*, Nov 15th, 1860

9 – As above

10 – As above

11 – As quoted and reported by *Manchester Guardian*, Nov 22nd, 1860

12 – As above

13 – From the broadside *God's Revenge Against Murder*, published November 1860, now held in Museum of London collections ref: 2002.76/50h

14 – As reported in the *Evening Standard* Nov 21st, 1860

Chapter Twenty-One

1 – As reported in the *Evening Standard*, Nov 20th, 1860

2 – As reported in *Reynold's News*, Nov 25th, 1860

3 – As reported in *The Times*, Nov 20th, 1860

4 – As reported in the *Evening Standard*, Nov 20th, 1860
5 – As above
6 – As above

Chapter Twenty-Two

1 – Article in the *Illustrated Times*, Nov 24th, 1860
2 – As above
3 – Elizabeth Goetz's letter to *East London Observer*, June 1st, 1861
4 – As reported in *East London Observer*, Aug 31st, 1861

Chapter Twenty-Three

1 – 'The Debatable Case of Mrs Emsley' by Arthur Conan-Doyle,
   The Strand magazine, May 1901
2 – From 'Literary Reminiscences', the later 1851 edition of
   'Autobiography of an Opium Eater' by Thomas de Quincey

Chapter Twenty-Four

1 – 'The Debatable Case of Mrs Emsley' by Arthur Conan-Doyle,
   as above
2 – As above
3 – As above
4 – C Donovan, as quoted in *Manchester Guardian*, Nov 25th, 1860
5 – As above
6 – Advertisement from *East London Observer*, January 1861
7 – Letter in *Morning Advertiser*, Dec 8th, 1860

Picture Credits

Index

Index

Index

Acknowledgements

First of all, countless thanks to the brilliant archivists at the Tower Hamlets Archives. This wonderful library – to be found in Bancroft Road, Mile End – is a treasure store of rare local documents, 19th century parish records, minutes of vestry meetings, property deeds and so much else. What is more, all are welcome there. Countless thanks also to my fantastic literary agent Anna Power, whose judgements are unfailingly acute and wise. Profound gratitude also to Richard Green and Jennifer Barr for seeing the potential and guiding the book into harbour with such style; Jessica Axe and Jessie Sullivan for letting the world know about it; David Jøgensen, with his learned and raptor-eyed editing; and Ru Merritt, not only for excellent production but also great patience.